Bedroom and Bathroom
GLASSWARE
of the
Depression Years

Margaret & Kenn Whitmyer

COLLECTOR BOOKS

A Division of Schroeder Publishing Co., Inc.

The current values in this book should be used only as a guide. They are not intended to set prices, which vary from one section of the country to another. Auction prices as well as dealer prices vary greatly and are affected by condition as well as demand. Neither the Author nor the Publisher assumes responsibility for any losses that might be incurred as a result of consulting this guide.

Additional copies of this book may be ordered from:

Collector Books
P.O. Box 3009
Paducah, Kentucky   42001

@ $19.95 plus $2.00 for postage and handling.

Copyright: Margaret & Kenn Whitmyer, 1990
P.O. Box 30806
Gahanna, OH   43230

DEDICATION

To our parents,
Mr. and Mrs. Robert C. Johnson
and
Mr. and Mrs. Wilbur Lesher,
for their encouragement and enlightenment,
and above all,
for just being there and offering gentle guidance.

ACKNOWLEDGMENTS

Bedroom and Bathroom Glassware of the Depression Years has been made possible through the generous efforts of many dedicated collectors and dealers throughout the country. These persons have given us encouragement and inspiration when the problems involved with a project of this magnitude seemed endless. They have also unselfishly shared their knowledge and collections with us, and have helped to check the finished copy for accuracy. To both old friends who have helped in the past, and new ones acquired in this undertaking, we offer our warmest "thank you."

We are expecially grateful to two couples who helped us tremendously with our research - Joyce and John Baden and Marjorie and Arlan Stokes. They opened their homes to us and allowed us to interrupt their busy lives for an extended period of time. Our visits with both of you will be fondly remembered. Don and Mary Henderson, Helen and Jim Kennon, Jim and Rose Cornutt, Marti DeGraaf and Tobi Mack also allowed us to visit. We enjoyed learning more about their interests, and our readers will certainly benefit from their contributions.

Lorraine and David Kovar and Don and Sally Davis took the time to make a long drive to meet with us and work on this project. Bonnie Koeninger, Kevin and Barbara Kiley, Woody Griffith and Gerry Macke packed and shipped numerous items for us and were the source of much encouragement.

We would like to thank Barbara and Bill Adt for sharing much of their patent information with us. Also their extensive knowledge of Fostoria and other elegant glassware aided us tremendously.

We also appreciate the efforts of the following people who either loaned us pieces for photography, supplied needed information, or helped with pricing:

Warren C. Anderson
Joyce and Parke Bloyer
Dennis Bialek
Bill Cass
Austin and Shirley Hartsock
Audrey and Joe Humphrey
Shirley Imholte
Ann Kerr
Ziggy and Pat Kurz
Jim La Mareoux
Mary Sue Lyons
Nancy and Jim Maben
Ted Mansfield
Janet and Wendell Martin

Jimmy McCrae
Fred and Jeannette McMorrow
Randy Moles
George Muraskevics
Marty Pruzzo
Mary Scharf & Tony Vimmer
Bill and Phyllis Smith
Rick and Ruth Teets
Dan Tucker and Lorrie Kitchen
Emma Ward
Lynn Welker
Clarke and Carol West
Delmer and Mary Lou Youngen
Jerry and Geraldine Zwisler

TABLE OF CONTENTS

PART III: Bathroom Accessories

PART IV: Lamps and Clocks

PART V: Guest Sets

FOREWORD

The primary consideration of this reference is vanity and powder room containers made by American glass companies during the first half of the twentieth century. The most prolific period of production was the era from the mid-1920's until the mid-1930's - a time in America's past which is often referred to as the "Great Depression." Products of interest to today's collectors, which are examined here, include both figural and non-figural containers for face and body powder, perfume, bath salts, soap, cold cream and lotions.

Part I covers the major American-made puff boxes which usually have no other associated vanity articles, such as perfumes or trays. The struggle for survival of the various major glass companies during the lean times of the "Great Depression" resulted in fierce competition which produced a proliferation of cheap, machine-made colored glassware. During this time, designers created numerous powder containers with interesting shapes to persuade a cash starved society to splurge on non-essentials. Manufacturers produced these interesting containers in a multitude of colors. One of the major selling points was the fact that the containers were reusable for any number of other purposes once the original contents were consumed.

The puff boxes are arranged in an order according to type of finial. Boxes with animal finials are first. These are followed by boxes with human figure finials, and the last part of the powder jar section features boxes without figural finials.

Vanity sets are pictured and described in Part II. These sets will have a puff box and one or more colognes. Sometimes, a tray or other accessories will also be part of the set. Sets featured in this section will be listed alphabetically according to manufacturing company. One exception here is some of the perfumes produced for DeVilbiss by other companies and will be listed under "DeVilbiss." DeVilbiss was a finishing and decorating company which used glass blanks from a number of different manufacturers.

Part III illustrates articles used primarily in the bathroom. This includes bath salt containers, soap dishes, toothbrush holders, jars and bottles for mouthwash, astringents, lotion and cold cream.

Part IV describes a sampling of the numerous styles of electric lamps and wind-up clocks available for use on vanities during the era. It is impossible to show all of the hundreds of different lamps which were produced, therefore, examples from various categories which were most popular have been included. Since there are already excellent references available on such subjects as oil lamps and Aladdin lamps, we have chosen not to give these categories the extensive coverage which would be necessary to represent them properly. Although a few American companies such as Fostoria and McKee produced glass clocks, the majority of the glass clocks were made in Europe. Some of the clocks came as part of sets and will have matching accessories such as vases and candlesticks.

Part V illustrates and prices various styles of guest sets which were produced. Many of the lesser quality sets were retailed as bath salts containers. When the contents were used the container could be used as a bedside water container.

Over the years various researchers have given names to numerous items which the original companies have chosen to identify by a number. Their reasoning has been that names are easier for collectors to associate with and remember than a multitude of meaningless numbers. Whenever possible, we have used original company names. If original names could not be determined for items which would be difficult to identify without one, we have either used names created by other researchers, or have supplied names created by ourselves or other collectors. All names which have been created are in quotation marks.

PRICING

The prices in this book represent retail prices for mint condition pieces. Items which are excessively worn, chipped or cracked will only bring a fraction of the listed price. A price range has been included to help account for regional differences in prices. Also, be aware that certain currently rare items, which are now valued at several hundred dollars, may prove hard-to-sell if a quantity of these items is discovered. The values of a few items, which are currently one-of-a-kind, may be omitted from the price guide if a retail value has not been established. In these cases, the letters "UND" for undetermined will appear in the listing.

All items are priced "each." Items which have lids or stoppers are priced "complete." Any exceptions to this will be noted in the individual listing. Prices of items in all categories may vary considerably according to color. Wherever possible, an attempt has been made to reflect these different valuations. However, any attempt to list and price the numerous colors in which some of the pieces may be found is impossible in a guide of this type. An effort has been made to give the reader general guidelines about rarity and desirability of various pieces and colors. Thoughtful consideration of these guidelines should produce a qualitative value for most any item.

Pricing information has been obtained from dealer listings, flea market and show observations, trade publications and from collectors. Remember, prices in this guide should only be used as a reference. Prices may vary in the marketplace, and it is not the intention of the authors to try to establish or control prices.

REPRODUCTIONS

Fortunately, collectors have experienced the reproduction of only a small number of the collectible items within the scope of this reference. Items produced from new molds during and after the 1960's appear to be more abundant. However, some of these later issues had short production runs and are now becoming collectible.

If proper caution is exercised, most collectors should have few problems identifying new or reproduction items in any of the categories included in this book. Two categories - current productions and reissues - concern modern collectors.

Products from new molds, in the majority of cases, involve import items which may often be found in gift shops which specialize in imported wares. Well-informed collectors often find a walk through an import store or the glass department of the local variety or discount store is very educational. Veteran collectors are usually careful to not be fooled by the sudden appearance of an item they have never seen before. They can rely on years of experience to guide them as they check for mold detail, color, and quality of glass as they view the new find with suspicion. New items are most troublesome to novice collectors who are more unfamiliar with the look and feel of older glass.

The second type of new product involves reproductions from old molds. In many cases, these reproductions are produced by a small American hand house. Since original molds are involved, detail on the new item is the same as on the original. Collectors must educate themselves and be aware of the colors the item was made in originally. Any unusual colors should then be initially suspected as being reproductions.

Since the major emphasis of this book is Depression Era collectibles, very few new products made later than the 1950's will be shown in this reference. An exception is items which have been made from old molds that have been made either continuously or intermittently. An attempt has been made to verify the period of production for the items shown. References have been included to identifiy items which have been reproduced or made sporadically over a long period of time.

PART I:
VANITY BOXES

ANIMAL FIGURAL POWDER JARS

There are two styles of the large size elephant powder jars shown in the top photograph - trunk down and trunk up. The elephant with the trunk down will be found in both frosted and transparent colors. Generally, the frosted colors of this jar are plentiful, and the transparent colors are more difficult to find. The elephant jar with the trunk up is very difficult to find and is only known in frosted colors. Belief in the old adage that an elephant with the trunk up brings good luck, has made this jar very popular among collectors.

Patent information shows the elephant jar with the trunk down was designed by Charles H. Oestreich of Brooklyn, New York. An application for a patent on this ornamental design for use as a toilet powder container was filed on November 4, 1930. The patent was granted on January 13, 1931.

The bottom of both styles of jar is the same. Notice the bottom has ripples and bulges to a diameter of 6" at the center. The top of the base has a series of slanted ridges over which the lid fits. This same type bottom is used for the seated German shepherd shown in the photo on page 11, but differs from the bottom used with the large owl finial. The top of the owl base has a single screw-like thread over which the lid fits. Also, there is no outward center bulge. Instead, it curves gradually to a flat bottom with a diameter of 6¾".

The figure of a large seated German shepherd decorates the lids of four of the powder jars shown in the bottom photo. The outer surfaces of both the lid and the bottom have embossed ripples. Known colors include transparent green, frosted green, frosted pink, frosted light turquoise, transparent amber and frosted crystal. A matching vanity lamp base was made from the lid of this jar by adding four small feet to the bottom rim. A hole drilled behind the finial accepts the lamp attachments. According to an ad in the Paramount Salesman Supplies Catalog, the wholesale price for the frosted crystal version of this lamp was 65¢ in 1938.

A small standing terrier finial also has been found atop the large-size rippled lid and round rippled base used with the elephant and the seated German shepherd. This jar is shown in the photo at the top of page 13. The finial is the same as the one which is more commonly found on the smaller powder jar shown in the photo on page 15.

The large-size owl powder jar has been found in frosted crystal and transparent green. The owl has large embossed eyes which are usually accented with yellow and black paint. The wings and ears may also be outlined in black. Both the top and bottom are embossed with ripples. Notice, however, both the shape of the bottom and the style of rippling are different from that of the German shepherd and elephant powder jars. This same style bottom is used with the "Lillian IV" jar shown on page 31.

	Crystal/ Frosted Crystal	Frosted Green/Pink	Transparent Green/Pink	Transparent Amber	Frosted Turquoise
* Elephant, trunk down	$20.00-25.00	$35.00-40.00	$65.00-75.00	$75.00-85.00	
Elephant, trunk up	$30.00-35.00	$75.00-85.00			
** "Rin Tin Tin"	$40.00-45.00	$70.00-75.00	$80.00-90.00	$100.00-110.00	$80.00-95.00
"Woodsy" owl	$90.00-100.00		$125.00-135.00		

* Lavender (sun-turned) $35.00 - $40.00
** Lavender (sun-turned) $50.00 - $60.00

Row 1: (a,b,c) Elephant with trunk down on ripple base, large-size, frosted lavender (sun-turned); transparent pink; frosted green.
Row 2: (a, b) Elephant with trunk down on rippled base, frosted pink, transparent amber; (c) Elephant with trunk up on rippled base, frosted pink.

Row 1: (a,b,c) "Rin Tin Tin," frosted lavender (sun-turned), transparent green and frosted green.
Row 2: (a) "Rin Tin Tin," frosted crystal; (b,c) "Woodsy" owl, transparent green and frosted crystal.

The "Standing Terrier" powder jar in the photo at the top left is an example of a small-size finial on a large-size jar. This combination is very unusual, and the crystal frosted jar illustrated is the only color which has been reported. The rippled-style lid and base are the same as the ones on the jars shown on the first three rows with the large finials on the previous page.

The jar shown at the top right has the miniature seated bulldog, "Butch," finial. The bottom is round with three tab-like feet. There is a raised panel the width of the foot which runs upward on the bottom and continues onto the lid, tapering at the base of the finial. Both the top and bottom have vertical ribbing positioned between each raised panel. Frosted crystal is the only color that has been found.

Due to the small size of the finials of the powder jars in the bottom photograph, these jars are often called miniatures. With the exception of the right jar on the bottom row, all have the same style base. The base is a small version of the one used with the "Mother Elephant with Babies" jar on page 15. It has two bands of stippling separated by a smooth central band and measures 4¼" in diameter. This stippling matches the stippling found on the lids. The finials available include a miniature German shepherd, miniature bulldog, and a miniature elephant with its trunk down.

The German shepherd jar has been found in a 1935 advertisement for Ramses powder. Known colors are transparent green, frosted green, and frosted pink. The miniature bulldog is in a sitting position and is wearing a spiked collar. The bulldog has been seen in frosted crystal and frosted pink.

Both powder jars on the bottom row have the same style finial. However, the remainder of the lids and the two bases are entirely different. The jar on the left has the stippled exterior surface which matches the jars on the row above it. The jar on the right has a rippled surface. It is a smaller version of the elephant powder jars shown on page 11. Both jars are available in frosted crystal, frosted green and frosted pink.

	Crystal/ Frosted Crystal	Frosted Green/Pink	Transparent Green
"Standing Terrier", large-size base	$85.00-95.00		
"Mascot", small-size base	$35.00-45.00	$60.00-65.00	$75.00-85.00
"Butch", footed base	$95.00-110.00		
"Butch", flat base	$35.00-40.00	$50.00-60.00	
Min. elephant/stippled base	$25.00-35.00	$50.00-60.00	
Min. elephant/rippled base	$25.00-35.00	$50.00-60.00	

Small "Standing Terrier," on large-size powder jar base, frosted crystal.

Miniature bulldog, "Butch," on unusual lid and footed base, frosted crystal.

Row 1: (a) Miniature seated German shepherd, "Mascot," frosted pink; (b,c) Miniature bulldog, "Butch," frosted crystal and frosted pink.
Row 2: (a) Miniature elephant with stippled base, frosted pink; (b) Miniature elephant with rippled base, frosted pink.

The two different powder jars shown on the top row both have the same shaped bottom. This bottom, which is 4¼" in diameter, features a recessed horizontal center panel which is intersected by four evenly spaced vertical recessed panels. See page 33 for other powder tops which utilize this same bottom.

Three different shaped lids are found on this bottom: (a) a smooth round type, (b) an octagonal style and (c) a round shape with four vertical panels which match the style of the bottom.

The first powder jar has a finial consisting of two elephants with joined upraised trunks. A weak area exists at this junction, since many of these jars are found with cracks at this point. Collectors have been calling this jar by two names - "Kissing Elephants" and "Battling Elephants." In addition to the frosted pink color shown, other known colors include frosted green, a light transparent green, crystal and crystal flashed with light pink, light green or light blue. The shape of this lid is octagonal.

The second and third powder jars are known as the "Three Birds." The finial features three perched birds - two with their heads turned toward each other with their beaks touching, and the other one looking straight ahead. The top has recessed panels which match the vertical recessed panels on the bottom. Colors, in addition to the frosted green and frosted pink shown in the picture, include transparent pink, transparent green, crystal, and flashed pink and flashed green over a crystal base.

A similar shaped base is used for the three different powder jars shown in the second row. The bottom features a flat horizontal center panel - not recessed as in the row above. The diameter of these jars is about 4½". Both the top and bottom sections have an embossed rippled surface. All three finial representations are found in frosted green and frosted pink colors. The bulldog in the center has also been found in a very dark frosted orange-pink color. The finial on the first powder jar is a seated cat. The finial of the middle jar is a standing bulldog wearing a spiked collar, and the dog finial on the third jar is a standing terrier. The small standing terrier finial may also be found atop the large-size rippled jar. See page 13.

The first powder jar in the top row of the bottom photo has a finial with a mother elephant and two baby elephants. The two babies are standing on either side of the mother and all three have their trunks curled upward. The outer surface of the lid is smooth, but part of the outer surface of the bottom is stippled. This stippled area slopes outward and is divided by a smooth, flat middle band which is about one inch wide. The diameter of the bottom is about six inches. This same bottom will also be found with other tops - "Jackie," the flapper girl in a seated position, shown on page 41, and "Gretchen," the finial torso of a semi-nude with her arms folded over her chest, which may be seen on page 41. This style bottom was also used with a flower frog top, many of which have disappeared. Therefore, powder jar collectors will find an abundance of these bottoms and a shortage of lids. In addition to frosted green, this jar will be found in frosted pink, transparent green, transparent pink and crystal.

The elephant carousel powder jar has an elephant finial with its trunk down similar to the powder jars in the top photo on page 11. However, there are no ripples on the top of this style jar. Instead, the finial is resting on a raised pad which features six radiating spokes. The bottom is 5½" in diameter and is supported by twelve small feet, and there are six elephants on parade around its center. This jar also exists in frosted pink.

The black powder jar with the elephant finial is a medium-size jar. It is 4⅞" in diameter and 3¾" high. Traces of gold remaining on the finial attest to its original decoration. Black is the only color we have seen, therefore, we are calling it the "Lonesome Elephant."

The Scottish terrier powder jars on the bottom row have been dubbed "My Pet." A central begging Scotty is supported by a seated pup on each side. The base is encircled by a series of intricately embossed eight-sided stars, which are separated by vertical ribbing toward the bottom and a fine line asterisk-like shape at the top. The same base is also used with a lid which has a simple knob finial. See page 59. The jar is 4½" in diameter and measures 5" in height. Known colors include transparent pink, green, cobalt and crystal. A frosted version of this jar is not known, however, some crystal jars have been found with flashed-on colors.

	Crystal/ Frosted Crystal	Frosted Pink/Green	Transparent Pink/Green	Flashed Colors	Black/ Cobalt
"Battling/Kissing Elephants"	$20.00-25.00	$50.00-60.00	$55.00-65.00	$20.00-25.00	
"Three Birds"	$18.00-20.00	$35.00-40.00	$55.00-65.00	$20.00-22.00	
"Seated Felix"		$75.00-85.00			
"Spike"		$45.00-50.00			
"Standing Terrier," small-size base		$40.00-45.00			
"Elephant with Babies"	$35.00-45.00	$75.00-85.00	$95.00-110.00		

	Crystal/ Frosted Crystal	Frosted Pink/Green	Transparent Pink/Green	Flashed Colors	Black/ Cobalt
"Elephant Carousel"		$45.00-55.00			
"Lonesome Elephant"					$90.00-110.00
"My Pet" Scotties	$20.00-25.00		$65.00-75.00	$20.00-25.00	$90.00-110.00

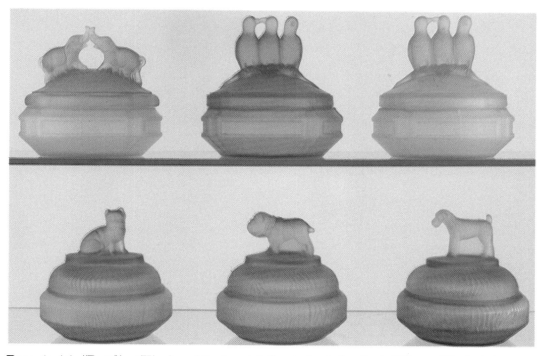

Row 1: (a) "Battling/Kissing Elephant," frosted pink; (b,c) "Three Birds," frosted green and frosted pink.
Row 2: (a) "Seated Felix," frosted green; (b) "Spike," frosted green; (c) "Standing Terrier," small-size base, frosted green.

Row 1: (a) "Mother Elephant with Babies," frosted green; (b) "Elephant Carousel," frosted green; (c) "Lonesome Elephant," black.
Row 2: (a,b,c) "My Pet," transparent pink, cobalt and transparent green.

The transparent green seated squirrel shown on the top row is a powder jar which many collectors are still seeking. The finial on the top portrays a very large seated squirrel clutching an acorn in its front paws. The surface of the lid is etched with a trellis-like design embellished with flowers. The 6½" wide squatty-shaped bottom is smooth except for lightly-molded, evenly-spaced vertical panels. This powder jar is also known to exist in transparent pink.

The two transparent pink powder jars shown on the top row appear to be of foreign manufacture. The jar with the squirrel finial is being called "Resting Squirrel." It features a squirrel in the resting position with an acorn in its front paws. This powder jar is a 3½" by 4¼" rectangular shape with a four-footed base and has an overall embossing of intricate fleur-de-lis and scrolls. The hexagonal jar with the six-footed bottom has a Cecropia moth finial. Three panels on the base are embossed with an oak leaf design. These alternate with three other panels embossed with a crane wading in a pond, a song bird perched on a tree, and two butterflies in flight. The jar is 4" in diameter and stands 4" high. "Rites of Spring" is a name which has been suggested for this jar.

The diamond-shaped frosted pink powder jar on the second row of the top photo has a "Basset Hound" finial. Its dimensions are 5½" long by 4¼" high. This playful-looking hound also may be found atop jars in frosted green.

The "Bowser" powder jar sports a recessed Scottish terrier in the center of the lid and in the bottom of the 3½" by 5" rectangular-shaped jar. All the sides of the top and bottom have vertical ribs with interlocking sawtooth edges. "Bowser" is also available in crystal.

The animal powder jars shown in the bottom photo were made by the Jeannette Glass Company from the 1930's through the 1950's. Many were sold to various distributors of cosmetics and candy. They were retailed by various "five and tens" around the country. The crystal donkey on the top row still contains the original powder and the label reads "Spicy Apple Blossom Body Powder; Landers Distributors, 5th Ave., N.Y."

"Bambi" the deer, and the Scotty may be found in crystal, transparent pink and marigold iridescent. The donkey and the elephant with the upraised trunk exist in crystal and transparent pink, but the French poodle has only been found in marigold iridescent.

	Crystal	Transparent Pink/Green	Frosted Pink/Green	Marigold Iridescent
"Seated Squirrel"		$110.00-125.00		
"Resting Squirrel"		$40.00-50.00		
"Rites of Spring"		$50.00-60.00		
"Basset Hound"			$45.00-55.00	
"Bowser	$18.00-20.00	$25.00-30.00		
"Bambi"	$10.00-12.00	$20.00-22.00		$12.00-15.00
French Poodle				$15.00-18.00
Donkey	$10.00-12.00	$20.00-22.00		
Elephant	$10.00-12.00	$20.00-25.00		
Scotty	$10.00-12.00	$20.00-22.00		$15.00-18.00

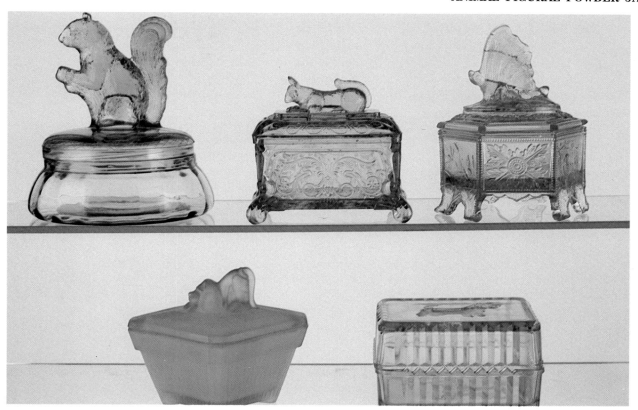

Row 1: (a) "Seated Squirrel," transparent green; (b) "Resting Squirrel," transparent pink; (c) "Rites of Spring" moth, transparent pink.
Row 2: (a) "Basset Hound," frosted pink; (b) "Bowser" Scottish terrier, transparent pink.

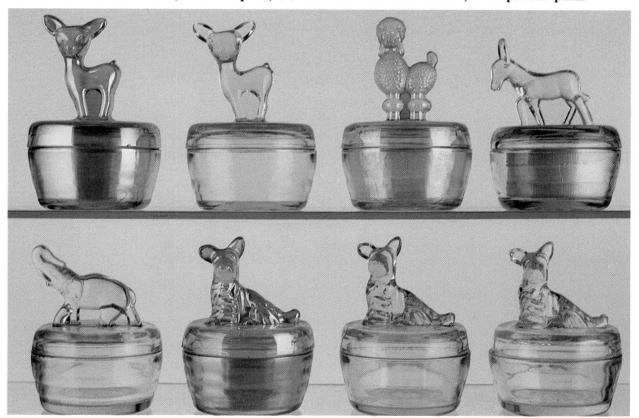

Row 1: (a) "Bambi," marigold iridescent; (b) "Bambi," transparent pink; (c) French poodle, marigold iridescent; (d) Donkey, crystal with original powder.
Row 2: (a) Elephant/trunk upraised, crystal; (b) Scotty, marigold iridescent; (c) Scotty, transparent pink; (d) Scotty, crystal.

The first and third jars on the top row are the same shape. These powder jars are 4" in diameter and feature a "lovebirds" finial. The finial features two dove-like kissing birds with slender beaks and short tails. Both the bottom and top parts are embossed with a delicate five-petal flower.

The center powder jar in the top row has a finial which consists of two parakeet-like birds. These birds have long tails and short curved beaks. The lid and bottom are both embossed with large fluffy flowers.

The finials of the first and third powder jars in the bottom row are the same. However, the remainder of these jars is vastly different. The penguins on the first jar are sitting on an almost square flat lid. The bottom of this jar is flat, and a large penguin protrudes from the center of each side. In addition to the black and frosted yellow colors pictured, this jar may be found in frosted green, frosted pink and jadite. The two loving penguins on the third powder jar are perched at the peak of a steeply sloping lid. The bottom of this jar is footed, and the two penguins appear on each side of a protruding center panel. This jar may also be found in frosted green. The base and lid of the "Egyptian Fountain" jar shown on page 37 is the same shape as this "Peaked Penguin" jar.

The crystal frosted powder jar in the center of the bottom row has two large parrots embossed on a slightly domed lid. The bottom of this jar is unembossed. Currently, this powder jar is being reproduced and sold by A & A Imports in transparent pink, cobalt, ruby and crystal. Other new colors may appear at any time. The only known original color is crystal. Many times the crystal jar was frosted, and the birds were enameled. Some frosted jars will also be found decorated with gold trim.

The pink frosted "Rabbit" puff box pictured at the bottom is very unusual. The narrow stylized rabbit head finial rises from the top of the flat rectangular-shaped lid. The head has a grain-like texture, and details include an embossed eye and whiskers on each side. Remaining features of the lid include a small raised tail on the rear center and several raised stylized embossed diagonal panels at the front of the right side and at the rear of the left side on the top surface. The base of the jar is footed. The front legs are styled in the shape of the rabbit's front feet, but the raised feet at the back of the jar lack any detail. Remaining detailing on the base consists of raised stylized embossed panels which match the ones on the lid. These are located on the sides of the base - on the rear half of the right side and on the front half of the left side. The underside is embossed "Dermay - Fifth Avenue - New York - 970." The puff box is 4½" long, 3¼" wide and 4½" high. The only colors we have seen are the frosted pink and frosted blue.

For information on the ruby Westmoreland elephant, see page 20.

	Crystal/ Frosted Crystal	Frosted Pink/Green	Black/Jadite Frosted Topaz
"Lovebirds"	$25.00-30.00	$35.00-40.00	
"Parakeets"	$70.00-80.00		
"Flat Penguins"		$75.00-85.00	$100.00-125.00
"Parrots"	$18.00-20.00		
"Peaked Penguins"		$75.00-85.00	
* "Rabbit"		$200.00-250.00	

* Frosted blue, $250.00-295.00

Row 1: (a,c) "Lovebirds," frosted pink and frosted green; (b) "Parakeets," frosted crystal.
Row 2: (a) "Flat Penguins," frosted topaz; (b) "Parrots," frosted crystal; (c) "Peaked Penguins," frosted pink.

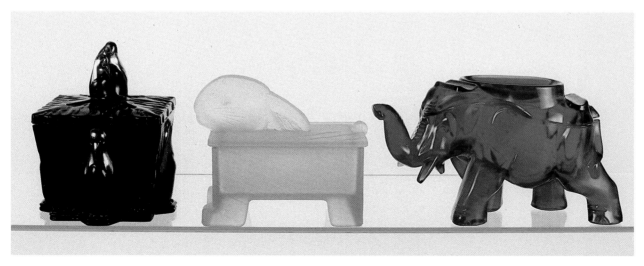

Left to right: (a) "Flat Penguins," black with silver trim; (b) "Rabbit," pink frosted; (c) "Jumbo," ruby with cigarette rest and ashtray back.

Two-piece animal figural boxes were very versatile utility items which glass companies produced for numerous marketing concerns. These containers were retailed containing such items as bubble bath, bath salts, bath powder, candy and cigarettes. Ads also touted the usefulness of these jars in the home when the contents were used.

The two-humped camel produced by Westmoreland in the 1930's is called "Humphrey." This camel is 6¼" long by 5½" high and was originally made in transparent pink, frosted pink, white milk glass and blue milk glass. In the late 1970's and early 1980's, Westmoreland reissued this camel in frosted amber, blue milk glass and white milk glass. These reissues were marked on the inside of the lid with the Westmoreland trademark - a "G" superimposed over a "W." Camels made in the 1930's do not have this trademark. After Westmoreland closed in 1985, the mold was obtained by Summit Art Glass.

"Jumbo" is a covered elephant container with a colorful history. It was originally made in the 1920's and 1930's by the Co-Operative Flint Glass Company. Two sizes - 4" x 7" and 6" x 13" - were produced. Colors available include: crystal, amber, cobalt, pink, black, white milk glass, green, ruby and crystal with fired-on colors. The lid shown on the elephant in the picture is referred to as the natural back. In addition, other styles of lids will be found. These include a top with holes for use as a flower frog, and one with cigarette rests and an indentation in the center for ashes (see page 19). In the early 1980's, Indiana Glass Company started reproducing the smaller elephant with the natural back lid. In 1981, these elephants were made in crystal and filled with jelly beans for distribution to members of the National Federation of Republican Women. In 1983, the Tiara Exclusives Division of Indiana Glass Company marketed this elephant in pink, blue, green and crystal with etching. Recently, the use of the mold has been acquired by a midwestern importer and reproductions have been seen in pink and green from this source.

"Kermit" - a sitting frog - was produced by the Co-Operative Flint Glass Company during the 1920's and 1930's. Transparent pink and transparent green are the most commonly found colors, but the jar may be found in the same array of colors as "Jumbo."

Other covered figural animal boxes were made during the same time period by the Co-Operative Flint Glass Company. These include a whale, a walking bear, a standing bulldog and a cat. The various colors of these animals are usually about the same as the colors for "Jumbo."

The frosted pink cosmetic jar in the top left of the bottom photo has a pair of snuggling, chubby ducklings on the lid. This design is repeated three times on the base. The jar is 4" in diameter, 4" tall and has been dubbed "Ducklings."

The name "Swallows" has been suggested for the small, squat powder jar in the center of the top row. It is 5" wide, but only 3½" tall. The knob, lid, and base of the frosted pink jar are embossed with multiple flying birds.

The third powder jar on the top row has a 3¾" square base with a round lid that is topped with a dove-like finial. All sides of the base are embossed with birds in flight and decorative lines, and the bottom is marked: "Dermay, Inc.; 5th Ave., N.Y." This frosted pink jar is part of a vanity set and has been named "Tweety Bird." Frosted green and frosted blue versions of this powder can also be found. See page 133 for the complete dresser set.

The small, three-footed, frosted green powder jar in the second row is 4¼" in diameter, 3" high and has an embossed swan on the lid. It is being called "Swimming Swan" and will also be found in frosted pink.

The frosted crystal swan powder jar was produced by the Jeannette Glass Company. The swan finial has a groove in its back which is designed to hold lipstick. The 4½" diameter jar was designed and patented in the 1920's and has been produced sporadically through the years. Original production colors were crystal, frosted crystal and marigold iridescent. In the 1960's, Jeannette made this jar in flashed-on colors - "amber-glo, amberina, and aquamarine." In the 1970's, flashed-on colors included red/amber and blue/green combinations. The Jeannette Glass Company closed in 1983, but this swan is still being produced for a midwestern importer. Present colors include flashed-on pink, light blue and amber. The detail of the feather embossing on the newer swans is not as sharp as on the older swans.

The large 6" long crystal duck, fondly called "Mama Quack" by collectors, came packaged with bubble bath for ladies and shaving soap for men. The duck was made by the Jeannette Glass Company from 1941 through the early 1950's. It will also be found in flashed-on iridescent marigold. The crystal ducks were sometimes decorated with handpainted eyes and bills.

	Crystal/ Frosted Crystal	Transparent Green/Pink	Frosted Green/Pink	Blue/White Milk Glass	Marigold Iridescent
* "Humphrey"		$125.00-150.00	$125.00-150.00	$125.00-150.00	
** "Jumbo"	$18.00-20.00	$35.00-45.00			
"Kermit"	$25.00-30.00	$80.00-90.00			
"Ducklings"			$45.00-50.00		
"Swallows"			$35.00-40.00		
*** "Tweety"			$35.00-40.00		
"Swimming Swan"			$35.00-40.00		
**** Jeannette swan	$8.00-10.00				
"Mama Quack"	$10.00-12.00				$12.00-15.00

* Camels with Westmoreland trademarks, $45.00 - $55.00
** Ruby, $175.00 - $225.00; black, $135.00 - $150.00; amber, $75.00 - $85.00; cobalt, $125.00 - $150.00; fired on colors, $85.00 - $95.00
*** Frosted Blue, $45.00 - $50.00
**** Older iridized colors, $12.00 - $15.00

Left to Right: (a) Westmoreland "Humphrey," frosted pink; (b) Co-Operative Flint "Jumbo," transparent blue; (c) Co-Operative Flint "Kermit," transparent pink.

Row 1: (a) "Ducklings", frosted pink; (b) "Swallows", frosted pink; "Tweety Bird", frosted pink.
Row 2: (a) "Swimming Swan", frosted green; (b) Jeannette swan, frosted crystal; (c) "Mama Quack", crystal.

AKRO AGATE SCOTTY PUFF BOXES

The Akro Agate Company of Clarksburg, West Virginia produced a heavy glass Scotty dog puff box for the dime store trade between 1939 and 1942. The two-part jar has a base with a slightly scalloped bottom. Four Scotties on a leash are embossed around the side of the base - two are seated and two are running. The underside is embossed "Made in U.S. of America" around the edge and also has the Akro Agate symbol - a flying crow with marbles in its beak and claws - in the center. A seated Scotty rises from the center of the domed lid and four more Scotties are embossed in a circle at the base of the finial. The jar is 3½" in diameter and 6½" tall.

As may be seen in the photo, both opaque and transparent colored puff boxes exist. The various shades of opaque blue are almost endless. These range from a light powder blue through turquoise to cobalt. Opaque colored boxes in white, pink, and lighter blues are seen most often. The opaque Scotty dog powders in lime green, dark green, and cobalt are more difficult for collectors to find than the opaque ones. The more desirable transparent jars are the ice blue and amber ones, but the crystal dog is equally hard to find.

For information on the Akro Agate Colonial Lady, see page 24.

	Opaque White/Pink	Opaque Light Blues	Opaque Cobalt/Green	Transparent Colors
Scotty Dog	$45.00-50.00	$55.00-65.00	$155.00-185.00	$185.00-225.00

Row 1: (a) Opaque pink Scotty; (b) opaque white Scotty; (c) opaque medium-blue Scotty; (d) opaque turquoise blue Scotty.
Row 2: (a) Lime green Scotty; (b) crystal Scotty; (c) transparent amber Scotty.

Left to right: (a) Transparent ice blue Scotty; (b) opaque pumpkin Colonial Lady; (c) opaque cobalt Scotty.

AKRO AGATE
COLONIAL LADY PUFF BOXES

The Colonial Lady puff boxes shown here were produced by the Akro Agate Company of Clarksburg, West Virginia. These jars are similar in composition to the heavy glass Scotty dog jars shown on the previous page. The base completes the skirt of the Colonial Lady. It is 3½" in diameter and is slightly ruffled at the bottom. The underside is marked in the center with the Akro trademark - a flying crow with marbles in its beak and claws - and around the edge with the embossed "Made in the U.S. of America." The domed lid has a finial with a Colonial Lady bust. Her head is tilted to the side, and her hands are clasped across her chest.

Jars in opaque white and opaque pink are easily found. A wide range of opaque blue colors is available - from a light powder blue to dark cobalt. Opaque green Colonial Lady jars are difficult to find. Transparent amber jars are rare, and the opaque pumpkin jar shown on the previous page is currently one-of-a-kind. The coloring of the jar shown on the right side of the top shelf is very unusual. It has a green marbleized effect on an opaque white background.

The opaque green Colonial Lady in the bottom photo still has its original powder insert. The attractively decorated box contains 4 oz. of Lavender dusting powder and was distributed by Lander of Fifth Avenue, New York.

	Opaque White/Pink	Opaque Light Blues	Opaque Cobalt/Green	Transparent Amber	Pumpkin Green Mar
Colonial Lady	$35.00-45.00	$43.00-55.00	$150.00-185.00	$185.00-225.00	UND

Top Row: (a) Opaque lime green Colonial Lady; (b) opaque white Colonial Lady; (c) opaque pink Colonial Lady; (d) opaque green marbleized Colonial Lady.

Bottom Row: (a) Opaque cobalt Colonial Lady; (b) opaque medium-blue Colonial Lady; (c) opaque turquoise Colonial Lady.

Opaque medium-green Colonial Lady with original powder.

HUMAN FIGURAL POWDER JARS

The large 3¾" wide by 5½" long by 6½" high rectangular-shaped powder jars on the top row are known as "Martha Washington's Trinket Box." The finial is comprised of three figures - a colonial style lady in the center accompanied by a young boy on one side and a young girl on the opposite side. The four-footed base is embossed with garlands of roses. The manufacturer of this powder jar has been identified as the New Martinsville Glass Manufacturing Company during the period 1937 - 1944. The frosted pink and frosted green jars are found more commonly, but transparent crystal, green, and pink ones also exist. A jar with a jadite lid and black base will also be found occasionally.

A 1931 Sears ad provides information about the powder jar on the second row. The jar came filled with Ramses body powder and featured a "frosted bowl made to represent a crinoline girl." Therefore, "Crinoline Girl" appears to be the perfect name for this jar, which orginally retailed for 59¢ - complete with powder. The lid consists of a lady wearing an off-shoulder hoop skirt gown. Her arms are by her sides, and she is holding a bouquet of flowers in one hand and a large round hat with flowers is hanging from her other arm. The bottom of the jar, with its prominently embossed bows, completes the skirt. This jar is 4½" in diameter and has been found in frosted pink, frosted green, frosted blue, crystal and transparent pink. The base of some of these powder jars will be marked "Ramses - Paris - N.Y."

At first glance, all the powder jars in the bottom photo appear to be the same style. However, upon closer examination, differences between the jars on the top row and those on the second row become apparent. The powder jars shown on the top row are being called "Curtsy." Their maker is unknown. The jars on the second row were called "Dancing Girl" by their maker - U.S. Glass. These U.S. Glass jars were produced between 1925 and 1936 and were sold as part of a dresser set, which includes two perfumes, a powder jar, and a matching tray. For an example of this set, see the U.S. Glass part of the perfume section.

Distinguishing features which allow collectors to differentiate between the two jars include:

1. The "Curtsy" finial's head is more upright than the "Dancing Girl's" head.

2. The facial features of "Curtsy" are somewhat crude and masculine, whereas the face of "Dancing Girl" is detailed and feminine.

3. On the lid of the "Curtsy" jar, there is a row of four embossed beads between the puffs in the skirt near the lady's downward extended arm.

4. The base of the "Curtsy" jar is usually marked "Toussant Glass." This may also be spelled "Taussaunt" or "Taussant." The base of the "Dancing Girl" jar is unmarked.

5. The top edge of the base of the "Curtsy" jar is smooth, while the top edge of the base of the "Dancing Girl" jar has a rope rim.

The "Curtsy" powder jar has been found in frosted pink, frosted green, frosted blue and jadite. The "Dancing Girl" jar is found in the three frosted colors, but the colors are generally a little brighter than those of the "Curtsy" jar. In addition, the "Dancing Girl" powder was advertised as being available in transparent colors. A transparent pink jar is shown in the photo.

	Frosted Crystal/ Crystal	Transparent Pink/Green	Frosted Pink/Green	Frosted Blue
* "Martha Washington"	$40.00-45.00	$95.00-110.00	$85.00-95.00	
"Crinoline Girl"	$30.00-40.00	$75.00-85.00	$50.00-60.00	$90.00-110.00
** "Curtsy"			$50.00-55.00	$60.00-70.00
"Dancing Girl"		$75.00-85.00	$55.00-65.00	$75.00-85.00

* With jadite top and black base, $110.00 - $135.00
** Jadite, $90.00 - $125.00

Row 1: (a) "Martha Washington Trinket Box," jadite top with black base; (b) "Martha Washington Trinket Box," crystal; (c) "Martha Washington Trinket Box," frosted pink.
Row 2: (a) "Crinoline Girl," frosted pink; (b) "Crinoline Girl," crystal; (c) "Crinoline Girl," frosted green.

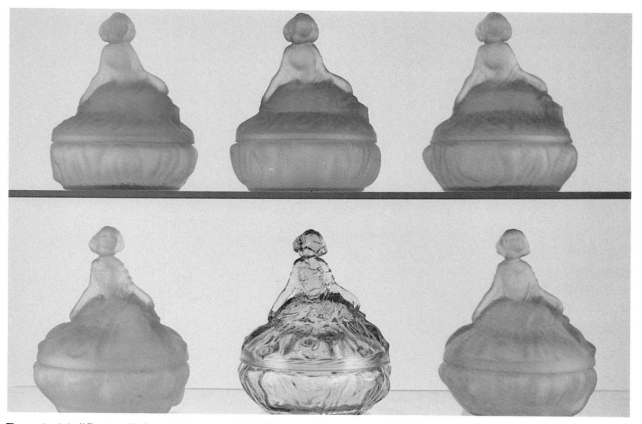

Row 1: (a) "Curtsy," frosted green; (b) "Curtsy," frosted pink; (c) "Curtsy," frosted blue.
Row 2: (a) "Dancing Girl,", frosted pink; (b) "Dancing Girl," transparent pink; (c) "Dancing Girl," frosted green.

The powder jar in the top photo with the finial head and shoulders of a lady with short bobbed hair is called "Babs I." This is a round jar, 4½" in diameter, with a three-footed bottom, which has been found in frosted pink and frosted green. The orginal label on the frosted green jar reads "Dermay - Fifth Ave. - N.Y. - Bath Powder." This same finial is also found on a different style powder jar, which is shown on the bottom row of the photo at the bottom of the page.

The "Lillian I" powder jar pictured in the center of the top row, we have only seen in frosted crystal. The short-haired "Lillian I" torso is atop a gently curved and paneled top. The bottom is smooth, 5½" in diameter, and the underside is marked with an "HA" - the trademark of the Hazel Atlas Glass Company. Other styles of powder boxes with the "Lillian" finial are shown on the next page.

The first two powder jars on the second row have a finial head and shoulders depicting a rather classy-looking Flapper named "Liz." She has a long elegant floral scarf draped over her shoulders, which gracefully swirls around and covers the entire surface of the lid. The bottom is 5½" in diameter and is covered with multiple embossed flowers. This jar is known to exist with a frosted crystal lid and frosted green bottom, a frosted crystal lid and a frosted pink bottom, and a jadite lid and bottom.

"Annabella" is the name which has been given to the jar with the finial head with her hair pulled back into a chignon. The amber powder jar pictured has an Art Deco design etched in gold on the lid surface. The plain round bottom is made of very heavy glass and has a deep well for the powder and puff. The jar measures 3½" high and is 4¾" in diameter. Transparent amber and transparent pink are the colors which have appeared. In addition, a modified version of this jar exists in which the head finial has been replaced with a Deco-looking triangular knob. See the miscellaneous powder jars for custard and jadite examples of this jar.

In the bottom photo, powder jars "Lillian II" and "Lillian III" have the same torso on top of different styles of lids and bottoms. The lid and base of the first jar have all-over ripples. The second powder jar has a lid with a stippled surface and a base with a smooth hexagonal center band which separates areas with a stippled surface. The bases of the jars are like the ones used with the animals with the miniature finials shown on page 13. Both powder jars have been found in frosted crystal and frosted pink.

The name "Joker" has been given to the transparent green powder jar with the finial head wearing a skull cap. The surface of the lid has embossed stipples, and the base has a smooth hexagonal middle which separates two areas of embossed stipples. The jars on the bottom row in this picture have the same shape and style of body.

The seated lady wearing a bathing suit is called "Minnie." The full-figure female finial has her arms folded across her waist and her legs outstretched along the top of the lid.

"Babs II" is a smaller version of the three-footed jar shown on the top row of the photo above. This jar is found in frosted crystal and transparent cobalt, which is somewhat of an unusual color for powder jars.

	Frosted Crystal/ Crystal	Transparent Green/Pink/ Amber	Frosted Green/Pink	Jadite	Cobalt
"Babs I"			$40.00-45.00		
"Lillian I"	$60.00-65.00				
* "Liz				$95.00-110.00	
"Annabella"		$40.00-50.00			
** "Lillian II"	$25.00-30.00		$40.00-45.00		
"Lillian III"	$25.00-30.00		$50.00-60.00		
"Joker"	$20.00-25.00	$60.00-65.00	$45.00-55.00		
"Minnie"	$25.00-35.00		$57.00-62.00		
"Babs II"	$20.00-35.00		$45.00-55.00		$90.00-110.00

* Frosted crystal lid with frosted pink or green bottom, $40.00 - $50.00
** Frosted Lavender, $40.00 - $45.00

Row 1: (a) "Babs I," frosted green; (b) "Lillian I," frosted crystal; (c) "Babs I," frosted pink.
Row 2: (a) "Liz," frosted crystal lid/frosted green bottom; "Liz," jadite; (c) "Annabella," amber.

Row 1: (a) "Lillian II," frosted lavender (sun-turned); (b) "Lillian III," frosted crystal; (c) "Joker," transparent green.
Row 2: (a) "Minnie," frosted green; (b) "Babs II," frosted crystal; (c) "Babs II," transparent cobalt.

The finial of the "Three Sisters" powder jar is formed by the figures of three ladies seated with their backs to each other. The balance of the lid is in the form of their large ruffled, tiered skirts. The base has an embossed ripple design and is the same as the one used with the large 6" diameter standing elephant with the trunk down. The colors which have been found are frosted green and frosted pink.

"Lillian IV," who was marketed by the George Button Corporation of New York in the late 1920's, is wearing a three-tier skirt. Two of the tiers are formed by the lid, and the third tier is completed by the 6¾" wide base. The torso of a lady with short curly hair who is holding a large bouquet of flowers to her chest forms the finial. This same finial will be found atop six other different style powder jars. The base of this powder jar is the same as the one used with "Woodsy," the large owl. Colors available include frosted pink, frosted blue, frosted green and frosted crystal.

The "Victorian Lady" powder jar features the torso of a lovely girl wearing a fancy hoop skirt. The girl has a bonnet on her head, her arms are folded at her waist; a basket is hanging from one arm and a parasol is in her other hand. Garlands of flowers and bows encircle the bottom edge of the skirt above a row of ruffling. The bottom is 4½" in diameter, embossed with a trellis-like design and is marked "Dermay, Inc. - 5th Ave - N.Y." along with the number "972." Frosted pink and frosted green are the colors which have been found.

The "Southern Belle" powder jar has the finial torso of a bonneted lady wearing a hoop skirt. The lady has both arms extended outward at a downward angle and is holding a nosegay in her left hand. The upper part of the skirt has floral panels and a scalloped edge which forms the rim of the lid. The lower portion of the skirt is completed by the base of the jar which is 5" in diameter. Frosted green and frosted pink are the known colors. Three different styles of lamps were also produced using the lid to this jar. See the lamp section for more information.

The "Lillian" finial keeps showing up on additional powder jars. Three different jars which have been found recently are shown in the pictures at the bottom of these two pages. The "Lillian V" jar, below, has the same lid as "Lillian I," but the base has been modified to include three feet. There is also a Greek key design embossed around the center of the bottom and both the top and bottom are accented with gold.

The "Lillian VI," shown in bottom photo on page 31 is also similar to "Lillian I." The base is the same but the top lacks panels. This jar has only been seen in frosted crystal. The pink frosted cone-shaped jar is "Lillian VII." The jar appears to be shaped more like a candy jar than a powder jar. It is 8" tall and has also been found in frosted green and frosted crystal.

	Crystal/ Frosted Crystal	Transparent Green/Pink	Frosted Green/Pink	Frosted Blue
"Three Sisters"			$75.00-85.00	
"Lillian IV"	$40.00-50.00		$80.00-90.00	$100.00-125.00
"Victorian Lady"			$60.00-70.00	
"Southern Belle"			$75.00-90.00	
"Lillian V"	$70.00-$75.00			
"Lillian VI"	$60.00-65.00			
"Lillian VII"	$90.00-100.00	$125.00-150.00		

"Lillian V," frosted crystal with gold encrusted decoration.

Row 1: (a) "Pandora," frosted pink; (b) "Pandora," frosted green.
Row 2: (a) "Godiva," frosted green; (b) "Simone," crystal finial with black base; (c) "Godiva," frosted pink.

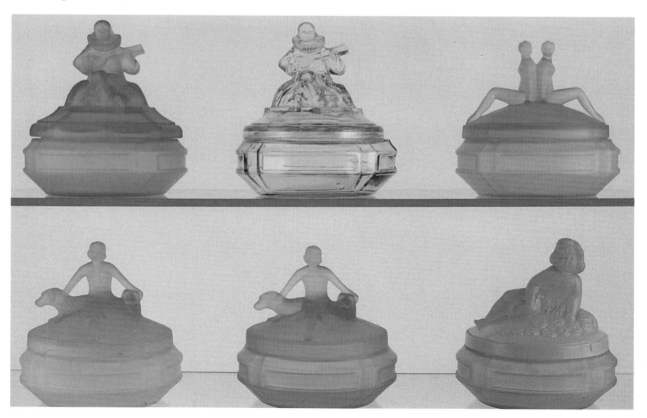

Row 1: (a) "Minstrel," frosted green; (b) "Minstrel," crystal; (c) "Twins," frosted green.
Row 2: (a) "Annette," frosted pink; (b) "Annette," frosted green; (c) "Cherub," baked-on pink lid frosted pink bottom.

The powder jar shown in the top photo is called "Lovers." The finial consists of a man and woman embracing. The base is a 5" oval with varigated vertical ridges. This jar is found most often in frosted green and frosted pink, but other combinations such as crystal frosted tops with black, frosted green or frosted pink bases may also be found. The lid of this jar was also used to produce a lamp. A hole was drilled behind the finial and four small feet were added. For more information, see the lamp section.

The frosted pink powder jar in the center of the top shelf of the bottom photo has been named "Wendy." The finial is comprised of a flapper girl with outstretched arms, which appears to be holding her skirt down. She is wearing a low-cut gown with a double strand of beads around her neck. The base is a four-footed 5½" oval. Other colors, in addition to the frosted pink shown, include frosted green, frosted crystal and crystal with flashed colors. "Wendy" may also be found in crystal with elaborate paint. An example is shown on the right side of the top photo.

The emerald green powder jar is known as "Cabbage Patch Baby." The 5¼" diameter round powder jar has large overlapping embossed leaves which look like a head of cabbage. The finial torso of a chubby baby appears to be emerging from the center of the cabbage head. The idea for this style jar possibly evolved from the old fable which told of finding babies in a cabbage patch.

The frosted pink powder jar on the bottom row has a base which is 4½" long and is divided into two compartments. It is marked, "Dermay - Fifth Ave. - N.Y. - 971." The lid is rectangular and sports a small child on an elevated platform who is leaning over hugging a puppy. "Puppy Love" has been suggested as a name for this jar.

The jar in the middle of the bottom row is called "Flappers." The round lid is plain with a ball knob. The bottom is decorated with the figures of three evenly-spaced flappers who are kneeling to form the feet of this jar. The jar's diameter is 4¼", and its height is 4". Frosted pink and opaque black jars with handpainted floral decorated lids will also be found.

The name "Antoinette," has been given to the jar on the right side of the bottom row. The finial is comprised of a Colonial lady who is wearing a hoop skirt gown, which is completed by the base of the jar. Her hair is swept up and is accented with a band around her head and by the addition of a flower above one ear. Her right arm is upraised at the elbow to cradle a long floral garland. Matching perfumes exist, and other colors which have been found include a frosted crystal top and transparent amber base, transparent pink base, or transparent blue base. See page 144.

	Crystal/ Frosted Crystal	Frosted Green/Pink	Frosted Emerald	Fired-on Colors	Black
* "Lovers"		$80.00-90.00			
"Wendy"	$35.00-40.00	$75.00-85.00		$65.00-75.00	
"Cabbage Patch Baby"			$70.00-80.00		
"Puppy Love"		$110.00-125.00			
"Flappers"		$40.00-50.00			$75.00-85.00
** "Antoinette"					

* Frosted crystal top with black base, $100.00 - $110.00.
* Frosted crystal top with frosted green or pink base, $70.00 - $80.00.
** Frosted top with clear green, pink, blue or amber base, $25.00 - $30.00.

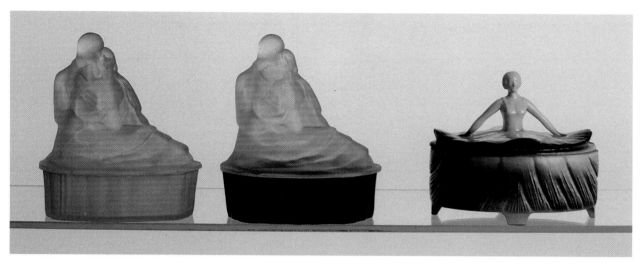

Left to right: (a) "Lovers," crystal top with green base; (b) "Lovers," frosted crystal top with frosted green base; (c) "Wendy," crystal with elaborate paint.

Row 1: (a) "Lovers," frosted green; (b) "Wendy," frosted pink; (c) "Cabbage Patch Baby," frosted emerald.
Row 2: (a) "Puppy Love," frosted pink; (b) "Flappers," frosted green; (c) "Antoinette," frosted lavender top with transparent green base.

The large 3½" wide by 6½" long by 5¼" high rectangular powder jar with the reclining draped nude finial is called "Cleopatra I." The partially draped figure is lying with one arm propped on a cushion, and the other arm is stretched outward resting on an urn. A different sport scene - golf, polo, football and tennis - is depicted in intricate detail on each side of the bottom. Known colors of this jar are black, frosted crystal, frosted pink and frosted green.

The crystal jar ("Delilah I") on the left side of the second row and the transparent pink powder jar ("Delilah II") in the center of the row have the same style lids. The finial is composed of a draped nude in a reclining position with one arm resting on a cushion, and her other arm behind her body. One leg is outstretched with its toes touching the front corner of the lid, and her other leg is bent at the knee and tucked under the outstretched leg. The bottom of the crystal jar has seven convex vertical panels across the front and back. In the April, 1976 "National Depression Glass Journal," author Mary Van Pelt attributes this powder jar to the American Glass Company. It was shown in a 1940's catalogue published by General Glassware. The base of the pink jar has six flat vertical panels across the front and back and rests upon four feet. Each of the panels contains a single embossed flower with its accompanying stem and leaves. This same base in frosted pink is used with the coach puff box pictured on page 47. A reprint in "Collecting Glass - Volume 3" by William Heacock shows this jar in a mid-1930's Nestle's Milk Products premium book. Jars in black and frosted green have also been found. The "Delilah" lid was also modified by adding four feet and drilling a hole behind the knee of the extended leg to produce a lamp. See the reprint shown on page 172 in the lamp section.

The crystal jar on the right side of the second row is a variation of the larger jars on the top row. This jar is "Cleopatra II" and features a more shallow base and a deeper lid to produce a jar which is only 4¾" high. The detailing on the finial is undefinable, and the position of the legs is altered in relation to those on the "Cleopatra I" jar above it. The outstretched legs of "Cleopatra I" trail to the side of the lid and her toes point toward the center. The legs of the crystal "Cleopatra II" are positioned so her toes point toward the front corner of the lid. This jar was pictured in a catalogue by General Glassware in the 1940's and was produced by the American Glass Company according to Mary Van Pelt.

"Cleopatra III" is similar to "Cleopatra II." It has the same increased depth to its lid, and the toes of the lady are again pointed toward the front corner of the lid, but the details of the finial are more intricate. The base has been redesigned to include six feet. An example may be seen in the bottom photo which shows a black jar with a gold-colored finial. This jar is 6½" long, 3¼" wide and 5¼" tall. Additional colors found include jars in frosted green and frosted pink.

The frosted pink "Egyptian Fountain" four-footed powder jar with the high peaked lid is the same shape as the penguin jar pictured on page 19. A pair of long stem flowers adorns each of the four corners of the lid. Eight kneeling nudes with upraised forearms grace the corners of the base. An elaborate fountain spewing streams of water is featured on each of the four protruding center panels of the base. The underside of the base is marked "Ramses - Paris - New York." The jar is 4½" square and 5¾" tall. According to an ad in a 1930-31 Montgomery Ward catalogue this jar was marketed with Ramses scented bath powder and the retail price was 85¢. The "Egyptian Fountain" has only been found in frosted pink but should also exist in other frosted colors.

The tall black powder jar in the lower photo on the right is called "Carrie." For more information on this jar, see page 38.

	Crystal/ Frosted Crystal	Frosted Green/Pink	Transparent Green/Pink	Black
"Cleopatra I"	$75.00-85.00	$100.00-125.00		$150.00-175.00
"Cleopatra II"	$45.00-55.00			
"Cleopatra III"		$80.00-90.00		$110.00-125.00
"Delilah I"	$40.00-50.00			
"Delilah II"		$75.00-85.00	$90.00-100.00	$95.00-110.00
"Egyptian Fountain"		$85.00-95.00		

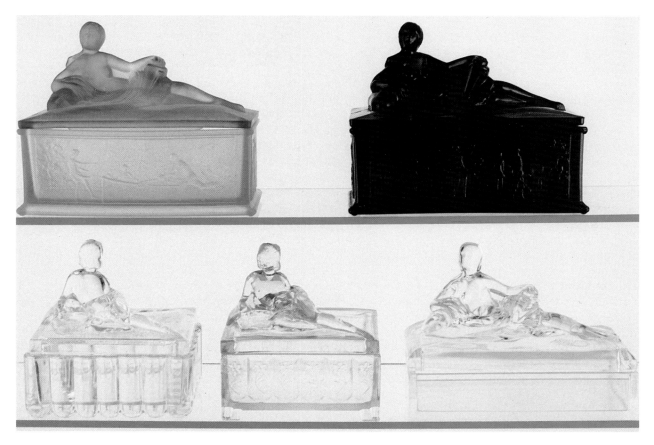

Row 1: (a) "Cleopatra I," frosted pink; (b) "Cleopatra I," black.
Row 2: (a) "Delilah I," crystal with convex ribbed base; (b) "Delilah II," transparent pink with four-footed, flat, floral-paneled base, (c) "Cleopatra II," crystal.

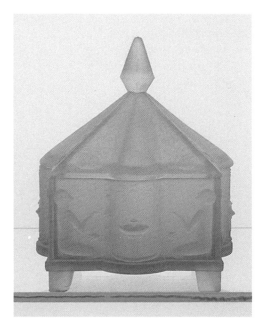

"Egyptian Fountain," frosted pink.

Left: "Cleopatra III," black with gold painted finial.
Right: "Carrie," black with handpainted flowers.

"Carrie" is the name associated with the draped nude figure with the round powder bowl balanced on her head. This 9¾" tall jar is found most often in frosted colors with handpainted flowers on the lid and round pedestal foot. The bottom of the base is marked "DERMAY - 5th Ave. - New York," but this will usually be obscured on the frosted jars. Known colors include frosted green, frosted pink, frosted cobalt, frosted yellow, black and white milk glass.

An importer is currently having the base of these powder jars reproduced in various frosted and transparent colors. This lidless version is being marketed as a tall compote. Currently, all handpainted jars are old.

The middle powder jar in the top photo is 8½" high. It features a "Spring Nymph," under a garland of flowers. The finial is comprised of a kneeling nude with a drape across her lap. The urn-shaped base has curlicue handles, a pedestal foot and is marked "940." The colors which have appeared are frosted green, frosted crystal, frosted blue and white milk glass. A lamp has also been found in frosted crystal. The base has four small feet added to allow clearance for the cord, which is typical of other lamps of this type. The interior of the base is also lacquered with an opaque green color which causes most of the light to be emitted through the frosted lid and finial. See page 171.

The powder bowl of "Prima Donna" forms a large round tutu. The 7¾" tall standing figure has her hands crossed, and she is clutching a bouquet of flowers to her chest. The ballerina's legs extend from the base of the bowl and rest on a round base. Correct alignment of the lid and base is assured through the utilization of a bar and slot on the interior surface. The base is marked "Ramses, Inc. - N.Y. - 411." In addition to the frosted green jar shown, frosted pink will also be found. An ad in an early 1930's Montgomery Ward catalogue shows the jar was originally sold filled with Ramses perfumed bath powder and a velour puff. The price, including shipping was 98¢. The lid of this jar with the addition of five tiny feet was also used to form the base of a lamp. The original shade is made of glass and has a band of ribbing at the top with a large beaded edge. See page 171.

The 8" tall "Lady Cameo" powder jars shown to the left in the bottom photo, have an oval bowl and an oval foot. The finial is the profile of a head of a lovely lady with short, curly hair. A headband crosses the top of her head with a flower positioned over each ear. The surface of the lid has twelve narrow embossed bands of overlapping leaves which radiate outward from the finial. Between each band of leaves is a single embossed flower. The powder compartment has four plain recessed embossed hearts. The area between the hearts is embossed with multiple-sized leaves. The pedestal stem contains an embossed cameo which matches the finial of the lid, and the bottom of the pedestal is flanked by two curlicues. The only two colors we have seen are frosted green and frosted pink.

The "Ballerina I" powder on the right in the bottom photo is similar to "Prima Donna." However, the 8¼" "Ballerina I" is wearing an oval ruffled tutu. Her hands are crossed and resting on her chest. According to patent information, this jar was designed in 1930 by Milton Sierad of New York. It was designed as a face powder container, and the rights to the design were assigned to the George W. Button Corporation of New York. The known colors are frosted crystal, frosted green and frosted pink. Another powder jar, "Ballerina II," will be found. This jar is identical to the ones pictured, except the arms of the figure are extended outward. This jar is found in the same colors as "Ballerina I."

	Frosted Crystal	Frosted Green/Pink	Frosted Blue/ Cobalt	White Milk Glass	Black
"Carrie"		$50.00-65.00	$80.00-90.00	$90.00-110.00	$110.00-125.00
"Spring Nymph"	$35.00-40.00	$75.00-85.00			
"Prima Donna"		$100.00-125.00			
"Lady Cameo"		$50.00-65.00			
* "Ballerina I"	$35.00-45.00	$70.00-80.00			
"Ballerina II"	$40.00-50.00	$90.00-110.00			

* Frosted lavender (sun-turned), $45.00 - $55.00

Left to Right: (a) "Carrie," frosted pink; (b) "Spring Nymph," frosted green; (c) "Prima Donna," frosted green.

Left to Right: (a) "Lady Cameo," frosted pink; (b) "Lady Cameo," frosted green; (c) "Ballerina I," frosted lavender; (d) "Ballerina I," frosted green.

The powder jars at both ends of the top row with the kneeling nude finial are being called "Rapunzel." The girl is leaning forward and has a beaded entity cascading from her hands to the top of the lid. Identification of the cascading beads has perplexed numerous collectors. They have been called many things, including water, a rope, flowers and even the nude's hair. The base of the jar is round, 4½" in diameter, and has four small feet. Its bottom is marked "Dermay Inc. - 5th Ave. - N.Y. - 973." Colors which have been found are frosted green, frosted pink, frosted blue, black and white milk glass.

The name "Dolly Sisters" has been suggested for the large powder jar in the center of the top row. The jar consists of two kneeling nudes who are facing outward with their backs supporting a large, round covered powder container. The lid is round, cone-shaped, with concentric ribs on the outer surface. Frosted green and frosted pink are the two colors which have been found.

"Camellia" is a powder jar with a finial comprised of a seated nude figural who has one leg extended and the other leg bent at the knee and turned to the side. One of her arms is by her side, and her other arm is draped across her waist. The general shape of the jar is a gently rounded square. Each of the corners contains a large camellia blossom - half the blossom is on the lid, and the other half of the blossom is completed by the upper portion of the base. Mary Van Pelt attributes this jar to the Phoenix Glass Company in her book "Fantastic Figurines." The known colors are frosted green and frosted pink. This lid is also shown on a different-shaped base in a 1933 Montgomery Ward catalogue. This combination is advertised as a lamp in which the "light glows through the artistically modeled amber glass figure on top." The metal base is described as being finished in a brown lacquer, and the reprint shows the top of the base is embossed with a floral design which completes the floral pattern of the lid. This lamp is pictured on page 171.

The powder jar with the finial of the seated flapper who is hugging her legs is called "Claudette." She is wearing a flowing gown and has a headband across her forehead which continues around her head. The bottom has four oval panels with sailboat scenes. Each panel is separated by a double fan design. The sailboat scenes and the double fan designs are embossed in transparent glass, but the remainder of the jar is frosted. This frosted vaseline jar is the only example of this style we have seen.

The powder jars in the bottom picture are shown on two different variations of the same shaped base. Both bottoms have the hexagonal center panel and are large-size with a diameter of 6". On most of the jars, two areas of embossed stipples are separated by the smooth hexagonal center panel. The jar on the right side of the first row illustrates the second style of embossing. Both the lid and base of this jar are covered with embossed ripples. The stippled base also may be found with a stippled-style lid in which the figural finial has been replaced with a plain knob. An example of this type jar in transparent pink may be seen on page 59.

The jar with the semi-nude torso finial is called "Gretchen." The young lady is posing with her arms crossed over her chest. Her hair is pulled into a bun over both ears and is parted down the middle of her head. This powder jar has only been found with a stippled background and is known to exist in frosted green and pink and in transparent green. A seated flapper girl named "Jackie" shares the same style stippled base as "Gretchen." She has also been found on rippled background as shown on the powder jar at the right of the top row. The finial portrays a seated young lady with her legs bent upward at the knees. She has short, curly hair, and her head is leaning slightly toward one side. One arm is bent upward at the elbow with her hand resting on her chest, and her other arm is resting on her leg. She is wearing a short, hip-length jacket with its collar turned up. This powder jar has been found with both styles of backgrounds in frosted green and frosted pink. It has been found with the stippled background in transparent pink, pink flashed over crystal, jadite and jadite lid with a black base.

	Frosted Green/Pink	Frosted Vaseline	Frosted Blue	Black/White Milk Glass
"Rapunzel"	$75.00-85.00		$100.00-125.00	$110.00-125.00
"Dolly Sisters"	$90.00-110.00			
"Camellia"	$85.00-95.00			
"Claudette"		$75.00-85.00		
* "Gretchen"	$55.00-65.00			
** "Jackie"	$50.00-57.00			

* Transparent green or pink, $75.00 - $85.00.
** Jadite or Jadite/Black combination, $100.00 - $125.00.

40

Row 1: (a) "Rapunzel," frosted pink; (b) "Dolly Sisters," frosted green; (c) "Rapunzel," frosted green.
Row 2: (a) "Camellia," frosted green; (b) "Camellia," frosted pink; (c) "Claudette," frosted vaseline.

Row 1: (a) "Gretchen," frosted green; (b) "Gretchen," transparent green; (c) "Gretchen, frosted pink; (d) "Jackie," frosted green with rippled background.
Row 2: (a) "Jackie," frosted pink with stippled background; (b) "Jackie," jadite stippled lid with black stippled base; (c) "Jackie," jadite stippled lid with light jadite stippled base.

The two powder jars on the left side of the top row in the bottom photo have the same lid. The finial features a reclining nude, called "Salome," with her legs bent toward the back of the jar. One arm is supporting her, and her other arm is bent over her head. Long hair flows down one side of the nude's back and arcs onto the rear surface of the lid. A flowing drape on the front of her body extends onto the front surface of the lid. The different shapes of the bases provide collectors with an opportunity to collect two similar, but uniquely different, attractive powder jars. Both styles of jars are available in frosted green and frosted pink.

The right side of the top row is completed by two jars called "Mermaid and Cockleshell." The finial has a mermaid seated in front of a large cockleshell. One of her arms is extended down to her side, and her other arm is slightly bent with her hand resting in her lap. The mermaid's tail is curled toward the back side of the jar. The base of the jar is embossed with swimming fish, waves and bubbles. The jar is probably of foreign origin and will be found as part of a vanity set with other matching accessory pieces which also includes two cold cream jars, a ring holder and a tray. Colors which have been found are frosted green and frosted pink.

All the powder jars on the bottom row have the same embossing on the base. The only difference in the bases is the jars with the celluloid lids have feet and the jar with the glass lid has a flat base. The base has eight panels which alternate in size. The four small panels contain an embossed nude, and the four wide panels have embossed sweeping vertical lines which produce a woodgrain effect. The jars with the celluloid lids are part of a vanity set which also contains a narrow rectangular celluloid tray and two rectangular glass perfume bottles encased in celluloid. The colors which have been found are frosted green, frosted pink, and frosted amber.

The jar with the glass lid has been named "Roxana." The finial depicts a nude in a seated position with her arms outstretched. A graceful draping covers most of the nude. This draping flows onto the lid and covers its entire surface. The underside of the base is marked "Ramses - Paris - New York." An ad in an early 1930's Montgomery Ward catalogue lists this jar filled with Ramses perfumed bath powder and a velour puff for 49¢ postpaid. Colors which have been seen are frosted green and frosted pink.

The powder jar featured in the drawing in the bottom photo was designed by Helen Hileman according to U.S. Patent Office information. The patent was filed October 20, 1924 and was assigned to the Phoenix Glass Company.

Although the article was supposed to have been produced in frosted pink and green, none of the collectors we know has this jar in their possession. We are supplying this drawing in the hope that a reader will be able to help us locate a jar of this design.

	Frosted Green/Pink
"Salome I"	$80.00-90.00
"Salome II"	$80.00-90.00
"Mermaid and Cockleshell"	$35.00-40.00
*Celluloid lid/"Roxana" base	$20.00-25.00
"Roxana"	$45.00-50.00
"Phoenix Sunbather"	UND

*Amber, $25.00 - $30.00

Row 1: (a) "Salome I," frosted green; (b) "Salome II," frosted green; (c) "Mermaid and Cockleshell," frosted pink; (d) "Mermaid and Cockleshell," frosted green.
Row 2: (a) Footed "Roxana" base with celluloid lid, frosted amber; (b) "Roxana," frosted green; (c) Footed "Roxana" base with celluloid lid, frosted green.

"Phoenix Sunbather" from U.S. Patent Office drawing.

POWDER JARS WITH FIGURAL FINIALS

"Court Jester" is the name of the powder jar displayed in the top picture. The finial is comprised of a jester head with the typical ruffled collar around his neck. The bottom is round, 5¼" in diameter, and contains twelve square tab-like feet. Most of the bases also bear the mark "Taussaunt Glass" on the bottom. This jar has been found in a variety of colors which include frosted green, frosted pink, frosted blue, frosted yellow, frosted black, shiny black, jadite and transparent green. According to an article in the February, 1977 "Depression Glass Daze" by Sophia Papapanu, the patent for this jar was obtained by Jerome E. Baum in 1929. The "Court Jester" has been found with a "Dermay Bath Powder" paper label and also with a "Wrisley Quality" paper label. This suggests that more than one powder company used this jar to promote their products.

The "Vamp" powder jar on the left side of the top row in the bottom photo has a finial with an upward tilted flapper's head with short, bobbed hair. The base is a hexagonal-shaped jar with a four-footed bottom. The underside is marked "Ramses." The embossing on the panels of the base alternates between panels with a nude with outstretched arms and panels with a single large daisy-like flower. Colors which have been found are frosted green and frosted pink. The jar has been found advertised with Ramses Bath Powder in an early 1930's Montgomery Ward catalogue. Original cost of the jar complete with bath powder and a velour powder puff was 59¢ postpaid.

The 7¾" tall "Roly-Poly Clown" protrudes prominently from the center position of the shelf. This is a large two-piece bubble bath container with a clown head finial and clown suit base which has been reported in frosted green and frosted pink.

The "Lotus" powder jar has a flower bud finial and an eight-pointed, star-shaped base with four feet. This jar is 3¾" high and 5" in diameter and is found most often in frosted crystal, but it has also been seen in frosted green, frosted pink and transparent pink.

The "Sphinx" powder jars shown on the bottom row are also called "King Tut" by some collectors. The finial is comprised of the head of a sphinx, and the jar is a cone-shaped hexagon with a three-footed unembossed base. Some jars have been found marked "Taussaunt" and one has been found with an original paper label, inscribed "Dermay - 5th Ave. - N.Y. - Bath Powder." Colors which have been found include frosted green, frosted pink, frosted yellow, frosted blue and black.

	Frosted Crystal	Frosted Green/Pink	Frosted Black/Blue	Frosted Yellow	Black Trans. Green
"Court Jester"		$45.00-55.00	$55.00-75.00	$60.00-70.00	$80.00-85.00
"Vamp"		$55.00-65.00			
"Roly-Poly Clown"		$80.00-100.00			
"Lotus"	$30.00-35.00	$50.00-55.00			
"Sphinx"		$50.00-60.00	$85.00-95.00	$85.00-95.00	$90.00-110.00

Row 1: (a) "Court Jester," frosted black; (b) "Court Jester," frosted yellow; (c) "Court Jester," frosted blue.
Row 2: (a) "Court Jester," frosted pink; (b) "Court Jester," frosted green.

Row 1: (a) "Vamp," frosted green; (b) "Roly-Poly Clown," frosted green; (c) "Lotus," frosted crystal.
Row 2: (a) "Sphinx," frosted pink; (b) "Sphinx," black; (c) "Sphinx," frosted yellow.

COACHES

According to patent information, the "Royal Coach," shown below, was designed as a face powder container by A.E. Sierad. The patent application was filed on November 6, 1930, and rights were assigned to the George W. Button Corporation of New York. The coach has a rectangular base with its two ends curved slightly upward. The lid sports a crown finial and has only been found in black. The various colors for the base include black, frosted green, frosted pink and transparent green.

The large crystal coach on the top row of the bottom photo has been named "Cinderella's Coach." It has essentially a rectangular body which narrows at one end where there is a small protrusion for the coachman's feet to rest. The underside of the base is marked with the numbers "452." The coach was made by the L.E. Smith Glass Company from the 1930's to the 1970's. During the 1930's, the coach was produced in frosted green and frosted pink with black lids. Later, during the early 1950's, the coach was reissued in white milk glass, and department store customers in the mid-1970's were treated with its reappearance in crystal. The cost of the new crystal coach in 1976 was about $7.00.

The small coaches on the bottom row are miniature versions of L.E. Smith's "Cinderella's Coach." They have the same details as the larger coach and were made in the same colors during the same eras, with the exception that they were not reissued in crystal during the 1970's. The underside of the base will be marked with the numbers "222," and some of the white milk glass coaches from the 1950's may be found with a silver and blue label which reads "Handmade by L.E. Smith."

Two different styles of "Horse-drawn Coach" may be found - round and square. The finial is a stagecoach pulled by a two-horse team. Many times, the finial will be painted, featuring a gold coach and white horses with a black harness. The round base has six half-circle feet which are embossed with spokes. The top half of the wheel is embossed into the base of the powder jar. Also, embossed around the base are prancing horses with coachmen who are wearing top hats and knee-length coats. The square base is the same as the one used with the "Delilah II" jar shown on page 37. This base has six flat vertical panels on each side, all containing a single flower.

	Crystal	Frosted Green/Pink	Transparent Green	White Milk Glass	Black
"Royal Coach"		$85.00-95.00	$110.00-140.00		$120.00-150.00
"Cinderella's Coach" large version	$18.00-22.00	$90.00-110.00		$60.00-80.00	
"Cinderella's Coach" small version		$80.00-90.00		$60.00-80.00	
"Horse-drawn Coach" round version		$125.00-150.00			
"Horse-drawn Coach" square version		$125.00-150.00			

Left: "Royal Coach," black.
Right: "Royal Coach," transparent green with black lid.

Row 1: (a) "Royal Coach," frosted green with black lid; (b) "Cinderella's Coach," large-size, crystal.
Row 2: (a) "Cinderella's Coach," small-size, frosted pink with black lid; (b) "Horse-drawn Coach," round, frosted green; (c) "Cinderella's Coach," frosted green with black lid.

"Horse-drawn Coach," square, frosted pink.

COACHES AND AUTOS

The large blue auto has three windows and a door on each side. It also has a rear window. The front end has a radiator grill and headlights, and there is a louvered air vent on each side of the hood. The chassis is supported by two metal axles which fit into tabs on the underside of the body. The axles have metal wheels with solid white rubber tires, much like those found on toy cars and trucks from the 1920's and 1930's. The passenger compartment of the vehicle is covered with a removable glass lid. The hood area is another compartment which probably was covered with a lid at one time, however, the lid is missing on this example. The underside of the body is marked, "D.R.G.M., Nr. 1068431" and has the trademark of the Saxony Glass Company, which is a crown enclosed in a circle with a cross at the top center of the crown and the letters "S" and "G" inside the crown. The car measures 3½" wide by 7¾" long by 4" high.

The "Conestoga Wagon" is a two-piece covered glass jar with the wagon bed used as the base and the canvas top and ribs acting as the lid. This jar is 6" long and was produced by the L.E. Smith Glass Company. It has been reissued several times since it first appeared in frosted colors in the 1930's. The undersides of the bases of the frosted green and frosted pink puff boxes are marked "RAMSES" in large letters. During the 1950's, it was made in white milk glass, and during the 1970's, it was sold in crystal. This covered wagon, made by Smith, is identified by its sway-back canvas top which is supported by eight ribs, and the wagon bed has an axle grease bucket and a chain hanging in front of the rear wheels.

The white milk glass "Stagecoach" was made during the 1950's by the Fostoria Glass Company. This 3½" wide by 7" long by 5½" high two-piece coach is a replica of the ones from the early West. The lid is comprised of a luggage rack which contains a turtleback trunk and other luggage and boxes in various shapes and sizes.

The small white milk glass "Prairie Schooner" on the right side of the second row was made by the Kemple Glass Company. It can be easily distinguished from the larger wagon above it since it only has five ribs which support its non-sagging top, and there are no accessories hanging from the wagon bed. Other colors which were made include amber, green and crystal. Lamps were also made from this puff box. A hole was drilled through the bottom, and a small light fixture was inserted to produce a night light. For an example of a crystal frosted lamp, see page 185.

The four-door "Touring Car" shown in the bottom picture is similar to autos produced in the late 1920's and 1930's. It has a glass lid which lifts off of the passenger compartment to reveal its contents.

	Crystal/ Crystal Frosted	Frosted Green/Pink	White Milk Glass	Blue
"Sedan"				$85.00-95.00
"Conestoga Wagon"	$20.00-25.00	$85.00-95.00	$60.00-80.00	
"Stagecoach"			$85.00-95.00	
"Prairie Schooner"	$35.00-45.00	$60.00-65.00	$60.00-80.00	
"Touring Car"	$80.00-90.00			

Row 1: (a) "Sedan," blue; (b) "Conestoga Wagon," crystal.
Row 2: (a) "Stagecoach," white milk glass; (b) "Prairie Schooner," white milk glass.

"Touring Car," crystal frosted.

MISCELLANEOUS POWDER JARS

Two different styles of powder jars with the same style bottom are shown in the top picture. Four stylistic "bow ties" are evenly spaced on the side of the bottom. The center of the "bow tie" is diamond-shaped, and each side of the diamond is accented with seven radial lines.

"Art Deco Pleated Fan" jars are pictured on the top row. The high-domed lid has a fan-like finial with a series of steps at its base. The round bottom of the lid has a crimped edge. These jars are found more commonly in transparent pink, green and crystal, but will also be seen in cobalt blue, flashed pink and flashed green colors. Although a complete black jar has not been found, black bases and transparent colored lids will be seen. An example is shown on the right side of the top row.

The "Sailboat" powder jar has a round, gently curved lid with embossed waves which is topped by a finial comprised of a sailboat with a very large sail. Commonly found colors are transparent green and transparent pink. "Sailboat" jars in cobalt are unusual and desirable as is indicated by the price below.

The powder jars on the top row of the bottom photo were named "Bark" by Hazel Weatherman. Both the bottom and lid are embossed to give the appearance of an old wooden tub. The bottom has two solid vertical handles, and the round lid is slotted to fit between the handles. Colors which have been found are transparent green, transparent pink and crystal.

The "Military Hat" pictured on the bottom row was made by the Paden City Glass Manufacturing Company. According to Jerry Barnett, who is an authority on Paden City glass, two sizes - 3" and 5" - were made. Information in the patent application filed by the inventor, Harry S. Berk, in 1942, indicates the design was originally intended for use as both an ornamental jar and an ash receptacle. The tops of some hats have a recessed area for a mirror and others are flat. The bottoms have a center front and two side insignia which consist of a spread eagle encircled by stars within a disc. Bottoms may be found with three slightly different background designs. The first style has a smooth visor and crown. Another has a stippled visor and a crown with encircling lines, and the third version has a visor and crown which both have encircling lines. Colors which have appeared include crystal, flashed amber, flashed medium blue, transparent amber, and cobalt. The flashed amber jar in the picture still has a paper label attached to its mirror which reads: "Lady Berkshire - U.S. Pat. D-13458."

	Crystal/ Flashed Colors	Transparent Green/Pink	Amber	Cobalt
* "Art Deco Pleated Fan"	$18.00-20.00	$40.00-45.00		$80.00-90.00
"Sailboat"	$20.00-22.00	$55.00-65.00		$90.00-110.00
"Bark"	$15.00-18.00	$20.00-25.00		
"Military Hat"	$15.00-18.00		$25.00-30.00	$40.00-45.00

* Pink with black base, $55.00 - $60.00
* White milk glass with black base, $50.00 - $55.00

Row 1: (a) "Art Deco Pleated Fan," transparent pink; (b) "Art Deco Pleated Fan," cobalt; (c) Art Deco Pleated Fan," transparent pink lid with black base.
Row 2: (a) "Sailboat," transparent green; (b) "Sailboat," cobalt; (c) "Sailboat," transparent pink.

Row 1: (a) "Bark," transparent pink; (b) "Bark," transparent green.
Row 2: (a) "Military Hat," crystal with plain lid and smooth visor and crown; (b) "Military Hat," flashed amber with mirror lid and smooth visor and crown; (c) "Military Hat," transparent amber with stippled visor and lines encircling crown.

Ruba Rombic powder bottom, jungle green.

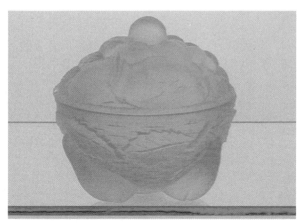

Powder box, embossed fruit, foreign, frosted green.

The Ruba Rombic powder jar was introduced in 1928 by the Consolidated Lamp and Glass Company. The style consists of twisted, distorted, angular features which are very cubist. The jar may be found in crystal, and various shades of green, lavender and brown. Some jars will also be found with flashed or fired-on colors over a crystal body.

The "Fruits" powder jar shown at the top right is frosted green and appears to be foreign. The three feet on the bottom are formed from three embossed pears which extend downward from short stems which are topped by two embossed leaves. The domed lid is formed from various types of embossed fruits, leaves and stems. Among the recognizable fruits are cherries, grapes and strawberries.

According to an ad in a 1931 Montgomery Ward catalogue, perfumed Ramses body powder was packaged in the "Spear" powder jars shown in the top photo on the next page. This peculiar type of glass, made by the L.J. Houzex Convex Glass Company, was called "onxglas" and came in pastel shades of blue, lavender, and green, a bright yellow and black. The jar was marketed with powder and a velour puff for 87¢. The top has a tall spear-like finial which tapers to a round edge. The base of the finial is adorned with a garland of roses. The bottom is plain, bowl-shaped and has a small foot.

A "Rose Blossom" powder jar is illustrated on the top row of the bottom photo. The embossed lid and bottom combine to form a single rose blossom. Colors which may be found include frosted pink, frosted green and black.

Jadite and black examples of a three-footed powder jar are shown on the bottom row. The lid is covered with embossed roses, and the side of the bottom has vertical ribs with three evenly spaced clusters of roses.

A "Pseudo-Rombic" powder jar is in the center position on the bottom row. This jar is often confused with the more collectible Ruba Rombic jar. The bottom of a Ruba Rombic jar is shown at the top left. The major distinguishing difference between the two jars is in the shape of the jar opening. The interlocking top and bottom edges of the "Pseudo-Rombic" jars are round, while the Ruba Rombic jars have a jagged opening.

	Crystal/ Frosted Crystal	Applied Colors	Frosted Green/Pink	Black	Blue/ Jadite
* "Spear"				$45.00-55.00	$45.00-55.00
"Rose Blossom"			$40.00-45.00	$55.00-65.00	
Rose, 3-footed				$40.00-45.00	
"Pseudo-Rombic"	$25.00-35.00		$45.00-55.00		
Ruba Rombic	$70.00-100.00	$125.00-150.00			
"Fruits"			$35.00-45.00		

* Lavender, yellow, $50.00 - $60.00

Left to Right: (a) "Spear," blue onxglas; (b) "Spear," black onxglas; (c) "Spear," green onxglas.

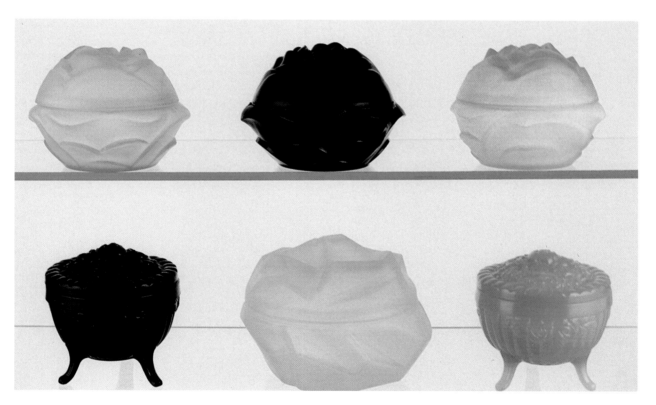

Row 1: (a) "Rose Blossom," frosted green; (b) "Rose Blossom," black; (c) "Rose Blossom," frosted pink.
Row 2: (a) Three-footed rose, black; (b) "Psuedo-Rombic," frosted green; (c) Three-footed rose, jadite.

The base of all the powder jars in the top photo is the same. It is 4¼" in diameter and has embossed ripples. The same type base is used with the miniature elephant shown on page 13. The jars on the top row have an elongated ball-shaped finial. Colors found include frosted crystal, frosted green and frosted pink.

The two jars on the bottom row of the top photo have an embossed four-leaf clover in the center of the lid in place of an elevated finial. The only colors we have seen are frosted crystal and transparent green, but other frosted colors such as pink and green should also exist.

Bridge set accessories are shown in the bottom picture on the opposite page. Originally, these items were sold with Dermay bath powder products. Afterwards, they could be used to decorate the bridge table.

The octagonal box with the flat lid has a cigarette rest on each corner of the lid. A single heart, diamond, spade and club is embossed in the center of each side of the recessed top of the lid. The same symbol pattern is repeated on the small corners of the octagonal-shaped base - one symbol is located on each corner. According to patent information, this article was designed as a toilet accessory container by Jerome E. Baum of New York. A patent was granted in July, 1929. The bottom of the base is marked: "Design Pat. No. 79009." The original paper on the frosted green jar reads: "Dermay Parfumer - Paris - New York - Narcisse - Super Quality Bath Fragrance." Colors which have been found are frosted green and frosted pink. Occasionally, jars will be found with the card symbols enameled with red and black paint.

The octagonal jar with the dome-shaped lid was also designed by Jerome E. Baum. He obtained a patent for this jar in May 1929. Original patent sketches show the finial as an ace playing card. However, we have only seen jars with a spade finial. Each of the four narrow octagonal sides of both the lid and base is embossed with a single card symbol. The bottoms of some bases will be marked: "Pat Pdg. D29403," and others bear the mark: "Design Pat No. 78433." A few jars have been found with the following paper label: "Dermay - Fifth Ave. - New York - Bath Powder." The color which is frequently seen is frosted pink, but frosted green jars should also exist.

A treasure chest and ring or trinket box are featured in the photo below. The treasure chest is a rectangular four-footed "turtleback" trunk. The lid and bottom have embossed hinges with a lock and decorative corners. The chest is known to exist in frosted pink and frosted green colors.

The trinket box is oval with a four-footed bottom. The flat rim of the lid is embossed with alternating circles and diamonds. The lower edge of the bottom is scalloped. The center of each side has an embossed half daisy-like flower with each foot of the jar formed by the middle of the flower. The underside of the jar is stamped in black ink: "Souvenir of Hilton Hotel Opening 1929 Plainview, Texas."

	Crystal/ Frosted Crystal	Frosted Green/Pink	Transparent Green
Ribbed box/ball finial	$15.00-18.00	$20.00-25.00	
Four-leaf clover box	$18.00-22.00	$27.00-32.00	$40.00-45.00
Flat octagonal bridge box		$30.00-35.00	
Domed octagonal bridge box		$40.00-45.00	
"Treasure Chest"		$40.00-45.00	
"Trinket Box"		$25.00-30.00	

**Left: "Treasure Chest," frosted pink.
Right: "Trinket Box," frosted green.**

Row 1: (a) Ribbed box with ball-shaped finial, frosted pink; (b) ribbed box with ball-shaped finial, frosted lavender (sun-turned); (c) ribbed box with ball-shaped finial, frosted green.
Row 2: (a) Ribbed bottom with four-leaf clover lid, frosted crystal; (b) ribbed bottom with four-leaf clover lid, transparent green.

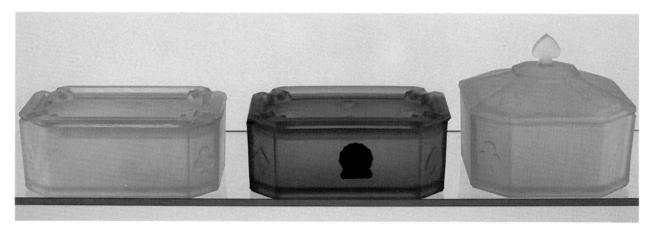

Left to Right: (a) Flat octagonal box, frosted pink; (b) flat octagonal box, frosted green; (c) octagonal box with domed lid, frosted pink.

The pink frosted "Sphere with Tower" powder jar on the top row is a souvenir from the 1933 Chicago "Century of Progress" World's Fair. The sphere represents the world, and the tower is a symbol of one of Chicago's famous skyscrapers. The jar may also be found in frosted green and is sometimes seen with a handpainted floral decoration applied over the frosted body.

The center jar on the top row has a bottom with three feet. The top rim of the base is embossed with a "Greek Key" design. The only decoration on the lid consists of three raised ribs which radiate from the central knob and divide the lid into three equal sections. Original paper labels on this style jar indicated the contents were supplied by Dermay. Other colors found include frosted pink and frosted crystal.

The frosted yellow octagonal powder jar has an eight-faceted finial and a four-footed base. Other known colors include jadite and frosted green. Some of these jars have been found with "Royal Furniture Co., Morgantown, W. Va." stamped in black ink on the underside of the base.

The frosted pink three-footed "Triangle" powder box is embossed "Ramses - Paris - N.Y." on the underside of the base. The gently sloping lid is topped by a three-tier triangular-shaped finial.

The frosted green "Pyramid" powder jar is resting on a three-tier base. The sides of the jar slope slightly outward from the top tier of the base. The slightly domed lid is topped with a triangular-shaped finial. Although this jar is not marked, it has been found with original powder puffs which have been marked "Ramses." Patent information indicates this jar was designed by Robert McEldowney in 1928. The patent was assigned to the New Martinsville Glass Mfg. Co. of New Martinsville, West Virginia.

The octagonal-shaped "Graduation Hat" has long center panels and short side panels. It has a silk tassel which is secured through a hole in the center of the flat lid. The jar will also be found in frosted pink.

The "Obelisk" powder jars on the top row of the bottom photo utilize a base which is the same as the one used with the "Court Jester" jar shown on page 45. The frosted blue jar is embossed "Taussaunt Glass" on the underside of the base. The other two jars are unmarked. The lid consists of a series of horizontal steps with a tall vertical-ridged tower forming the knob. Besides the colors shown, frosted green will also be found.

The square four-footed jars on the bottom row have an embossed "sunburst" in the center of the lids. The feet, corners of the lid, and "sunburst" are sometimes found decorated with gold. The underside of the base is embossed "Taussaunt Glass."

The frosted green "Pedestal Urn" powder jar shown on the bottom row is an oval-shaped jar with a pedestal foot. It is marked "Taussant Glass" on the underside of the foot. The jar may also be found in frosted pink.

Note in the above descriptions, "Taussaunt" has been found with more than one spelling.

	Frosted Crystal	Frosted Green/Pink	Clear Green	Frosted Yellow	Frosted Blue
* "Sphere with Tower"		$35.00-45.00			
"Greek Key" jar	$15.00-18.00	$18.00-22.00			
Footed octagonal jar		$22.00-25.00		$27.00-32.00	
Footed "Triangle"		$20.00-25.00			
"Pyramid"		$20.00-25.00			
"Graduation Hat"		$18.00-22.00			
"Obelisk"		$35.00-40.00	$40.00-50.00		$50.00-55.00
"Sunburst"		$35.00-40.00			$40.00-45.00
"Pedestal Urn"		$35.00-40.00			

* Frosted colors with handpainted flowers, $50.00 - $60.00.

Row 1: (a) "Sphere with Tower," pink frosted; (b) "Greek Key" jar, green frosted; (c) Footed octagonal jar, yellow frosted.
Row 2: (a) Footed "Triangle," frosted pink; (b) "Pyramid," frosted green; (c) "Graduation Hat," frosted green.

Row 1: (a) "Obelisk," frosted blue; (b) "Obelisk," clear green; (c) "Obelisk," frosted pink.
Row 2: (a) "Sunburst," frosted green; (b) "Sunburst," frosted blue; (c) "Pedestal Urn," frosted green.

The frosted green "Concentric Ridge" powder jar pictured on this page is foreign. The base has horizontal ridges and is three-footed. The domed lid has embossed leaves extending downward from the finial. The frosted crystal "Moderne" jar has triangular-shaped raised panels on the sides of the base which extend to form feet. Triangular panels on the slightly domed lid mirror the panels of the base.

Flat puff boxes are illustrated in the top photograph on the next page. The crystal frosted powder puff box with the handpainted "Forget-me-not" floral decoration on the left side of the front row is 4¼" in diameter. The lid fits into a rim formed by a ridge around the perimeter of the saucer-like base. The other box in the front row has three dragonflies embossed on the lid. The box is 5" in diameter, has a plain bottom, and the underside is marked "Made in France." The color is an opaque translucent clear which many collectors refer to as "clambroth."

The pink puff box to the rear has the Indiana Glass Sandwich pattern on the lid which also has a gold band decoration. The bottom is plain. The box is 4" in diameter and may also be found in transparent green, transparent amber, and crystal. The large green powder puff box in the center of the back row features a peacock with a fully spread tail. The bottom is plain. The box was made by Fostoria and is 5⅛" in diameter. The "Gothic Arches" design on the lid of the puff box on the right rear is a design produced by L.E. Smith in the late 1920's which Hazel Weatherman calls "Romanesque." The box has a plain bottom, is 4" in diameter, and may also be found in other transparent colors such as pink, canary, amber and crystal.

The unusual light color of the frosted green powder jar on the left side, top row of the bottom picture indicates it is probably of foreign origin. The lid and base have a matching horizontal band with an intricate paneled design at their juncture. The panels away from the central band are large and lack detail. The finial is a raised, rounded knob with panels which match the center band. The jar is 4" in diameter.

The second jar on the top row is crystal with a flashed lavender interior. It has an "Arrowhead" finial and is 4½" in diameter. The "pinwheel" design base of this jar is the same as the one which is usually found with the "My Pet" jar shown on page 15. Other colors we have seen are transparent pink and cobalt. The pink powder jar on the top row was made by L.E. Smith. It has a rippled lid and a rippled base with a plain center section on the base. The same style bottom, in two different sizes, may be found used with several of the figural powder jars. The large-size, 6" diameter bottoms to this jar are abundant, since they were also sold as decorative pieces with a flower frog insert.

The pagoda style lid adds character to the otherwise plain green frosted powder on the right side of the top row. The jar is 4" square, has recessed oval panels on the lid, and has a plain four-footed base. The original label reads "Les Bois de Senteur (Sweet Peas) Guimet."

The jars shown on the bottom row are heavy opaque colored glass. The jar to the left has two compartments and is 6" in diameter. The two smaller jars have a triangular finial. These jars have the same unusually heavy, shallow base as the "Annabella" jar shown on page 29.

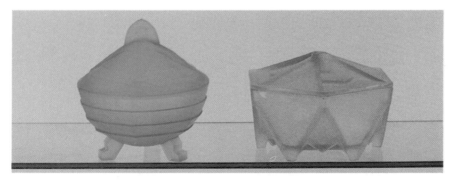

Left: "Concentric Ridge," frosted green.
Right: "Moderne," frosted crystal.

	Crystal/ Frosted Crystal	Frosted Green/Pink	Transparent Green/Pink	Opaque Jadite/Custard
"Concentric Ridge"		$25.00-35.00		
"Moderne"	$22.00-25.00	$27.00-32.00		
"Forget-me-not"	$18.00-20.00			
"Dragonfly"	$45.00-50.00			
Sandwich	$25.00-35.00		$32.00-37.00	

	Crystal/ Frosted Crystal	Frosted Green/Pink	Transparent Green/Pink	Opaque Jadite/Custard
"Peacock"			$65.00-75.00	
"Romanesque"			$35.00-40.00	
"Panel," foreign		$15.00-18.00		
"Arrowhead"	$15.00-18.00		$25.00-27.00	
Smith ripple			$18.00-20.00	
"Pagoda"		$23.00-35.00		
Two compartment, opaque				$45.00-55.00
Triangular, finial opaque				$35.00-45.00

Left to Right:
Front: (a) "Forget-me-not," crystal frosted; (b) "Dragonfly," opaque clambroth.
Rear: (a) Indiana Sandwich, transparent pink; (b) Fostoria "Peacock," transparent green; (c) L.E. Smith "Romanesque," transparent green.

Row 1: (a) Foreign "Panel," frosted green; (b) "Arrowhead," flashed lavender over crystal; (c) L.E. Smith ripple, transparent pink; (d) "Pagoda," frosted green.
Row 2: (a) Two compartment, jadite; (b) triangular finial, custard; (c) triangular finial, jadite.

The crystal and opaque pink jars shown at the top of the opposite page were produced by the Jeannette Glass Company. The opaque jars were part of the Pink Shell Milk Glass line, which Jeannette introduced in the late 1950's. The opaque pink jars were discontinued by the early 1960's, but crystal jar production continued. The jar is 3¾" high and 4¾" in diameter.

The black jar shown at the top is a stacking three-piece, two-compartment powder jar which was made by Westmoreland. There are two identical powder receptacles and a single lid. The top of the lid has a handpainted blue, pink and white floral decoration. The diameter of the jar is 4¼", and each compartment is 1½" deep.

Numerous shapes of glass powder bottoms may be found with celluloid covers. Generally, these powders were part of a larger dresser set which often consisted of accompanying combs, brushes, mirrors and cold cream jars. These sets were usually sold in attractive gift boxes, and the more elaborate sets included atomizers, nail files, scissors and picture frames. Sets like these were popular from the 1930's to the early 1950's. Today's collectors generally ignore the celluloid topped jars in favor of the more attractive figurals. However, some of the more elegantly decorated sets are beginning to find their way into collections.

The small round frosted pink container in the center of the second row is a compact. The bottom has indentions for rouge, lipstick and an eyebrow pencil. A powder puff also rests on top of these items.

A frosted crystal oval trinket box is on the right side of the second row. This small container could be used to hold rings, bobby pins, hair pins or other small items in milady's boudoir. The lid has an embossed diamond in the center with outlining beading inside the diamond. Alternating floral and plain panels radiate outward from the diamond.

The pink powder jar on the left side of the bottom row is made of very heavy glass. It has a plain lid topped by a mushroom-shaped finial with alternating cut and smooth ridges. The bottom has large vertical ribs. It is 4¼" in diameter at the junction with the lid and tapers to a diameter of 3" at its base.

The powder jar with the crystal base and ruby lid is 5" in diameter, and it has also been found in jadite.

The pink three-footed jar on the bottom row was produced by the Jeannette Glass Company between 1929 and 1933. Its pattern name is "Cubist", and it will also be found in crystal and transparent green. The pink acid etched powder jar on the bottom right was "Made in Germany - U.S. Zone" according to the stamp on the underside of the base. It has gold trim and a handpainted floral design on the lid. Without the backstamp, it would be very easy to confuse this powder with the Cambridge #582 powder shown on page 74.

Reprint of celluloid dresser articles from an early 1940's Levin Bros. catalogue of Terre Haute, Indiana.

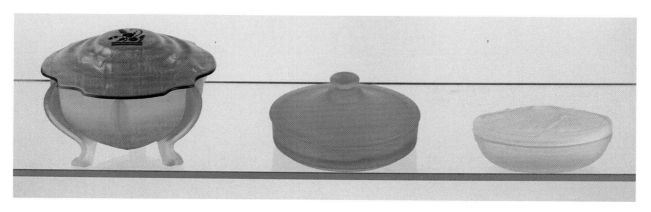

Row 1:
(a) Crystal Jeannette $8.00-10.00
(b) Pink Shell Milk Glass Jeannette $18.00-20.00
(c) Opaque black stack set $25.00-35.00

Row 2:
(a) Frosted green powder/celluloid top $12.00-14.00
(b) Frosted pink compact $14.00-16.00
(c) Frosted crystal oval trinket box $14.00-16.00

Row 3:
(a,c) Transparent pink
        cold cream jar/celluloid top $8.00-10.00

Row 3:
(b) Transparent pink
        hair receiver/celluloid top $12.00-14.00
(d) Transparent amber powder/
        celluloid top $10.00-12.00
(e) Transparent amber powder/
        celluloid top $10.00-12.00

Row 4:
(a) Transparent pink powder $20.00-25.00
(b) Crystal powder/ruby lid $10.00-12.00
(c) Transparent pink Cubist powder $15.00-18.00
(d) Frosted pink German powder $15.00-18.00

AKRO AGATE POWDER JARS

The Akro Agate Company of Clarksburg, West Virginia, produced several non-figural puff boxes, trinket boxes, and cold cream jars. Most of these items will not bear the company's trademark - a crow flying through the letter "A" with marbles in its claws and beak. These are most commonly seen in solid opaque colors, but marbleized and transparent examples also exist.

The opaque green six-sided covered box shown on the next page, top photo, has been attributed to Akro, but may have been produced by Westite. It has an ivy design and is marked "Ramses" on the underside of the base. The ruffled opaque green covered box was made by Akro. According to company records, it is pattern No. 724.

Akro's vertical ribbed powder jar is shown on the top row of the middle photo on opposite page. Generally, the solid opaque colors are easiest to find. Finding this jar in transparent colors, marbleized colors and black is quite a challenge. The second row features the Akro concentric ring powder jar. This jar may be found in opaque colors, both solid and marbleized.

Trinket boxes are shown on the top row of the bottom photo. The large crystal box is hard to find and is not known in any other color. It measures 4" wide by 5½" long by 2¾" high. The smaller opaque box is also difficult to find since it was only made for a few years in the early 1940's. It will usually be found in marbleized colors, but also came in a non-marbleized creamy white. It measures 3½" wide by 4⅛" long by 2⅝" high.

The large powder jars with the domed lid on the bottom row have an embossed ivy decoration. They are Akro pattern #723 and will be found most often in marbleized colors.

Akro Agate apple-shaped powder containers in opaque colors are both desirable and hard to find. Opaque apples are usually found in pumpkin or creamy white colors, although a few marbleized examples have surfaced. Transparent apples have only been found in crystal. These are the least desirable due to their reproduction in crystal at a later time.

	Crystal	Transparent Colors	Solid Colors	Marbleized Colors
Covered box, hexagonal			$20.00-25.00	
Covered box, No. 724			$18.00-22.00	
* Powder jar, apple shape	$18.00-22.00		$95.00-125.00	UND
Powder jar, concentric ring			$25.00-35.00	$35.00-45.00
** Powder jar, vertical ribbed		$40.00-45.00	$25.00-35.00	UND
Powder jar, ivy decoration			$45.00-50.00	$45.00-55.00
Treasure chest, domed lid			$50.00-60.00	$50.00-60.00
Trunk, large	$25.00-30.00			
Trinket box, flat, 3½" x 4"			$45.00-55.00	

* Opaque green, $300.00 - $350.00
** Opaque black, $55.00 - $65.00

Left: Covered box, hexagonal, opaque green.
Right: Covered box, ruffled, opaque green.

Row 1: Vertical rib powder jars: (a) opaque yellow; (b) opaque white; (c) opaque blue; (d) transparent pink; (e) black; (f) opaque green.
Row 2: Vertical rib powder jar, opaque pink; concentric ring powder jars: (b) opaque green; (c) blue marbleized; (d) green marbleized (e) orange marbleized; (f) opaque blue.

Row 1: (a) Large trunk, crystal; (b) treasure chest, oxblood marbleized; (c) treasure chest, creamy white; (d) treasure chest, green marbleized.
Row 2: (a) Ivy embossed powder jar, orange marbleized; (b) ivy embossed powder jar, orange marbleized; (c) apple powder jar, crystal; (d) apple powder jar, pumpkin.

Mexicali powder jars:
(a) orange marbleized; (b) green marbleized; (c) blue marbleized.

The Mexicali powder jar shown on this page was made for the Pickwick Cosmetic Corporation. It is embossed "Pickwick Cosmetic Corporation, Fifth Ave., New York" on the bottom of the base. One side of the base has an embossed figure of a seated Mexican taking a siesta under a cactus. The opposite side shows a seated Mexican man playing a guitar. The base is topped with a sombrero-shaped lid. These jars were originally distributed containing a spicy bath powder. After this was used, they became a handy cigarette holder. Three different basic colors of jars are normally seen. The most commonly found color is orange marbleized. Green marbleized is more unusual, and blue marbleized is the most difficult color to find. In addition, a few jars have been found without any marbleized color, and some jars will contain a blend of more than one marbleized color.

	Orange Marbleized	Green Marbleized	Blue Marbliezed	Solid Color
Jar, Mexicali	$25.00-30.00	$45.00-55.00	$45.00-55.00	$55.00-65.00

Akro produced the bell-shaped containers for distribution of Landers' powders and colognes. Notice there are two styles of bells. The more common bell has a basket-weave pattern on its side. The crystal bell shown on the right side of the second row has vertical ribs. The photo shows the bells were sealed by a cardboard cap, and they also held a smaller bell-shaped jar which contained perfume. The basket-weave style bells have been reproduced. Old bells produced by Akro Agate have six distinct panels at the end of the handle. Reproduction bells are round and smooth in this area. Most of the old bells are marked "made in U.S.A." near the area where the clanger is attached. In the early Bennet reproductions, this mark has been replaced by a "B." Later versions have no mark in this area.

During the mid-1940's, Akro Agate produced numerous items for the Jean Vivaudou Company of New York. Some of these are illustrated in the photo at the bottom of the opposite page. These toiletry items were often designed to look like porcelain and were usually handpainted. A 1942 ad proclaims "the hand-painted porcelain-white apothecary jars - each with a different motif - are artful adaptations of priceless antiques in America's oldest apothecary shop, now a national shrine in Fredericksburg, Va." The toiletries were accented with the fragrance "Attar of Petals."

The large round lighter colored apothecary jars were part of the Attar of Petals line and were sold with dusting powder, bubble bath and cream products for women. The sinister-looking black jars are from the Bergamot line and contained products for men such as shaving cream and talcum powder. Blue and pink jars were used for baby products.

The mortar and pestle style jar came with cream or flower potpourri. A label from the bottom of one jar reads, "Perfumed petals to sprinkle into vanity, bureau drawers, to perfume accessories, lingerie and linens. Impart a lovely garden-sweet fragrance to wearable in clothes closets, also to place in containers to perfume rooms."

The small bottle type jars were made by Brockway and styled to look like the larger Akro apothecary jars. They are usually found painted white or black over crystal. The bottles were filled with cologne, toilet water or talcum powder for women and after shave or hand dressing for men. These bottles are generally harder to find than the apothecary jars, but they are less collectible.

The small round puff box on the bottom row is usually found in white and features various handpainted decorations. The jar may also be found in blue and is 4" in diameter.

	Crystal	Opaque White	Opaque Blue	Trans. Blue	Pumpkin	Pink/ Black
* Bell, basket-weave	$12.00-15.00		$45.00-55.00	$50.00-60.00	$65.00-75.00	$75.00-85.00
Bell, vertical rib	$25.00-30.00					
Bottle, Brockway	$8.00-10.00					$8.00-10.00
Jar, apothecary	$12.00-14.00	$40.00-45.00				$25.00-30.00
Jar, mortar & pestle		$10.00-12.00	$25.00-30.00			$20.00-22.00
Puff box, round	**$20.00-22.00	$30.00-35.00				

* With end cap and perfume insert, add 20%.   ** Decorated, $30.00 - $35.00

Row 1: (a) Bell, light blue; (b) Bell, medium blue; (c) Bell, white; (d) Bell, transparent blue; (e) Bell, crystal with original tassel and cardboard cap.
Row 2: (a) Bell, crystal; (b) cardboard cap and bell-shaped glass perfume insert; (c) Bell, light pumpkin; (d) Bell, dark pumpkin; (e) Bell, crystal with vertical ribs.

Row 1: Apothecary jars: (a) pink, (b) white, (c) handpainted white with original label; (d) Brockway bottle, handpainted white; (e) Apothecary jar, black with gold trim; (f,g) Brockway bottles, black with gold trim and original labels.
Row 2: Mortar and pestles: (a) black with gold trim, (b) handpainted white; (c) blue; (d) handpainted pink. Round puff boxes: (e,f) handpainted white.

FENTON WAVE CREST COVERED BOXES

The Wave Crest boxes shown here were produced by the Fenton Art Glass Company of Williamstown, West Virginia in 1961. Although these are a relatively late production, they are not easy to find, and their beauty and desirability have kept their price relatively high. The Wave Crest boxes are larger than regular powder boxes but are included here since they can be used for a multitude of purposes on a vanity.

For those collectors who are unfamiliar with Fenton glass, "cased" may be an unfamiliar term. "Cased" glass results from the layering of two different colors of glass, one over the other, to produce the finished product. In the Fenton examples, a colored layer is usually applied over a white inner layer.

Top Row:
(a) Apple green, cased $90.00-100.00
(b) Coral, cased $100.00-110.00
(c) Powder blue, cased $90.00-100.00
(d) Honey amber, cased $90.00-100.00

Bottom Row:
(a) White milk glass with pink roses,
     signed Louise Piper $125.00-150.00
(b) Wild rose, cased $90.00-100.00
(c) White milk glass with
     "Violets in the Snow" $75.00-95.00
(d) Jamestown, not cased $80.00-90.00

ENAMELED CRANBERRY AND WAVE CREST VANITY BOXES

The two fancy creamy opaque boxes with the handpainted decorations are signed "Wave Crest." This is a trademark of the C.F. Monroe Company of New York which was in production from 1892 until 1916.

Top Row:
(a) Cranberry hinged box with
enameled flowers $120.00-140.00
(b) Cranberry hinged box in
footed metal base with
enameled dots $130.00-150.00
(c) Cranberry hinged jewelry casket
with "Lily of the Valley" cutting.....$140.00-160.00
(d) Cranberry hinged box with
"Mellon Rib" pattern $120.00-130.00
(e) Cranberry hinged box with
enameled colored flowers $120.00-140.00

Bottom Row:
(a) Wave Crest hinged box with
pink and white flowers $150.00-180.00
(b) Wave Crest hinged box with
colorful floral design $160.00-185.00
(c) Cranberry box with glass lid,
vertical stripe pattern,
signed "Steuben" $140.00-160.00
(d) Cranberry enameled box with
silver lid..$115.00-130.00
(e) Cranberry enameled box with
glass lid...$115.00-130.00

COMPACTS

The large 4¼" by 9" rectangular emerald compact is a "Gentleman's Shaving Compact." According to patent information, it was designed in 1927 by Wilbur L. Orme who was vice-president of the Cambridge Glass Company. The underside of the base is marked, "Pat. No. 1643171." The decoration on the top has a single flower with a spray of leaves on the two long sides. The short sides have a series of dots connected by lines. The center of the knob has a hole to provide ventilation for the interior. The bottom has multiple compartments for a shaving brush, shaving cream, a package of safety razor blades, a safety razor and a styptic pencil.

The 8½" long milk glass oval compact on the top row has been named "Alexandria." The finial consists of the torso of a lady with her arms folded at her waist and a bouquet of flowers held to her side. Her hair is pulled into a bun at the back of her head and curls cascade down over each ear. The lady's gown billows outward from her waist like a hoop skirt and covers the entire surface of the lid. A bow is located at the center of both sides near the lower edge of the lid. The bottom has compartments for powder and a puff, lipstick, an eyebrow pencil and rouge. The underside of the base is stamped in black "Made in Czechoslavakia."

The diamond-shaped pink compact also has a diamond-shaped finial. It is 6½" wide by 8½" long and has a small foot at each corner of the base. The top of the lid has a decoration which consists of two stylized flowers with long pistils, long stems and leaves. The bottom has compartments for powder and a puff, lipstick, an eyebrow pencil and rouge.

The oval compact is 4¾" wide and 8½" long and was introduced by the Cambridge Glass Company in 1926. The lid has an intricately etched floral design. The bottom is marked on the underside "Pat. Appl'd For" and has compartments for powder and a puff, lipstick, an eyebrow pencil and rouge.

All the compacts in the bottom photo were made by the Cambridge Glass Company. They have the same compartments as the Cambridge compact above, but they are 8½" long and 3¾" wide. The pink compact has an emerald rose finial. The bluebell color compact has a gold encrusted floral decoration, and the ivory compact has an enameled Iris decoration.

Top Photo:

(a) Emerald, Cambridge shaving $85.00-100.00
(b) "Alexandria,"
   made in Czechoslavakia $75.00-80.00
(c) Diamond-shaped with etched
   floral design $35.00-45.00
(d) Amber oval Cambridge with
   etched flowers $30.00-37.00

Bottom Photo:

(a) Pink Cambridge with emerald
   rose finial .... * $45.00-55.00
(b) Bluebell Cambridge with gold
   encrusted floral decoration $45.00-55.00
(c) Ivory with enameled
   Iris decoration $90.00-110.00
*Without rose finial, 20% less.

Row 1: (a) Shaving compact, emerald Cambridge; (b) Make-up compact, white milk glass with pink decoration, made in Czechoslavakia.
Row 2: (a) Make-up compact, pink; (b) Make-up compact, amber Cambridge with etched floral design.

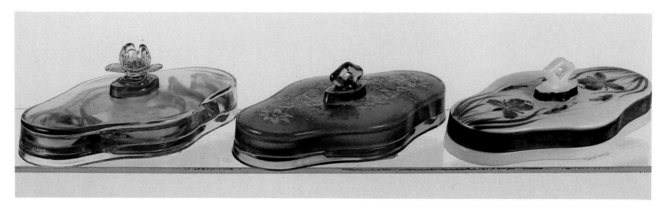

Left to right: (a) Make-up compact, pink Cambridge with emerald rose finial; (b) Make-up compact, bluebell Cambridge with gold encrusted floral design; (c) Make-up compact, ivory Cambridge with enameled Iris decoration.

The blue fan-shaped compact has a lid with a fleur-de-lis style finial. The bottom has compartments for powder and a puff, lipstick, an eyebrow pencil and rouge. The compact was made by the Fostoria Glass Company during the 1920's and will also be found in green and pink.

The black base with the gold-colored metal lid and afghan dog finial has the same shape as the previous blue compact. This suggests the glass part was made by Fostoria for the W.B. Mfg. Co., who supplied the metal lid and marketed the finished product. Silver colored lids have also been found with this black base.

The green three-piece powder/rouge container was introduced by New Martinsville in 1926 as part of its No. 1926/2 "Mysterious Vanity Set." A covered rouge compartment is positioned on the center of the puff box lid. The inside of the rouge compartment is marked "Pat. Apld. For." For more information on the vanity set, see page 120.

The oval three-piece compact has a covered rouge compartment on the top center of the compact lid. The compact base has areas to hold a puff and powder, lipstick and an eyebrow pencil.

	Green/Pink Amber	Blue	Metal Lid Black Base
Compact, Fostoria	$25.00-35.00	$35.00-40.00	
Compact, dog finial			$55.00-70.00
Compact, round	$18.00-20.00	$20.00-22.00	
Compact, oval	$20.00-25.00	$25.00-27.00	

DRESSER SETS

McKee's transparent glass "Shari" dresser set is pictured on the top row. The base is 2" wide by 7" long and has four slots to hold make-up compacts and perfume bottles. The base is marked "Shari" in the center of both sides and decoration consists of a single floral band. The slots hold two metal compacts of different sizes and two different size miniature perfume bottles. The compacts are marked "Shari" on one side and "Langlois, New York" on the opposite side. The eight-sided perfume bottles are glass with long glass stoppers which have flat tops with the same floral design as the holder. Paper labels on the bottles identify them as "Shari." The narrow oval cover has an intricate embossed floral design with two perched birds and three fluttering butterflies on both sides. Colors which have been found are pink and vaseline.

The jadite octagonal shaped box is 5" in diameter and is embossed "Shari" on the cover. It has indentions in the base for the two compacts and two perfume bottles described above. They lie flat in this base. The floral design is embossed on the lid and on alternating panels on the side of the base. The design on this case lacks butterflies, but a bird is featured in an oval on the alternate panels of the base.

The dresser set in the pink holder contains six crystal jars with metal caps. The pink three-footed holder is 3" deep by 6½" long and has a plain flat back panel. The curved front contains three narrow panels and two wide panels. The three narrow panels contain the figure of a nude lady holding a drape between her two outstretched arms. The large panels are covered with embossed flowers. The bottles contain products of the "Charme Volupte" line by Doris Dorie of New York - Paris. Included are nail lustre, lustre remover, vanishing cream, toilet water and two bottles of perfume.

	Pink	Vaseline	Jadite
Dresser set, "Shari" rectangular	$100.00-125.00	$125.00-145.00	
Dresser set, "Shari" octagonal			$75.00-85.00
* Dresser set, "Doris Dorie"	$85.00-90.00		

* Without bottles, $15.00-18.00

PART II:
VANITY SETS

At some time in their history, most of the major American glass companies produced vanity sets. These basic sets normally contain two colognes with stoppers, a puff box and lid, and some type of tray. Some of the more elaborate sets might also have one or more of the following matching articles: an atomizer, hair receiver, pin tray, cold cream jar, trinket box, glove box, clock or mirror.

The vanity sets in this section are arranged alphabetically according to company of manufacture. Whenever possible, the perfumes and puff boxes illustrated are described and priced in all their known colors. However, some companies produced perfumes in highly unusual colors or with exotic decorations. In these cases, only the pictured items will be priced, since prices for items in different colors or with another decoration may vary considerably.

Some of the colognes produced by different companies are so similar they almost appear to have been made from the same molds. In the cases where the similarities are confusing, we have included detailed descriptions of body parts and stoppers and recorded various measurements to help with identification.

A few pages at the end of the section include a sample of some foreign vanity sets. There are literally hundreds more sets which were produced in Europe. Czechoslavakia was especially active in the manufacture of scent bottles. Anyone interested in more detailed information on these perfumes should consult Ruth Forsythe's book "Made in Czechoslavakia."

A Double Set At One Price! $3.00 Set

Think of it! A six-piece Dresser Set where each unit makes all the others indispensable and they all sell each other. The two torchier dresser lamps have stable, attractive crystal clear glass bases with bright, non-inflammable acetate shades. The harmonizing table set includes two crystal perfume bottles with combination stoppers and applicators, a generous size, yet utterly feminine crystal powder box and charming cover. Both rest on a trim mirror glass tray that reflects the beauty of the entire ensemble. It measures 7½ by 15 in. The lamps are 14 in. high. The assorted colors include Rose, Green, Blue, White, Gold, and Orchid, all good sellers. Sold only in set of 6 pieces in a carton. (Mfrs. 492).

S3815—Ship. wt. 8 lbs. Complete Set...... **$3.00**

Reprint of a dresser set with matching lamps from an early 1940's Levin Bros. wholesale catalogue of Terre Haute, Indiana.

CAMBRIDGE PERFUMES AND PUFF BOXES

The Cambridge Glass Company of Cambridge, Ohio produced handmade glassware from 1902 until the factory closed in 1958. At that time, many of the molds still in existence were acquired by the Imperial Glass Company of Bellaire, Ohio. When Imperial Glass ceased production, numerous molds were acquired by private individuals and many of the old molds are again being used to produce glassware. However, if molds for the perfumes and puff boxes exist, they are not being used, and currently reproductions from these old molds are not a problem for collectors. The only original Cambridge item within the scope of this reference which is being made currently is a Mt. Vernon pattern 3" toilet box. This piece is shown on page 84.

Most of the items shown here were made during the late 1920's and early 1930's. During this period, Cambridge produced numerous colognes and puff boxes with various decorations in colors with unique names. Some of the colors are very similar, with just a shade of difference between two or more colors. Extreme care should be taken in determining the proper name for the purpose of identification.

The value of each shape vanity article varies greatly with both style of decoration and color. Therefore, an attempt has been made to illustrate as many examples of each shape in as many colors and decorations as possible. Some of the patterns and decorations were given names by Cambridge; others were named later by researchers. Other patterns or decorations are only known by numbers, and some still have not been identified.

The #575 perfumes will also be found with atomizer fittings. An example may be seen on page 81. The flat #579 puff box is also listed in 3" and 5" sizes. The #584 flat puff box without a knob also comes in a 3" size.

Top Row:

(a) Perfume, #575, emerald $45.00-55.00
(b) Perfume, #575 amber with
    metal collar and stopper top $40.00-45.00
(c) Perfume, satin emerald with gold
    encrusted foot and
    top of stopper $40.00-45.00
(d) Perfume, plate etch # 704,
    bluebell with gold band $55.00-65.00
(e) Puff box, #582, bluebell with
    plate etch # 704 .... $35.00-40.00
(f) Perfume, bluebell with
    plate etch # 704 .... $55.00-65.00

Bottom Row:

(a) Perfume, topaz $30.00-35.00
(b) Puff box, #579-4", topaz with
    plate etch # 704 .... $40.00-45.00
(c) Perfume, satin peach-blo
    with gold band $30.00-35.00
(d) Puff box, #584-4" peach-blo with
    Medallion etching $30.00-35.00
(e) Perfume, peach-blo
    with plate etch # 704 .... $55.00-60.00
(f) Puff box, #582 emerald with
    plate etch # 704 .... $35.00-40.00
(g) Perfume, topaz $30.00-35.00

CAMBRIDGE PERFUMES AND VANITY SETS

Row 1: Various colors and decorations of the #198 Cambridge cologne are pictured on the top row. The total height of the perfume is 5". The stopper is 3¼" long, and the bottom is 4⅛" high. The head of the stopper has eight flat sides which are separated by four curved scallops. The top is also ground and polished. The perfume bottom has three series of concentric rings. One set is on the foot, another is on the narrow part of the perfume, just above the foot, and the third is just below the neck. The powder jar on the top row is the Cambridge #581 (square knob) jar which is 4" in diameter. The lid of the green jar has an etching depicting two oriental birds seated on an ornamental urn.

(a) Perfume, #198 ivory with
    enameled Iris decoration $100.00-125.00
(b) Perfume, #198 peach-blo with
    wheel cut decoration $35.00-40.00
(c) Perfume, #198 cobalt with
    gold decoration $45.00-55.00
(d) Puff box, #581 cobalt
    (square knob)..$20.00-25.00
(e) Perfume, #198 cobalt............................$40.00-45.00
(f) Perfume, #198 emerald with
    gold band decoration $30.00-35.00

(g) Puff box, #581 emerald (square knob)
    with oriental bird
    plate etching No. 733 ....$30.00-35.00
(h) Perfume, #198 emerald with paper label:
    "Superb Perfume -Kingham Bros. -
    Indianapolis" .... * $25.00-35.00
(i) Perfume, #198 bluebell with
    floral etch on bottom $35.00-45.00
(j) Perfume, #198
    experimental color $125.00-150.00

* With original label, $45.00-50.00

Row 2: The first perfume is shape #198 in topaz with a handpainted enamel decoration. It is accompanied by a matching enameled #582 dome top powder. Displayed in the center of the shelf is a frosted Peach-blo vanity set. The set consists of a four-part 7¼" x 11¼" vanity tray, two ½ oz. #585 perfumes, and a #582-4" diameter powder jar. In the photo, two different enamel decorations are shown on the perfumes. The height of the bottom of the perfume is 3", the length of the stopper is 3", and the overall height of the complete perfume is 4". The perfumes with the beehive stoppers are similar to the Paden City perfume shown on page 128.

(a) Perfume, #198 topaz $40.00-45.00
(b) Puff box, # 582 topaz with
    handpainted decoration $20.00-25.00
(c) Vanity tray, frosted peach-blo
    four-part # 660 ....$25.00-30.00
(d,f) Perfume, # 585 sponge acid decorated
    peach-blo, beehive stopper $30.00-35.00

(e) Puff box, # 582 sponge acid
    decorated peach-blo................................$20.00-25.00
(g) Perfume, # 585 frosted topaz with
    beehive stopper $30.00-35.00
(h) Puff box, #589
    transparent amber.................................$18.00-20.00
(i) Perfume, transparent amber $20.00-25.00

Row 1:

(a) Perfume, #198 transparent amber
with plate etched band $35.00-40.00

(b) Perfume, #198 transparent amber
with celluloid holder $30.00-35.00

(c) Perfume, #198 amethyst $30.00-35.00

(d) Perfume, #198 emerald with
handpainted floral decoration $40.00-45.00

(e) Perfume, #198 crystal $18.00-20.00

(f) Perfume, #198 peach-blo with gold
encrusted floral decoration $40.00-45.00

Row 2: The bell-shaped azurite cologne with the gold encrusted basket decoration is similar in shape to colognes produced by Fostoria. For examples of the Fostoria colognes, see page 103.

(a) Perfume, # 585 mulberry with
beehive stopper $25.00-30.00

(b) Perfume, #585 bluebell with
sponge acid decoration $35.00-40.00

(c) Perfume, #585 peach-blo with
beehive stopper $30.00-35.00

(d) Perfume, azurite bell-shaped cologne
with gold encrusted Basket motif
from "Dresden" etching $90.00-125.00

(e) Perfume, crystal cut with
gold encrusted stopper top $30.00-35.00

The first four perfumes shown are the same style and were probably produced by Cambridge for the S.S. Kresge Co. Bottles may sometimes be found with the Kresge paper label still intact on the top of the stopper. The bottom is 4" high and has many narrow panels which extend from the foot toward the neck. These panels end at the widest part of the bottom, and the remainder of the area to the collar is plain. The bottle is capped with a beehive stopper which is about 3½" long and is ground and polished on the top. These perfumes will be found in many of the more popular Cambridge colors. The last perfume in the row, which is amber with handpainted flowers, is a combination of the Kresge perfume and the # 198 perfume described on the previous page. It has the interior panels of the Kresge perfume. The rings on its foot and its stopper are like the # 198 perfume.

(a) Perfume, cobalt Kresge $55.00-65.00
(b) Perfume, peach-blo Kresge $27.00-30.00
(c) Perfume, emerald Kresge $27.00-30.00

(d) Perfume, amber Kresge $25.00-30.00
(e) Perfume, amber handpainted $25.00-30.00

The amber dresser set shown on the left is a Cambridge pattern known as Wetherford. The bottle is 4" tall, the stopper is 3" long and has a ground and polished top, and the stoppered bottle is a total of 5⅛" high. The powder box is 4" in diameter and has a peaked lid which is topped with a pointed knob. The perfumes and powder box are setting on a # 488-9½" tray. This same underplate will be found with some of the Cambridge tumble-ups pictured elsewhere in this book. The four perfumes on the right illustrate two different sizes of perfumes with the same style body. They appear to have been made from the same mold as the # 396 style shaker, but we have been unable to find this shape perfume in

Cambridge catalogues. Closure is effected with the # 682 stopper. The two larger perfumes are 5" high, and the smaller ones measure 4½" with their stoppers.

(a) Tray, amber #488-9½" $18.00-20.00
(b,d) Perfume, amber Wetherford $30.00-35.00
(c) Puff box, amber Wetherford $22.00-27.00
(e) Perfume emerald Wetherford $30.00-35.00
(f) Puff box, emerald Wetherford $25.00-30.00
(g) Perfume, amber large
    straight-sided $35.00-38.00

(h) Perfume, emerald large
    straight-sided $40.00-45.00
(i) Perfume, frosted topaz handpainted
    small straight-sided $40.00-45.00
(j) Perfume, emerald handpainted,
    small straight-sided $40.00-45.00

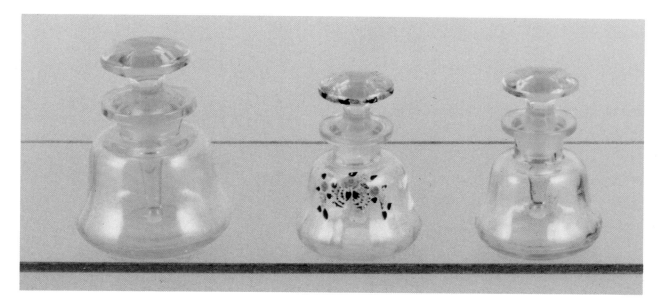

Perfumes in these sizes and styles were made by Fostoria, Cambridge and Heisey. Many of the Heisey perfumes are marked with a "diamond H" on the side of the collar. However, unless there is an identifiable pattern or etching, it is virtually impossible to distinguish the difference between Cambridge and Fostoria perfumes of this shape.

(a) Perfume, topaz $40.00-45.00
(b) Perfume, emerald with handpainted decoration $35.00-40.00
(c) Perfume, emerald $30.00-35.00

Various patterns and decorations of the Cambridge 2 oz. #3400/97 perfume are illustrated. Notice all perfumes of this style have long stoppers.

Top Row:

(a) Perfume, #3400/97 heatherbloom
Diane plate etching $100.00-125.00
(b) Perfume, #3400/97 amber plate
etched Apple Blossom
in metal filigree holder......................$95.00-110.00

(c) Perfume, #3400/97 topaz
with gold filigree casing $65.00-75.00
(d) Perfume, #3400/97 peach-blo plate
etched Apple Blossom $100.00-125.00

Bottom Row:

Some Cambridge perfumes and powder jars have ornate metal filigree holders. One example of this type holder is shown with the Gold Krystol Apple Blossom powder and perfume at the left. Gold Krystol is a light yellow which was introduced in 1929. The powder jar is available in two sizes - 3½" #3400/94 and 4½" #3400/95. The #3400/97 perfume holds 2 ounces.

(a) Puff box, #3400/94 gold krystol
Apple Blossom with metal lid
and holder $75.00-85.00
(b) Perfume, #3400/97 gold krystol
Apple Blossom in gold filigree
metal holder $100.00-125.00

(c) Vanity set, gold krystol
Apple Blossom with metal holders
and tray $175.00-225.00
(d) Puff box, #3400/94 willow blue
plate etched Portia $75.00-85.00
(e) Puff box, #3400/94
heatherbloom $40.00-45.00

Photo, Next Page:

The Willow Blue Cambridge color is illustrated by the #3400/97 plate etch Gloria perfume in the center. The second perfume from the right is the Gloria pattern in the heatherbloom color. Notice these are actual perfumes with long stoppers. Without the long stoppers, these pieces are considered an oil bottle.

Top Row:

(a) Puff box, gold krystol #3400/94
Apple Blossom in
metal filigree holder $75.00-85.00

(b) Perfume, gold krystol #3400/97
Apple Blossom in
metal filigree holder $100.00-125.00

(c) Perfume, willow blue #3400/97
Gloria pattern $100.00-125.00

(d) Perfume, heatherbloom
#3400/97 Portia etch $100.00-125.00

(e) Perfume, cobalt #3400/97 ....$95.00-110.00

Bottom Row:

According to Cambridge catalogues, the vanity set shown on the left was sold two different ways. The #683 three-piece set came as shown in the picture - a large 5" x 8" two compartment tray and two different size lids. In the #665 four-piece set, the small footed perfume shown to the right was inserted in the cavity covered by the small lid. Thus, the new set consisted of a large tray, a single lid, a perfume body and a perfume stopper. The amber powder jar in the center is oval and measures 2¾" x 4½". This jar has also been seen in pink. Although they cannot be seen in the picture, the 1½" oz. Nautilus-shape perfumes have long stoppers. Note the Cambridge name for red is "carmen."

(a) Vanity set, 3-piece
#683-3 peach-blo $75.00-85.00
Peach-blo #665, 4-piece vanity $85.00-95.00

(b) Puff box, amber oval $18.00-20.00

(c) Perfume, cobalt Nautilus $85.00-95.00

(d) Perfume, carmen Nautilus $95.00-110.00

Perfume for #665 - four-piece vanity set

CAMBRIDGE PERFUMES AND ATOMIZERS

The first three perfumes are a variation of the standard 1½ oz. #206 perfume. The bottom of the perfume has an added blown area which increases its capacity. The large amber perfume is 8" tall. All of the examples in the picture on this page are hand blown.

Top Row:

(a) Perfume, #206 ivory with distended base and floral sprig decoration $100.00-125.00

(b) Perfume, #206 ivory with distended base and enameled Iris decoration $95.00-125.00

(c) Perfume, #206 amber with distended base $55.00-65.00

(d) Perfume, #199 Helio with gold band decoration $85.00-90.00

(e) Perfume, #206 crystal with cut and gold Etta decoration $40.00-45.00

(f) Perfume, #206 satin peach-blo, early variation Wildflower, gold decorated body with transparent stem and foot $80.00-90.00

(g) Perfume, #206 emerald with gold encrusted Rockwell decoration $45.00-55.00

Bottom Row:

Some Cambridge perfumes will be found with stoppers which are a different color from the body. This will be especially true for some of the crystal cut perfumes. An example is the crystal perfume shown on this row with the primrose stopper. The amber perfume shown on the right has also been found with a primrose stopper.

(a) Perfume, #206, emerald with gold filigree holder $55.00-65.00

(b) Perfume, #206 jade with gold band decoration $60.00-80.00

(c) Perfume, #206 azurite with gold band decoration $75.00-85.00

(d) Perfume, #206 Helio with handpainted floral decoration $95.00-110.00

(e) Perfume, #206 cobalt blue 1 with gold encrusted Adam decoration $75.00-85.00

(f) Perfume, #206 emerald with early plate etched Apple Blossom variation $50.00-55.00

(g) Perfume, #206 crystal with cut design and primrose stopper................ $45.00-55.00

(h) Perfume, #206 amber with cut design $45.00-50.00

Top Row:

Various Cambridge tall perfumes are shown on the top row. These tall perfumes consist primarily of the 1 oz. #199 and 1½ oz. #206 perfumes. Close examination will reveal the blown perfumes are much thinner than the ones which were molded. Molded perfumes on the top row of this photo are distinguishable by their thick collars - the first, fifth, ninth and eleventh ones are molded. Two different stoppers were used with these perfumes. One type has a rosebud end, and the other style has a round top with six distinctive panels which are flattened by a definite ground and polished area in the center. Note the rosebud stopper is very difficult to find, and the price difference between the frosted emerald perfume and the transparent emerald perfume in the photo is attributed to the presence of this style stopper. Both sizes of perfumes, with either stopper, measure between 6½" and 7" high. Some of the different decorations were applied at independent decorating shops such as DeVilbiss. For more examples of Cambridge perfumes, see the section on DeVilbiss. Notice the Cambridge jade color is more turquoise than green.

(a) Perfume, #206 molded jade with multiple gold band decoration $60.00-80.00
(b) Perfume, #206 frosted green with bud stopper $100.00-125.00
(c) Perfume, #206 azurite with gold decoration and metal cap and collar $45.00-55.00
(d) Perfume, #206 azurite with stippled gold decoration $60.00-80.00
(e) Perfume, #206 molded ebony $60.00-70.00

(f) Perfume, #206 mulberry with distended bottom $40.00-45.00
(g) Perfume, #206 cobalt with gold floral decoration $95.00-110.00
(h) Perfume, #199 Helio with gold band decoration $75.00-85.00
(i) Perfume, #206 molded azurite with narrow gold band decoration $60.00-80.00
(j) Perfume, #206 emerald $30.00-35.00
(k) Perfume, #206 ivory with gold and black band decoration $40.00-45.00

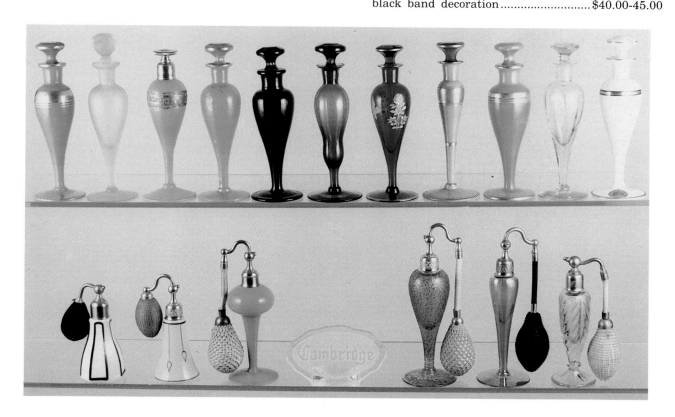

Bottom Row:

Cambridge produced numerous atomizer bodies which were finished by other companies. Examples are shown here and others will be found in the section on DeVilbiss.

(a) Atomizer, ivory eight panel with black panel outline decoration, 4¼" $40.00-45.00
(b) Atomizer, primrose bell-shaped with black enamel decoration, 4½" $40.00-45.00
(c) Atomizer, jade, 5¾" $90.00-110.00

(d) Atomizer, rose stain with sponge acid decoration using #206 blank, 6¾" $90.00-110.00
(e) Atomizer, iridized, made from #199 blank, 6¾" $70.00-75.00
(f) Atomizer, emerald made from #575 blank, 5¼" $55.00-60.00

Top Row:

(a) Atomizer, azurite, 6" $95.00-110.00

(b) Atomizer, primrose with
gold and black band decoration on
206 blank, 6½" $75.00-85.00

(c) Atomizer, ebony with gold
"Adam" decoration, 9" $95.00-120.00

(d) Atomizer, ivory with gold butterfly
and floral decoration, 9" $110.00-125.00

(e) Atomizer, primrose with black
floral band decoration, 9" $90.00-110.00

(f) Atomizer, helio with gold plate
etch # 532 decoration, 6¾" $90.00-110.00

Bottom Row:

Pairs of matching perfumes and atomizers will often be found. In many cases, standard perfume blanks were decorated and fitted with metal collars to form the perfumer. Matching atomizers were outfitted with hardware to produce attractive gift sets.

(a) Perfume, amber with metal collar
and metal cap, 5¾" $30.00-35.00

(b) Atomizer, amber, 6" $45.00-50.00

(c) Perfume, ebony with metal collar
and metal cap, 6" $45.00-55.00

(d) Atomizer, ebony using
#199 blank, 6½" $85.00-95.00

(e) Perfume, amber with metal collar and
metal cap from # 206 blank,
with plate etch # 704, 6" $50.00-55.00

(f) Atomizer, amber with plate etch # 704
matches above perfume, 6½" $60.00-65.00

(g) Perfume, ivory with metal collar and
metal cap from # 206 blank, 6" $50.00-55.00

(h) Atomizer, ivory
matches above perfume, 6½" $50.00-60.00

Top Row:

(a) Atomizer, helio with gold encrusted
   band decoration, 6½" $85.00-95.00
(b) Atomizer, helio with
   gold decoration, 6¼" $85.00-95.00
(c) Atomizer, jade with gold encrusted
   butterfly and floral decoration, 9" ..$125.00-145.00

(d) Atomizer, ivory with enameled
   basket of flowers, 9" $90.00-110.00
(e) Atomizer, azurite with black and
   gold decoration, 9" $100.00-120.00
(f) Atomizer, azurite, 6¼" $80.00-90.00

Bottom Row:

(a) Atomizer, jade with sponged
   gold decoration, 6" $95.00-110.00
(b) Atomizer, ebony with gold encrusted
   decoration, 6½" $75.00-85.00
(c) Atomizer, azurite with gold band
   decoration, 6½" $80.00-90.00

(d) Atomizer, azurite with gold and black
   decoration, 6½" $80.00-90.00
(e) Atomizer, helio with gold painted
   floral decoration, 4½" $75.00-85.00

CAMBRIDGE COLOGNES AND PUFF BOXES

The Mt. Vernon pattern will be found in most Cambridge colors. The cologne may be found in three different sizes. The Mt. Vernon round 3" diameter toilet box is currently being reproduced in various colors from the original molds. At present, it has not been made in any original Cambridge colors. Additional pieces of this pattern are pictured in the photo on page 85.

Top Row:

(a) Cologne, iridized # 2669
2 oz. Buzz Saw pattern $100.00-125.00

(b) Puff box, iridized # 2780
3¼" diameter Strawberry pattern $60.00-75.00

(c) Cologne, crystal # 2660
6 oz. Buzz Saw pattern $25.00-30.00

(d) Puff box, opaque yellow #2800,
4" diameter $40.00-45.00

(e) Puff box, crystal # 9 etched
Wedgewood, 4" diameter $40.00-45.00

Bottom Row:

(a) Puff box, Caprice, crystal with
Alpine decoration $50.00-60.00

(b) Cologne, crystal # 2675,
4 oz. Buzz Saw pattern $35.00-40.00

(c) Puff box, crystal,
4" diameter, marked "DeVilbiss" $45.00-50.00

(d) Cologne, crystal # 2912,
2½ oz. Mt. Vernon $20.00-22.00

(e) Toilet box, crystal, # 16
Mt. Vernon, 3" diameter $15.00-18.00

Top Row:
(a) Toilet box, azurite, #16 Mt. Vernon, 3" diameter $65.00-75.00
(b) Cologne, #2914, large Mt. Vernon $75.00-85.00
(c,d) Toilet bottle, #18, 7 oz. square Mt. Vernon $40.00-45.00

Bottom Row:
The "Agra Perfumes" display sampler was used in retail stores to allow customers to sample fragrances. The crystal sampler has the capacity to hold up to ten different fragrances.

"Agra Perfumes" ....UND

CONSOLIDATED VANITY SETS

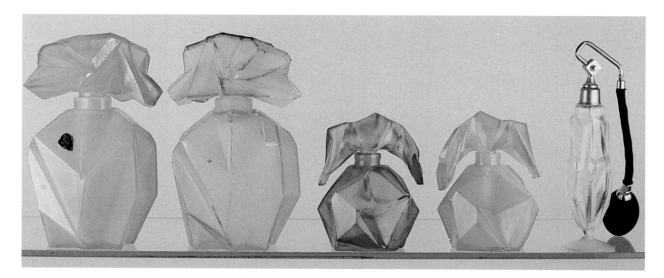

The Consolidated Glass and Lamp Company of Coraopolis, Pennsylvania introduced a new exotic angular line which it termed Ruba Rombic in 1928. Colognes, perfumes and powder jars with distinct angular lines may be found in transparent, satin and applied colors. Extraordinary colors were smokey topaz, jade, lilac, amethyst, silver grey, honey and jungle green. Consolidated went bankrupt in 1933, and the molds were lent to The Phoenix Glass Company. In 1936, production was resumed at Consolidated, and most of the molds were returned. The plant closed in 1967, but the availability of Ruba Rombic today, seems to indicate production of this pattern must have been limited to the early years. The Consolidated items shown here include a cologne, three perfumes and a powder base. The atomizer pictured is a very good Ruba Rombic look-alike made in Czechoslavakia. Note the angular lines comprising the opening of the powder jar. Other powder jars with round openings and very angular lines are sometimes mistaken as Ruba Rombic. Applied finishes are colored washes used over a crystal or cased base. These finishes are similar to, but more durable than, a flashed finish.

A smokey topaz Ruba Rombic powder jar is pictured in the photo below along with a pseudo-Rombic powder base. Notice the Ruba Rombic powder jar has an angular opening, and the opening of the look-alike jar is round.

Left to right:

(a) Cologne, applied sunshine wash over cased base, original paper label "Ruba Rombic - An Epic in Modern Art", 8" $130.00-150.00

(b) Cologne, crystal frosted, 8" $100.00-125.00

(c) Perfume, applied silver grey, 5" $90.00-110.00

(d) Perfume, applied sunshine wash, 5" $110.00-130.00

(e) Frosted crystal Ruba Rombic look-alike atomizer, 7½" $90.00-110.00

**Left: Ruba Rombic powder jar, smokey topaz, 5¼", $150.00-175.00
Right: Pseudo-Rombic powder jar base.**

DeVILBISS PERFUMIZERS AND VANITY SETS

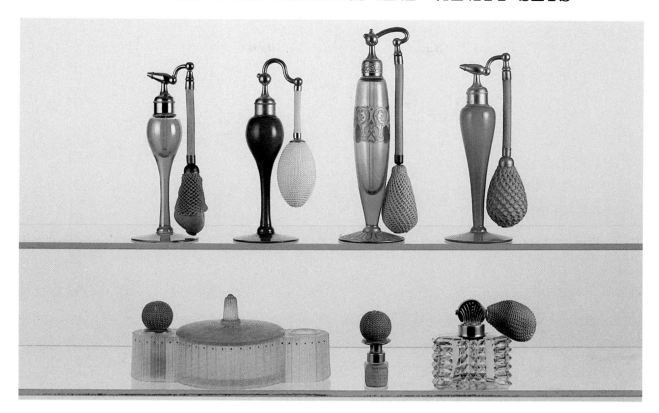

DeVilbiss is a hand decorating and finishing company which has been in operation in Toledo, Ohio since the early 1900's. They are most noted for their unique designs of atomizer fittings for perfume and toilet water bottles. Glass blanks were purchased from all the leading glasshouses for the purpose of decorating with enamel and gold. Most DeVilbiss products are signed on the bottom with a script "DeVilbiss" or "DeVilbiss, Made in U.S.A." However, some items were sold with paper labels, most of which were destroyed through use. For an example of a paper label, see the blue Coin Dot perfumizer on page 90.

Perfumizers and perfume droppers were always available in matched sets. Sometimes other matching accessory pieces such as puff boxes, pin trays and large dresser trays were available. These numerous intricately decorated perfumizers (as DeVilbiss called their atomizers) and perfume droppers are eagerly sought by today's collectors.

The pale blue and crystal frosted vanity set on the bottom row is unusual. The powder jar and holders for the perfumizers are a single piece of glass. A metal collar prevents the perfumizers from slipping through the hole. All three parts have DeVilbiss paper labels.

Devilbiss also designed and decorated colorful perfume lamps. For information on these, see page 186 of the lamp section.

Top Row:
(a) Perfumizer, orange stain over
   crystal base, 6" $75.00-80.00
(b) Perfumizer, green enamel, 6" $65.00-70.00
(c) Perfumizer, cranberry stain with
   gold decoration, 7" $95.00-110.00
(d) Perfumizer, lavender enamel, 6¼" $65.00-70.00

Bottom Row:
(a) Four piece vanity set*: $60.00-70.00
(b) Perfumizer, transparent blue, 3" $45.00-55.00

* Includes crystal frosted powder base and perfumizer holder with blue dot decoration, 3¾" x 6¾"; blue enamel powder lid with fancy multicolor floral decoration; perfumizers, crystal frosted, 2¾".

Top Row:

(a) Perfumizer,
enameled lavender, 6¼" $50.00-60.00

(b) Perfumizer, tangerine, 6⅜" $80.00-90.00

(c) Perfumizer, ebony, 6¼" $85.00-95.00

(d) Perfumizer, enameled dark green
with black enamel floral decoration,
octagon shape, 5½" $50.00-60.00

(e) Perfumizer, deep blue enamel
with black enamel
decoration, 5¼" $50.00-60.00

(f) Perfumizer, black body with
crystal stem and foot, 4¼" $50.00-60.00

Bottom Row:

(a) Perfumizer, emerald with gold
decoration, 7¾" $110.00-125.00

(b) Perfumizer, orange enamel body
with black and gold decoration,
crystal stem and foot, 7¾" $90.00-110.00

(c) Three piece vanity set:
Perfume dropper, green enamel body
with gold design and gold
encrusted stem and foot, 6¾".......$70.00-80.00
Puff box, green enamel lid with
gold design, gold encrusted
footed base, 4¾" diameter.............$45.00-55.00
Perfumizer, green enamel body
with gold design and gold
encrusted stem and foot, 7¾"..$110.00-125.00

(d) Perfumizer, frosted crystal stem,
orange satin enamel body and
foot with black enamel
decoration, 7" $100.00-125.00

(e) Perfumizer, gold decorated black
enamel body and gold encrusted stem
and foot over a crystal
frosted base, 7" $100.00-125.00

Top Row:

(a) Perfumizer, gold decorated crystal
  body and foot with gilded
  draped lady stem, 7¼" $200.00-250.00

(b) Perfumizer, gold decorated green
  enamel body over green base with
  green stem and foot, 6¼" $65.00-75.00

(c) Perfumizer, gold encrusted
  crystal, 10" $125.00-150.00

(d) Perfume dropper, orange
  enamel, 5⅝" $45.00-55.00

(e) Perfumizer, gold decorated orange
  enamel body over pink base with
  pink stem and foot, 6¼" $60.00-70.00

(f) Perfumizer, frosted crystal with
  black enamel decoration,
  octagonal shape, 4⅛" $45.00-55.00

Bottom Row:

(a) Perfumizer, orange enamel with black
  enamel decoration, 5¾" $80.00-90.00

(b) Three piece vanity set:
  Pin Tray, orange enamel with
    black enamel and gold
    decoration, 3¼" x 5⅝" $20.00-25.00
  Puff box, orange enamel with black
    enamel and gold decoration,
    4¾" $40.00-45.00
  Perfumizer, orange enamel with
    black enamel and gold decoration,
    gold encrusted stem and
    foot, 7½" $100.00-125.00

(c) Perfumizer, black enamel
  decorated orange enamel body over
  frosted crystal base with frosted
  crystal stem and foot, 6¾" $100.00-125.00

DeVILBISS PERFUMIZERS

Top Row:

(a) Perfumizer, pink opalescent $30.00-35.00
(b) Perfumizer, crystal with yellow
    and black enamel $30.00-40.00
(c) Perfume dropper, yellow opaque
    with black enamel, octagonal $35.00-40.00
(d) Perfumizer, orange opaque,
    octagonal with bulbous bottom $40.00-45.00
(e) Perfume dropper, crystal with
    blue floral decoration $20.00-25.00

Bottom Row:

All the perfumizers on this row were made for DeVilbiss by Fenton.
(a) Perfumizer, topaz opalescent $30.00-35.00
(b) Perfumizer, French opalescent
    Coin Dot $30.00-35.00
(c) Perfumizer, blue opalescent
    Coin Dot with original label $35.00-45.00
(d) Perfumizer, green hobnail $35.00-45.00

DUNCAN AND MILLER PERFUMES AND VANITY SETS

The Duncan and Miller Company was located in Washington, Pennsylvania. It was founded before the turn of the century, but the perfumes and vanity sets which attract the most attention among collectors were produced in the late 1920's and early 1930's. The coming of color and the addition of the Sandwich and Early American Hobnail patterns catapulted the company into national prominence. Opalescent colors were added in the 1940's. Duncan was sold to the United States Glass Company in 1955, and most of its molds were transferred to the Tiffin, Ohio plant.

In the above photo, the colognes and puff box pictured on the left are Duncan's popular Early American Hobnail pattern. This pattern was introduced in 1930, and colors made include crystal, amber, green, ruby, sapphire blue, rose, flashed applications and opalescents. The Duncan #118 Hobnail pattern is easily confused with several other hobnail patterns which were made by Imperial and Westmoreland. The height of the cologne and stopper is 6½". The height and diameter of the puff box are 4". There are small rays beneath the finial on the lid which radiate out toward four rows of hobs. The base has four rows of hobs on its side. The underside is similar to the top of the lid. It has a ring of rays in the center surrounded on the outside by four rows of hobs.

The crystal cologne with the green-colored stopper is Duncan's Astaire pattern. It is part of a five-piece dresser set which includes a tall bath powder box, a short puff box, two colognes, and a tray. The covers, stoppers and tray may also be found in cobalt and ruby.

	Crystal/ Crystal Flashed	Pink/ Green
(a,c) Cologne, Early American Hobnail	$25.00-30.00	$35.00-40.00
(b) Puff box, Early American Hobnail	$18.00-22.00	$25.00-35.00
(d) Cologne, Astaire	$40.00-50.00	
(e) Cologne, pressed quilted pattern, large	$35.00-45.00	
(f) Cologne, pressed quilted pattern, small	$30.00-40.00	

Right Photo:

(a) Puff box, topaz $25.00-30.00
(b) Cologne, topaz..........................$30.00-40.00

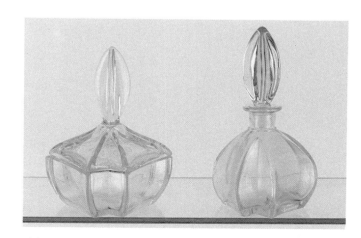

FENTON PERFUMES, PUFF BOXES, VANITY SETS

The Fenton Art Glass Company was organized in 1905 as a cutting and decorating shop in Martins Ferry, Ohio by brothers John and Frank Fenton. As business grew and the supply of glass blanks from glass companies became uncertain, the Fentons decided to construct their own glass manufacturing facility. Production of glass by Fenton began in January, 1907 at a new plant in Williamstown, West Virginia. This plant is still in operation today. Most of the collectible dresser pieces Fenton made were produced between the early 1930's and the mid-1960's. Some items which are shown in this section are still being made today. Articles manufactured after the early 1970's may be identified by the presence of a script "Fenton" signature in an oval on their underside.

As is often the case, color is an important criteria in determining the value of Fenton's pieces. Most of the items pictured on these pages have been made in a virtual spectrum of colors over the last fifty years. It is almost impossible to list, identify, and price each piece in every possible color. Items will be listed in the colors we have seen, and colors will be separated to the extent space permits. Price ranges will be given for groups of colors.

The No. 1502 perfume shown in ruby on the top row may be found either plain or with a Diamond Quilted pattern. It is pictured in Fenton catalogues as part of a dresser set, which includes two perfumes, a powder jar (shown in the photo at the bottom of the next page) and a tray like the lilac one shown in the second row. This perfume may be easily confused with a similar one made by Heisey. However, the Heisey perfume is usually signed with a diamond "H" in the bottom of its foot and is only supposed to have been made in crystal, Flamingo (pink), Emerald (light green) and Hawthorne. Unsigned perfumes in these colors require closer scrutiny to determine their origin. The diameter of the foot is Fenton - 2⅛"; Heisey - 2". Also, the foot of the Fenton perfume is thicker than that of the Heisey. The top of the Fenton stopper is a gently rounded oval; the top of the Heisey stopper is more pointed. The part of the stopper which fits inside the bottle also is different. The Fenton stopper tapers almost to a point, whereas the Heisey stopper is much thicker - about ¼" in diameter at its ground tip.

Several styles of the No. 53 puff box may be found. It may have either a flat or rounded knob finial, and the body may be smooth or have the checkerboard design like the No. 53 perfumes in the picture. Some puff boxes are entirely smooth, some have both lids and bases with the design, and others may have either the lid or the base with the pattern. The jade and black puff box has a smooth lid and a base with the checkerboard pattern on the inside. The No. 53 perfume may be found in two different sizes. Its stopper is scalloped much like some of the Cambridge stoppers. However, the Fenton stoppers are not ground on the top.

The Daisy and Button items are from a vanity set which includes two colognes, a puff box and a fan-shaped tray. The complete vanity set retailed for as little as $1.50 in the late 1930's. Commonly found colors are rose, amber, amethyst, sapphire blue and crystal.

The No. 55 one-half rose bud stopper shown on the No. 55 cologne at the bottom of the next page will also be found on the other shapes of early stretch glass perfumes.

	Rose/Amber Green	Light Blue	Orchid/ Amethyst	Jade/ Pekin Blue	Ruby/ Ebony	Stretch Colors
Cologne, #1502	$45.00-55.00		$45.00-55.00		$100.00-125.00	
* Cologne, #56			$55.00-65.00			$75.00-95.00
Cologne, #1900	$25.00-30.00	$35.00-40.00				
Cologne, #53	$35.00-45.00	$55.00-60.00	$45.00-55.00	$60.00-70.00		
* Cologne, #55						
* Cologne, #59			$50.00-60.00			$75.00-85.00
Fan tray, #957	$14.00-18.00	$18.00-20.00				
Puff box, #53	$20.00-25.00		$25.00-30.00	$25.00-30.00	$30.00-35.00	$40.00-45.00
Puff box, #1900	$18.00-20.00	$25.00-30.00				
** Puff box, #1502	$25.00-35.00		$27.00-32.00			
Tray, #53	$18.00-20.00		$25.00-30.00			

* With rose bud stopper, add 25%.
** Satin San Toy with tray, $45.00-55.00

Top Row: (a) Ruby #1502 cologne; (b) Celeste blue #56 cologne; (c) Celeste blue #53 puff box; (d) amethyst #56 cologne; (e) jade and ebony #53 puff box.

Bottom Row: (a) Sapphire blue #1900 Daisy and Button cologne; (b) sapphire blue #1900 Daisy and Button puff box; (c) amber #1900 Daisy and Button cologne; (d) green #53 cologne; (e) orchid #53 colognes and tray.

Left to right: (a) Puff box, #1502 diamond optic; (b) Cologne, topaz stretch, #59; (c) Cologne, #55, topaz stretch with #55 one-half rose bud stopper; (d) Fan tray, #957, blue opalescent Daisy and Button.

FENTON HOBNAIL VANITY SETS

The Hobnail pattern is probably the most recognized of all Fenton patterns. It was introduced in 1939 and all Hobnail produced before 1953 had the same number - 389. It is virtually impossible to date much of the older Hobnail. In some cases, color will help to establish the period of production, but some colors were introduced and discontinued periodically and other colors have been produced almost continuously. Therefore, most unsigned Fenton is collected as old without regard to exact age. Price differentials are based primarily on rarity of color.

The earliest perfumes had flat Hobnail stoppers with their color matching the color of the bottle. Puff boxes had an almost flat domed lid with only a slight indication of a raised point in the center. The mid-1940's perfume stopper is pointed like the stopper in the French opalescent bottle on the bottom row. The puff box lid also changed to the pointed knob finial. The three-piece vanity bottle which combines a perfume and puff box into one unit was introduced in 1953. This set is currently being produced in French Opalescent. The price indicated below is for older sets.

The mulberry Melon Rib and Diamond Optic puff box is shown on the left side of the bottom shelf. Mulberry is a color which is not easily found. Notice the box has a crystal Hobnail lid.

	French Opalescent	Blue Opalescent	Cranberry Opalescent	Green/Topaz Opalescent	Opaques/ White Milk Glass
Cologne, #389	$22.00-25.00	$27.00-32.00	$32.00-37.00	$32.00-37.00	$20.00-25.00
* Puff box; #389	$20.00-25.00	$25.00-30.00	$35.00-40.00	$35.00-40.00	$18.00-20.00
Vanity set, #3986	$45.00-55.00	$75.00-85.00	$80.00-90.00	$80.00-90.00	

* Melon Rib and Diamond Optic, mulberry with crystal Hobnail lid, $70.00-80.00

Top Row: (a) Topaz opalescent Hobnail puff box; (b) topaz opalescent Hobnail cologne; (c) French opalescent Hobnail #3986 combination perfume and powder vanity; (d) blue opalescent Hobnail #3986 combination perfume and powder vanity; (e) blue opalescent Hobnail cologne; (f) blue opalescent Hobnail puff box.

Bottom Row: (a) Mulberry Melon Rib and Diamond Panel puff box with crystal Hobnail lid; (b) lime green opalescent Hobnail cologne; (c) cranberry opalescent Hobnail cologne; (d) cranberry opalescent Hobnail puff box; (e) French opalescent Hobnail cologne; (f) turquoise Hobnail cologne with matching pointed stopper; (g) lime green opalescent Hobnail cologne with metal collar for DeVilbiss-style atomizer fitting.

FENTON COLOGNES AND VANITY SETS

Fenton's Swirled Feather pattern was introduced in 1953. Both the satin and shiny finish are shown in the photo. Note the satin sets have frosted crystal lids and stoppers and the shiny sets have clear crystal lids and stoppers. Colors which may be found are cranberry, green, blue and French opalescents. The satin red was originally introduced as rose, but collectors seem to prefer to call this color cranberry. None of the old vanity sets are easy to find. However, the pattern is currently being made in some of the old colors. The Fenton logo is not easy to see on the bottom of new pieces with a satin finish, but it can be found with careful examination.

Two different styles of atomizers have been seen. One style is shown in the photo and the other style has a metal cap which attaches the spray mechanism to the body. The cologne with the cranberry crest is a rare sample item which was made in 1986.

	Satin Blue Opalescent	Satin French Opalescent	Satin Cranberry/ Satin Green Opalescent	High Lustre Opalescents
Atomizer	$75.00-85.00	$50.00-55.00	$85.00-95.00	$85.00-95.00
Cologne	$65.00-75.00	$40.00-45.00	$80.00-90.00	$65.00-75.00
Puff Box	$42.00-47.00	$30.00-35.00	$62.00-67.00	$55.00-65.00

French opalescent Spiral cologne with cranberry crest, $85.00-95.00

Top Row: (a) Satin cranberry opalescent Swirled Feather vanity set; **(b)** satin blue opalescent Swirled Feather vanity set.
Bottom Row: (a) Satin green opalescent Swirled Feather atomizer; **(b)** French opalescent Spiral with cranberry crest cologne; **(c)** shiny cranberry opalescent Swirled Feather vanity set.

Several sizes of colognes and puff boxes may be found in the Melon Rib style. The pattern dates to the early 1940's and was produced in ruby overlay, blue overlay, rose overlay, peach crest, aqua crest, crystal crest and mulberry. The tall bottle and the large boxes were multipurpose items and will also be found advertised as parts of other sets or used in non-boudoir capacities.

The traditional Melon Rib shape was sometimes embellished with a Diamond Optic design. Examples are the ruby overlay pieces shown in the photo.

	Rose/Blue Overlay	Ruby Overlay	Peach Crest	Aqua Crest	Crystal Crest	Mulberry
Bottle, 7"	$22.00-27.00	$30.00-35.00	$22.00-25.00	$25.00-30.00	$20.00-22.00	$55.00-65.00
Bottle, 5½"	$20.00-25.00	$25.00-27.00	$18.00-22.00	$20.00-22.00	$18.00-20.00	$40.00-50.00
Cologne, 4¼"	$18.00-22.00	$20.00-25.00	$22.00-25.00	$27.00-30.00	$15.00-18.00	$50.00-55.00
Cologne, 5"	$18.00-22.00	$20.00-25.00	$25.00-27.00	$25.00-30.00	$18.00-20.00	$50.00-55.00
Puff box, 4"	$18.00-20.00	$25.00-30.00	$25.00-27.00	$27.00-30.00	$15.00-18.00	$40.00-50.00
Puff box, 5"	$25.00-27.00	$35.00-40.00	$27.00-30.00	$32.00-37.00	$18.00-20.00	$50.00-60.00

Top Row: (a) Blue overlay Melon Rib medium cologne; **(b)** Blue overlay Melon Rib large box; **(c)** Blue overlay Melon Rib tall bottle; **(d)** Ruby overlay Melon Rib tall bottle; **(e)** Ruby overlay Melon rib large box.
Bottom Row: (a) Ruby overlay Melon Rib medium cologne; **(b)** Ruby overlay Melon Rib puff box; **(c)** Ruby overlay Melon Rib small cologne; **(d)** Aqua crest Melon Rib puff box; **(e)** Aqua crest Melon Rib small cologne.

FENTON COIN DOT VANITY SETS

Vanity sets in Fenton's opalescent Coin Dot first appeared in 1947. The colors made include French opalescent, blue opalescent and cranberry opalescent. Several styles of stoppers and lids have been used in the set through the years.

Top Row:	French Opalescent	Blue Opalescent	Cranberry Opalescent
Bottle and stopper	$30.00-37.00	$45.00-55.00	$60.00-70.00
Cologne	$22.00-27.00	$45.00-55.00	$55.00-65.00
Puff box, 4"	$22.00-27.00	$60.00-70.00	$70.00-90.00
Large jar, crystal lid	$35.00-45.00	$65.00-75.00	$90.00-95.00
Bottom Row:			
Large jar, patterned lid	$45.00-55.00	$75.00-90.00	$90.00-110.00

Top Row: (a) Cranberry opalescent large jar; (b) Cranberry opalescent tall bottle; (c) Cranberry opalescent No. 1485 Coin Dot puff box; (d) Cranberry opalescent No. 1465 Coin Dot cologne. Bottom Row: (a) Blue opalescent No. 91 Coin Dot large jar; (b) Fenton logo from 1987; (c) Cranberry opalescent No. 91 Coin Dot large jar.

FENTON ATOMIZERS AND COLOGNES

The metal fixtures on glass atomizer bases pictured on the top row were fitted by companies other than Fenton. Companies such as DeVilbiss contracted with glass houses to produce the glass base. The independent companies then assembled and retailed the finished product. For more Fenton atomizers, see the section on DeVilbiss.

The French opalescent Hobnail perfume bottle Fenton produced under contract with the Allen B. Wrisley Company of Chicago is credited with lifting Fenton from the depths of the Great Depression. The #289 Wrisley cologne is a modification of an earlier barber bottle which Fenton made for the L.G. Wright Company. In order to reduce costs and make the bottle feasible for the lower priced perfume industry, the neck of the barber bottle was shortened and a wooden stopper was substituted.

Wrisley filled the Hobnail bottles with perfume and test marketed them in the spring and summer of 1938. The results of the tests were amazing, and Wrisley immediately launched a full campaign. As a result, Fenton could barely keep up with the avalanche of orders from Wrisley. However, by the early 1940's, Fenton's labor costs were becoming prohibitive for Wrisley, and Hocking was contracted to produce a similar machine-made bottle. The new bottle was made of opaline glass and had a cork encased glass stopper.

Besides the difference in stoppers, the bases of the Fenton and Hocking bottles differ slightly. An examination of the mold seams will identify the maker. Fenton used a six-part mold and Hocking's mold was four-part. Fenton also used a six-part mold for the puff box. Occasionally, lids are found with original paper labels which identify the contents as "Hobnail Dusting Powder by Wrisley." Gardenia, Apple Blossom and Honeysuckle fragrances were available.

A few Wrisley colognes made by Fenton have appeared in cranberry opalescent. The cologne base has also been found in green and blue opalescent with factory drilled holes to be used as lamp bases. These lamp bases were made for the Edward P. Paul and Company, Inc. in the early 1940's.

The pastel rose Swirl cologne is part of a vanity set Fenton produced in the mid-1950's. Fenton also made the set in pastel blue and pastel green.

Top Row:	French Opalescent	Blue Opalescent	Cranberry Opalescent	Rose Pastel
Atomizer, Horizontal Rib	$22.00-25.00	$25.00-28.00		
* Atomizer, Swirl			$65.00-75.00	
Atomizer, "Pearls"	$30.00-35.00	$45.00-55.00	$75.00-85.00	
Atomizer, "Pearls"	$30.00-35.00	$45.00-55.00	$75.00-85.00	
Bottom Row:				
Cologne and stopper, Fenton	$10.00-12.00			
Puff Box and lid	$8.00-10.00			
Cologne and stopper, Hocking	$5.00-8.00			
Cologne, Swirl				$20.00-25.00

Not pictured: Lamp base, French opalescent, $25-00-30.00

* Green Swirl, $50.00-60.00

Top Row: (a) Blue opalescent Horizontal Rib atomizer base made for DeVilbiss; (b) Cranberry opalescent Swirl atomizer base with metal collar; (c) Cranbery opalescent "Pearls" atomizer base made for DeVilbiss; (d) Cranberry opalescent "Pearls" atomizer base made for DeVilbiss.
Bottom Row: (a) French opalescent cologne with wooden stopper made for Wrisley; (b) French opalescent puff base with wooden lid made for Wrisley; (c) White milk glass hobnail cologne with cork encased glass stopper made by Hocking for Wrisley; (d) Pastel rose Swirl cologne.

FOSTORIA PERFUMES

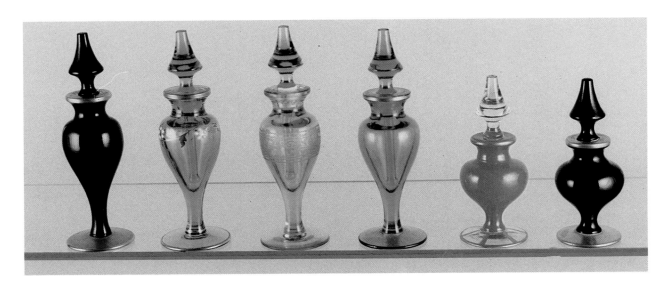

The Fostoria Glass Company was organized in Fostoria, Ohio in 1887. Initial production concentrated on lamps and lamp parts. In 1891, due to a shortage of natural gas, production was moved to Moundsville, West Virginia. Spurred on by the enthusiasm of an eager young chemist named W.F. Dalzell, who later became president of the company in 1945, Fostoria began to produce colored glass tableware and accessory pieces in the mid-1920's. The company ceased production in 1988.

Most of the colored glass perfumes such as the ones shown in the photo were produced between 1925 and the early 1940's. The tall perfume has a bottom which is 4¼" high. Its stopper is 4" long and has a ground and polished flat top. The complete perfume is 5¾" tall. The stopper of the short perfume is similar in shape to the large one, but it is only 3¼" long. The bottom is 2¾" high, and the complete perfume is 4½" tall.

Ebony, # 2322 with gold trim $60.00-70.00
Blue, # 2322 with gold leaf and white enamel
handpainted decoration $50.00-55.00
Green, # 2322 with acid etch Royal decoration $125.00-150.00
Blue, # 2322 with gold trim $50.00-55.00
Crystal, # 2323 with orange enamel and gold trim $25.00-30.00
Ebony, # 2323 with gold trim..$60.00-70.00

FOSTORIA VANITY SETS AND POWDER JARS

Beginning in the mid-1920's and ending in the early 1940's, Fostoria produced a popular three-piece vanity set which combined the perfume and powder jar in a single unit. The powder base is 4⅝" in diameter, and the total height of the vanity with the stopper in place is 7½". The length of the stopper is 4⅛". The exposed hexagonal shaped area of the stopper was ground to a sharp point. With this perfume, any lady who dared to carelessly reach for her chosen scent might risk leaving a little of her blood behind in place of the desired fragrance.

Several Fostoria powder jars are shown on the bottom row of the photo above. The first two blue jars with the flat lids are 4" in diameter. Other colors which have been found include crystal, green and amber. These powders will be found with various gold encrusted and wheel cut designs.

The green powder jar is from Fostoria's plate etching #288 pattern which is more commonly called "Cupid." Matching #2322 colognes and the three-piece #2276 vanity set may also be found. This pattern was only made for two years - 1927 to 1929 - so all pieces are in short supply. Other colors made were amber, blue and ebony. A matching clock and candle dresser set are shown on page 211. The blue puff box with the knob lid may also be found in crystal, amber, green, and ebony.

Top Row:
(a) Vaseline #2276 vanity with
    gold encrusted decoration $60.00-65.00
(b) Crystal #2276 vanity with
    orange and black enamel decoration
    and gold trim $40.00-50.00
(c) Green #2276 vanity with gold
    leaf and floral decoration $55.00-60.00

Bottom Row:
(a) Blue #2338 puff box with
    gold encrusted Royal decoration $55.00-65.00
(b) Blue #2338 puff box with
    wheel cut decoration $22.00-27.00
(c) Green, #2359 ½ puff box with
    #288 "Cupid" plate etching $75.00-85.00
(d) Blue #2347 puff box $22.00-26.00

(a) Blue #2776 vanity with wheel cut design $55.00-60.00
(b) Amber #2276 vanity with plate etch Vesper design $95.00-120.00
(c) Blue #2276 vanity with plate etch Royal design $100.00-125.00

(a) Blue #2276 vanity with wheel cut design..$55.00-60.00
(b) Ebony #2276 vanity...$70.00-75.00
(c) Green #2276 vanity with wheel cut design $47.00-55.00

FOSTORIA VANITY SETS AND COLOGNES

(a) Vanity, topaz $30.00-35.00
(b) Vanity, green with enamel decoration $30.00-35.00
(c) Vanity, amber $30.00-35.00

(a) Cologne, pressed crystal with wide neck $20.00-25.00
(b) Cologne, pressed crystal with narrow neck $20.00-25.00
(c) Cologne, crystal No. 444 .... $22.00-25.00
(d) Cologne, crystal No. 501 Hartford $45.00-55.00
(e) Cologne, crystal with gold bands and original label $20.00-25.00
(f) Cologne, crystal with satin bands $25.00-27.00
(g) Cologne, crystal bell-shaped No. 2243 with cut design $35.00-40.00

FOSTORIA AMERICAN PATTERN

Fostoria introduced the American pattern in 1915. Through the many years of production, some of the original pieces were dropped from the line, but many others were added. Several pieces were still being made when Fostoria discontinued operations, and a few items are still being made currently by another company. However, no item in the listing below is in current production.

A few pieces of the vanity set may also be found in amber, canary and blue. Some individual pieces in American were advertised with multiple functions. The puff box and the hair receiver utilize the same base. The lid of the puff box is solid, but the lid of the hair receiver has a hole in the center. Special sets were also sold which were comprised of regular stock items. For example, the Boudoir Set was composed of a one-quart jug, a 10½" x 7⅝" tray, an 8 oz. tumbler, a match box and a 7¼" tall square base candle. By convincing customers to buy special sets, Fostoria could sometimes sell duplicate items to the same individual.

American Vanity Set	Crystal	Amber	Blue
Cologne and stopper, 5¾"	$47.00-52.00		
* Cologne and stopper, 7¼"	$50.00-55.00	$250.00-295.00	$250.00-295.00
Comb and brush tray, oval 2-H 5" x 10"	$25.00-30.00		
Comb and brush tray, rect. 7½" x 10⅝"	$45.00-50.00		$125.00-150.00
Hair pin box and cover, 1¾" x 3½" x 1½"	$80.00-90.00		
Hair receiver, 3" x 3" x 2⅞"	$110.00-120.00		UND
Handkerchief box and cover, 4½" x 5½" x 2"	$120.00-140.00		
Glove box and cover, 3½" x 9½" x 2¼"	$140.00-160.00		
Jewel box and cover, 2¼" x 5¼" x 2"	$100.00-110.00		
Pin tray, oval 2-H 3" x 6¾"	$8.00-10.00	$100.00-110.00	$125.00-150.00
Pin tray, rect. 2½" x 5"	$10.00-12.00		
Pomade box, 2" x 2"	$160.00-180.00		
Puff box and cover, 3" x 3" x 2⅞"	$110.00-120.00	$225.00-250.00	$275.00-290.00

* Vaseline, $200.00 - $225.00

American Boudoir Set

	Crystal
Candle, 7¼" sq. base	$80.00-90.00
Jug, quart, 7¼"	$20.00-25.00
Match box, ¾" x 3½" x 1½"	$150.00-175.00
Tray, 7½" x 10⅝"	$45.00-50.00
Tumbler, 8 oz.	$10.00-12.00

FOSTORIA MILK GLASS BOUDOIR SET

All articles may be found with or without the Jenny Lind figure within the beaded oval. The items were issued originally without the figure and the head was added on a later reissue. Pink and powder blue colored pieces were also made in this later run. In addition to the items shown, there is a 10" long oval glove box, a 5" long pin tray, a 2⅛" high pomade and a 5¼" square handkerchief box. The glove box is the same shape as the jewel box, and the pomade is shaped like the puff box.

Top Row:	Without Figure	With Figure	Pink/ Blue
(a,b,c) Cologne flask, No. 827, 10¾" tall	$45.00-55.00	$40.00-45.00	$100.00-125.00
(d) Puff box and cover	$25.00-30.00		
Bottom Row:			
(a) Comb and brush tray, No. 824, 11½" long	$25.00-30.00	$20.00-25.00	$30.00-35.00
(b) Puff box, No. 829, 3⅛" high	$25.00-30.00	$25.00-30.00	$30.00-35.00
(c) Pin box, No. 829, 5" oval	$30.00-35.00	$27.00-32.00	$35.00-40.00
(d) Jewel box, No. 833, 6" oval	$35.00-40.00	$30.00-35.00	$40.00-45.00
Articles not shown:			
Handkerchief box, No. 831, 5¼" square	$40.00-45.00	$35.00-40.00	$40.00-50.00
Glove box, No. 832, 10⅜" oval	$50.00-60.00	$40.00-50.00	$50.00-60.00
Pin Tray, No. 826, 6" oval	$12.00-15.00	$12.00-15.00	$18.00-20.00
Pitcher, No. 834		$30.00-35.00	
Pomade, No. 830, 2⅛" high	$22.00-27.00	$20.00-25.00	$27.00-32.00
Tumbler, No. 835		$9.00-11.00	

FOSTORIA #2519 MILK GLASS VANITY SET

Fostoria's No. 2519 heavy milk glass cologne and powder jar may be found listed in catalogues from the 1960's. The cologne is 5½" high and is embossed with an all-over floral pattern. The matching puff box is 4⅜" high and 5" in diameter. The sets are usually found in white, but may also be found in blue and pink milk glass.

	White	Pink/Blue
Cologne	$45.00-55.00	$55.00-65.00
Puff box	$25.00-30.00	$35.00-40.00

HAWKES ATOMIZER

Thomas Hawkes established his glass company in Corning, New York in 1880. The company was soon recognized for its excellence in cutting and decoration. Many Hawkes pieces may be identified through the presence of the company logo - a three-lobed shape which encases a hawk in the two bottom lobes and has a fleur-de-lis in the center - which is etched into the glass.

Atomizer, green with cut decoration $90.00-110.00

HEISEY COLOGNE AND VANITY SETS

A.H. Heisey and Company of Newark, Ohio began production of glassware in 1896. The early years were devoted to the production of pressed wares which were suitable for the bar and hotel industry. Much of Heisey's glassware bears the identifying mark - an "H" within a diamond - which was designed by his son, George Duncan Heisey. Use of the trademark began in late 1900 and the mark was registered in late 1901.

HEISEY WINGED SCROLL TOILET SET

Winged Scroll was a pattern produced by Heisey between 1898 and 1901. The toilet set consists of a large 13" tray, a cologne, a puff box, a trinket box, a ring holder and one or more pin trays. The taller box is the puff box and the shorter one is the trinket box. Colors which may be found are emerald, custard, opal, vaseline, and crystal. Gold decoration is common. The trinket box is frequently found in clambroth and was issued as a souvenir in this color.

	Crystal	Emerald	Custard	Opal
Cologne	$60.00-75.00	$140.00-175.00	$125.00-145.00	$125.00-145.00
Pin Tray	$35.00-45.00	$75.00-100.00	$75.00-90.00	$70.00-90.00
Puff box	$35.00-45.00	$75.00-100.00	$80.00-90.00	$80.00-90.00
Ring holder	$175.00-200.00	$400.00-500.00	$325.00-375.00	$400.00-450.00
Tray, 13"	$75.00-85.00	$160.00-185.00	$135.00-150.00	$135.00-150.00
Trinket box	$25.00-35.00	$50.00-75.00	$45.00-65.00	$45.00-65.00
Not Pictured:				
Hair receiver	$35.00-45.00	$75.00-100.00	$70.00-90.00	$70.00-90.00

HEISEY COLOGNES AND VANITY SETS

Most of the colored colognes and vanity sets shown on this page were produced in the decade between 1925 and 1935. Heisey used a numbering system to identify the colognes. Over the years, collectors and researchers have given many of the numbered colognes names. These names are included in parentheses behind the number in the descriptions.

Top Row:

#515 (Taper)

The first three colognes illustrate the 1¼ oz. #515 (Short Taper) cologne with the #69 stopper. The three Heisey colors are Moongleam (green), Hawthorne (orchid) and Flamingo (pink). The cologne was produced both plain and with the diamond optic design. The colognes are usually marked with a diamond "H" in the center of the foot. This style cologne is similar to one produced by Fenton. For an explanation of the differences, see the Fenton section. This style cologne will also be found in crystal in a 2 oz. size called Tall Taper. These large crystal colognes will often be found with decorative cuttings.

#517 (Circle Pair)

The fourth cologne is #517 (Circle Pair) shown here in Moongleam with the #69 stopper. It was produced in the ¼ oz. size and has a diamond optic design. Other colors made were Flamingo and Crystal.

#4035 (Seven Octagon)

The last two colognes are Heisey's #4035 (Seven Octagon) with #77 duck stopper. The name is derived from the seven steps and eight sides of the cologne. The first cologne on the bottom row is similar, but it has round sides. This is a ¾ oz. bottle and may sometimes be found with the #69 stopper. In addition to Moongleam and Flamingo, Crystal examples may be found.

Bottom Row:

#4034 (Seven Circle)

The first cologne is a ¾ oz. #4034 (Seven Circle) with a #69 stopper. This bottle will also be found in Crystal and Moongleam, and it comes with the #77 duck stopper.

#4035 (Seven Octagon)

These two colognes are the same as the ones on the right side of the top row, but are shown here with the #69 stopper.

#516 (Fairacre)

The last two colognes on the bottom row are examples of the #516 (Fairacre) shape with the diamond optic design. This bottle was made in the 1 oz. size and used the #76 stopper. Examples will also be found without the diamond optic. Colors made were Moongleam, Flamingo, Hawthorne and Crystal.

#1186 Yeoman

The #1186 Yeoman powder puff may be found with or without the diamond optic design. It goes well with either the Fairacre or Taper colognes to produce a vanity set. The crystal insert for the powder puff is usually missing. An example is shown in the illustration at the bottom of page 109.

In the price guide below, the Seven Octagon and Seven Circle colognes are priced with the #69 stopper. With the #77 duck stopper, add $50.00.

	Crystal	Moongleam	Flamingo	Hawthorne
#515 (Taper) 2 oz.	$35.00-40.00			
#515 (Taper) 1¼ oz.	$30.00-35.00	$95.00-125.00	$85.00-95.00	$110.00-120.00
#517 (Circle Pair)	$30.00-35.00	$95.00-120.00	$90.00-110.00	
#4035 (Seven Circle)	$30.00-40.00	$80.00-90.00	$80.00-90.00	
#4034 (Seven Octagon)	$25.00-30.00	$80.00-90.00	$80.00-90.00	
#516 (Fairacre)	$25.00-30.00	$90.00-110.00	$85.00-95.00	
#1186 Yeoman puff box	$25.00-30.00	$50.00-60.00	$35.00-45.00	$110.00-125.00
Puff box insert	$18.00-20.00			

Row 1: (a) Cologne, #515 Taper, Moongleam; (b) Cologne, #515 Taper, Hawthorne; (c) Cologne, #515 Taper, Flamingo; (d) Cologne, #517 Circle Pair, emerald; (e,f) Cologne, #4035 Seven Octagon with #77 duck stopper, Flamingo and emerald.

Row 2: (a) Cologne, #4034 Seven Circle, Flamingo; (b) Cologne, #4035 Seven Octagon, Moongleam; (c) Cologne, #4035 Seven Octagon, Flamingo; (d) Cologne, #516 Fairacre, Moongleam; (e) Puff box, #1186 Yeoman, Flamingo; (f) Cologne, #516 Fairacre, Flamingo.

Puff box, #1186 Yeoman with crystal insert.

HEISEY COLOGNES AND PUFF BOXES

Top Row:

The colognes pictured on the top row illustrate several different sizes of the style called "Hexagon Stem" by collectors. Heisey catalogues list this cologne in various sizes and with several different stoppers. These colognes are crystal, but may be decorated with elaborate cuttings, colored stains or gold designs. The first cologne illustrates a cutting, the third cologne has a blue stain, and the second to last cologne is decorated with gold. The bottoms are generally marked with the "H" in a diamond trademark in the center of the bottom of the foot. Various stoppers were used to produce the finished products as follows:

The #485 cologne was sold with the pointed #64 stopper complete with long dauber in 1 oz., 1¼ oz., and 3½ oz. sizes. This style cologne is illustrated by the third through sixth colognes shown on the top row.

The #486 cologne uses the same cologne body as the #485, but has a pointed #66 stopper which lacks a long dauber. The sizes available are 1 oz., 2 oz., and 4 oz.

The #487 cologne uses a #63 stopper with a flat rounded top and a long dauber. This bottle came in three sizes - 1 oz., 1¼ oz., and 3½ oz. Examples are the two colognes on the left side of the top row.

The #488 cologne has the same body as the #487 cologne, but was listed with a #61 stopper, which is a flat rounded stopper which lacks a long dauber. This cologne was made in 1 oz., 2 oz. and 4 oz. sizes.

Bottom Row:

The first bottle is Heisey's #1503 Crystolite pattern 4 oz. cologne with #108 stopper. These bottles were usually sold with the matching Crystolite 4¾" diameter puff box to produce a vanity set. The second cologne is a tall crystal Horizontal Thread style with a flat stopper. Heisey's #1403 Ipswich cologne with a #91 stopper is illustrated in the center of the row. The fourth cologne is gold decorated. This same bottle was used with various stoppers to produce the following colognes:

The #489 2 oz. cologne used a #64 pointed stopper with a long dauber.

The #490 2 oz. cologne used a #66 pointed stopper which lacks a long dauber.
The #491 2 oz. cologne was sold with the #63 flat rounded top stopper with a long dauber.
The #492 cologne used a #61 flat rounded top stopper without a long dauber.

The short round 2 oz. cologne on the end was sold two different ways. It was a #493 cologne with the flat rounded #65 stopper with a long dauber. When it was sold with the #61 stopper, the cologne was designated #494.

Cologne	Crystal	Colored Stain	Crystal with Cutting
#485, #487 1 oz.	$20.00-25.00	$45.00-55.00	$50.00-55.00
#485, #487 1¾ oz.	$20.00-25.00	$45.00-55.00	$50.00-55.00
#485, #487 3½ oz.	$25.00-30.00	$45.00-55.00	$50.00-60.00
#486, #488 1 oz.	$20.00-25.00	$40.00-50.00	$50.00-55.00
#486, #488 2 oz.	$20.00-25.00	$40.00-50.00	$50.00-55.00
#486, #488 4 oz.	$25.00-30.00	$40.00-45.00	$45.00-50.00
#1503 Crystolite	$50.00-60.00		
Horizontal Thread, tall	$50.00-60.00		
#1403 Ipswich	$85.00-95.00		
#489, #492 2 oz.	$30.00-35.00		$40.00-45.00
#493, #494 2 oz.	$30.00-35.00		$40.00-45.00

(a) Cologne, Lariat $45.00-55.00
(b) Cologne, short Horizontal Threads with peaked stopper $45.00-55.00
(c) Puff box, pressed glass base with embossed silverplate top $55.00-65.00
(d) Puff box, clear base with enameled top $40.00-45.00

IMPERIAL GLASS COMPANY VANITY SETS

Production of glass began at Imperial's plant in Bellaire, Ohio in 1904. Initial capacity was filled producing pressed tableware, jelly glasses and hotel tumblers. Imperial was a pioneer in the world of colored glassware. Iridescent "Carnival Glass" was produced beginning in 1910. From there, Imperial progressed to stretch glass and finally to transparent colored glass by the mid-1920's. The Early American Hobnail vanity sets shown on the top row may be found in many of Imperial's vibrant colors, including opalescents. The more frequently found colors are pink, green, amber and crystal. Found less often are Ritz blue, black and ruby. A treatment called Sea Foam was introduced to the line in 1931. This consisted of the semi-transparent colors of moss green, Harding blue and burnt almond edged with opalescence. These opalescent colors are not commonly found.

The pink vanity set shown on the left side of the bottom row is commonly called "Twisted Optic." It may be found in amber, green and pink. The crystal colognes and puff box are Imperial's #699 Mt. Vernon pattern. This pattern was also called Washington in some Imperial ads and catalogues. The puff box is rectangular, measuring 2⅞" by 3½". The square colognes are 5½" tall. The three-piece amber set illustrates Imperial's #169 My Lady dresser set. This set may be found with various cuttings in amber, green and pink.

Top Row:	Crystal	Amber/Pink Green	Ritz blue Black/Ruby	Opalescent Colors
Early American Hobnail				
Cologne and stopper, #742	$8.00-10.00	$15.00-20.00	$25.00-35.00	$30.00-35.00
Puff Box, #742	$10.00-12.00	$18.00-20.00	$25.00-30.00	$25.00-35.00
Bottom Row:				
Twisted Optic cologne		$35.00-40.00		
Twisted Optic puff box		$8.00-10.00		
Twisted Optic tray		$8.00-10.00		
Mt. Vernon cologne	$15.00-18.00			
Mt. Vernon puff box	$15.00-18.00			
My Lady cologne		$30.00-35.00		
My Lady puff box		$12.00-15.00		
My Lady tray		$8.00-10.00		

The Imperial vanity sets shown here are distinguished by their unique stoppers. The stoppers are fan-shaped with narrow panels and do not have long daubers. A pink swirl No. 153 set is pictured on the top row and Imperial's basic No. 1300 Reeded pattern set is shown on the bottom row. Notice in the accompanying Imperial catalogue reprint, (shown on page 114) other stoppers may be found with these colognes. Both styles of colognes are 4½" tall, and both puff boxes are 4" in diameter.

	Green/ Pink	Black/White Combination
Top Row:		
Swirl cologne	$15.00-20.00	
Swirl puff box	$15.00-20.00	
Bottom Row:		
Cologne, #1300 Reeded		$20.00-25.00
Puff box, #1300 Reeded		$18.00-20.00

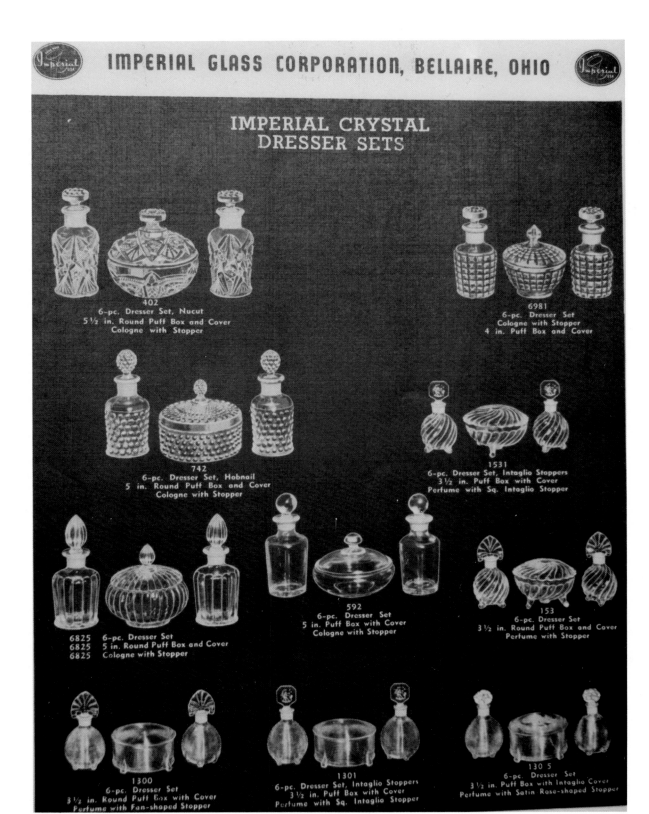

IMPERIAL GLASS CORPORATION, BELLAIRE, OHIO

IMPERIAL CRYSTAL
DRESSER SETS

402
6-pc. Dresser Set, Nucut
5½ in. Round Puff Box and Cover
Cologne with Stopper

6981
6-pc. Dresser Set
Cologne with Stopper
4 in. Puff Box and Cover

742
6-pc. Dresser Set, Hobnail
5 in. Round Puff Box and Cover
Cologne with Stopper

1531
6-pc. Dresser Set, Intaglio Stoppers
3½ in. Puff Box with Cover
Perfume with Sq. Intaglio Stopper

6825
6825   6-pc. Dresser Set
6825   5 in. Round Puff Box and Cover
            Cologne with Stopper

592
6-pc. Dresser Set
5 in. Puff Box with Cover
Cologne with Stopper

153
6-pc. Dresser Set
3½ in. Round Puff Box and Cover
Perfume with Stopper

1300
6-pc. Dresser Set
3½ in. Round Puff Box with Cover
Perfume with Fan-shaped Stopper

1301
6-pc. Dresser Set, Intaglio Stoppers
3½ in. Puff Box with Cover
Perfume with Sq. Intaglio Stopper

130 5
6-pc. Dresser Set
3½ in. Puff Box with Intaglio Cover
Perfume with Satin Rose-shaped Stopper

IMPERIAL'S CANDLEWICK VANITY SET

Imperial suffered severe cash problems during the depression and was forced into bankruptcy in 1931. Therefore in the mid-1930's, the company desperately needed a successful crystal pattern to compete with the other quality crystal products on the market. Upon the recovery of the general economy of the nation, the leaders of Imperial cast their fate and the fortune of the struggling company on the promising sales of their new Candlewick pattern. This line which had its modest start with a few simple trial pieces soon developed into one of Imperial's most successful products of all time. As a result, new pieces were designed and several cuttings were implemented. Among the new items in 1940 was a boudoir set made for the Irving Rice Company of New York. The set consisted of two cologne bottles, a puff box and clock. Some versions also included a 10" round mirrored tray. There are two sizes of cologne bottles - 6½" and 5¾". Both use a four-bead stopper, but they are not interchangeable. The colognes with the beaded foot are more desirable among today's collectors. The puff box was produced by using the regular line sherbet as the base and designing a lid to fit. The lid is slightly domed and has a three-bead finial. These pieces will occasionally be found with one of the various etchings.

The boudoir clock is round, 4" in diameter, and has a beaded edge like the mirror. The round 10" ribbed tray will be found both with and without a mirror since it was a multi-purpose item, used both for the boudoir set and as a serving tray and underplate in the kitchen.

The mirror is 4¼" in diameter and has a beaded edge. It is supported by two large beads on the bottom and a curled glass arm which extends downward from the center of the glass back. The mirror is held in place by glue and a tension spring.

	Crystal	Crystal with Cutting
Clock, 4"	$250.00-275.00	
Cologne, 6½"	$30.00-35.00	$45.00-55.00
Mirror, 4¼"	$75.00-85.00	
Puff box, 4"	$35.00-40.00	$55.00-60.00
Tray with mirror, 10"	$45.00-55.00	

LANCASTER GLASS COMPANY VANITY SETS

The Lancaster Glass Company was founded in Lancaster, Ohio in 1908. It became a subsidiary of the Hocking Glass Company in 1924, and was later operated as Plant #2 of the Anchor Hocking Corporation. Several styles of perfumes and puff boxes were produced from the mid-1920's through the mid-1930's. Vanity sets were produced by combining a small oval tray with two perfumes and a puff box.

Top Row: The bodies of all the bottles except the last one on the right have a wide neck with wide, rounded shoulders. The bodies taper to a small upraised ⅜" high pedestal above the foot and they are 4¼" tall. There are two types of stoppers - both with a long dauber. The top of one style looks like a beehive; the other has a cone-shaped appearance with a ground top. Both stoppers are 4¼" long. The green perfume on the right side has a hexagon stem base. The base is 5" tall and is fitted with a beehive stopper.

The blue puff box is decorated to match the perfumes. It is 4" in diameter and has a knob lid with a finial the same shape as the top of the perfume stopper. However, the top of this knob is not ground. As may be seen in the picture, cuttings, etchings and handpainted enamel decorations were popular. Some of these finishing touches may have been done at Lancaster's sister company - Standard.

Bottom Row: The first three perfumes are the same style as the shorter perfumes on the top row. The two bottles on the left side have a crackle appearance. The first one is flashed pink with a blue beehive stopper, and the second is flashed green over crystal with a crystal stopper. The base of the frosted green perfume on the right side is 4" high. It is wider than the taller bottles and has a shorter pedestal at its junction with the base.

The base of the green crackle puff box is the same as the blue one on the top row. However, the lid is slightly different. The side of the finial is more rounded and rests on a more pronounced collar.

	Crystal/ Flashed Crystal	Green/ Pink	Blue
Perfume, tapered	$15.00-18.00	$30.00-35.00	$40.00-45.00
Perfume, hexagon		$32.00-38.00	
Perfume, short wide		$45.00-55.00	
Puff box	$10.00-12.00	$18.00-20.00	$20.00-25.00

LIBERTY WORKS VANITY SET

The Liberty Glass Works Company was formed in Egg Harbor, New Jersey in 1903 as a cutting and decorating shop. Later, the company began making its own glassware, and by the Depression Era, it was producing numerous lines of colored glassware. One of the more notable tableware patterns was American Pioneer which was introduced in 1931. This line included a vanity set which was produced in crystal, pink, and green. The set consists of a round covered puff box, a round tray, and two round, flat colognes with long stoppers.

The Liberty Works plant burned in 1932 and was not rebuilt. As a result of the short production, American Pioneer vanity items are not easy to find.

	Crystal	Pink/Green
Cologne, 4¼"	$30.00-35.00	$70.00-80.00
Puff box, 4¼"	$30.00-35.00	$50.00-60.00
Tray, 7½"	$18.00-20.00	$30.00-35.00

NEW MARTINSVILLE VANITY SETS

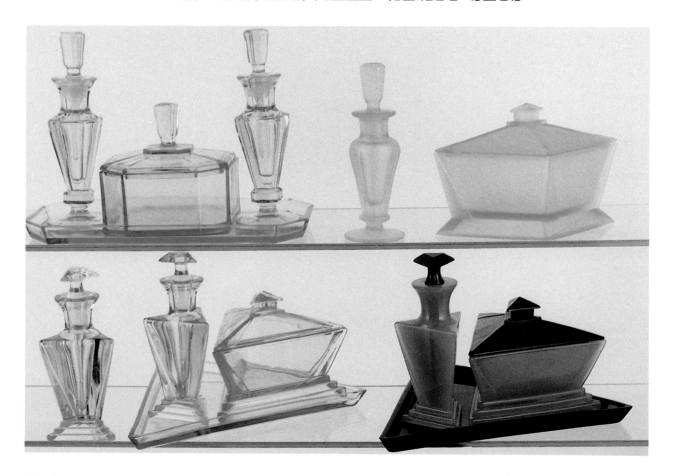

The New Martinsville Glass Manufacturing Company was formed in New Martinsville, West Virginia in 1901. Introduction of colored glass vanity sets occurred in 1926, and the company soon became a leader in the design and production of boudoir and toiletry articles.

Top Row: A vanity set with eight-sided articles is pictured on the left side of the photo. This set may also be found in transparent pink, frosted green, frosted pink and jadite with black stoppers and puff box top.

The perfumes to the vanity set are large and rather bulky looking. The body has eight sides with alternating large and small vertical panels. The body tapers to an enlarged stem which is also eight-sided and has panels of alternating size. The height of the body is 5⅛". The stopper is 4¼" long with an octagonal top, like the other New Martinsville perfumes with long tapers on the following pages.

The transparent green puff box is eight-sided with long panels in the center and narrow panels on the corners of the box. It is 4" square and has a lid with an octagonal shaped finial which matches the shape of the perfume stoppers.

The tray is eight-sided and measures 4¾" wide by 9½" long. Pie-shaped wedges are formed on the bottom by five lines which radiate from the center of the bottom toward the edge of the long sides.

The diamond-shaped powder jar illustrated by frosted green example was patented by New Martinsville in 1924. The jar is 4¼" wide and 6½" long. It is elevated slightly by a solid foot which flares out slightly. The lid has a diamond-shaped finial to match the form of the jar.

Bottom Row: The style of vanity set shown here is very difficult to find in good condition. The numerous sharp corners are quite easily damaged. In addition to the colors shown, sets may be found in transparent pink, frosted pink and frosted green.

The body of the perfume is triangular in shape and is 5" tall. The foot is also triangular and has three steps. The stopper is 4¼" long and has a triangular-shaped head that is grounded on the top.

The triangular-shaped puff box has three steps at its base to match the base of the perfumes. The length of each side is 5¼". The lid is slightly peaked and has a triangular-shaped finial. According to patent information, the jar was designed in 1928 by Robert McEldowney. This patent was then assigned to the New Martinsville Glass Manufacturing Company.

	Pink/Green	Jadite/Black
Perfume, octagonal	$40.00-45.00	$60.00-70.00
Perfume, triangular	$50.00-55.00	$60.00-70.00
Puff box, diamond shape	$25.00-30.00	
Puff box, octagonal	$22.00-27.00	
Puff box, triangular	$30.00-35.00	$60.00-70.00
Tray, octagonal	$12.00-15.00	
Tray, triangular	$18.00-20.00	$25.00-30.00

Reprint showing vanity sets from an early 1930's New Martinsville catalogue.

Top Row: The No. 1926 perfumes shown here illustrate New Martinsville's diverse colors. Two perfumes, the pictured puff box and a heavy ribbed rectangular tray were combined in a 1926 ad as the No. 1926/2 "Mysterious" vanity set. The perfume bottom is 3¾" high. The body is a gently rounded ellipse, and there is a slight outward round projection in the area of the stem. The stopper is 3¼" long. It has a round, flat top which has been ground in the center.

The 4¼" diameter puff box has two compartments. The larger bottom area was designed to hold powder and a powder puff. The smaller compartment formed on the top of the powder lid is 1½" in diameter and was designed to hold rouge or cold cream. Inside the rouge area is the mark "Pat. Apld. For." This puff box will also be found with a plain domed lid which lacks the rouge compartment.

Bottom Row: The tall tapered perfumes in this row all have a body with an interior swirl. The bottom is 4¼" tall and has a ⅜" high pedestal stem with a slight ridge at the top. Two styles of stoppers were used with this perfume. The stopper with the flat, scalloped top which is ground in the center is 3¾" long. The other stopper is 4¼" long and has a top which is octagonal shaped with a flat ground end.

The puff box is about 4" square, but appears to be rectangular in shape, since two sides are straight and the other two sides are scalloped and bulge outward at the center. The bottom is elevated slightly by the use of four small feet. The lid has a swirl design in the center area, and the flat knob has scallops which match the ends of the flat perfume stoppers. The puff box has been found in transparent green with a lid that has a tall octagonal-shaped finial.

Technically, the jadite and black perfumes should have flat ruffled stoppers if they are to match the powder box, but sets in these colors are always seen with the octagonal stoppers. If jadite or black flat stoppers were made, we have never seen one.

The matching tray is rectangular with slightly scalloped sides. It has ribs on the bottom which fan outward from the center to the edge. It measures 4¾" wide by 9¼" long.

	Crystal	Pink/Green Amber	Amethyst Blue	Jadite Black
Perfume, No. 1926	$15.00-18.00	$25.00-28.00	$37.00-40.00	
Perfume, swirl taper	$18.00-20.00	$28.00-30.00	$40.00-45.00	$50.00-55.00
Puff box, round		$18.00-20.00	$25.00-30.00	
Puff box, square		$18.00-20.00	$20.00-22.00	$27.00-30.00
Tray		$10.00-12.00	$15.00-18.00	$20.00-25.00

The perfumes shown in this photo are all the same style. They are a tall taper like the ones on the previous page, but lack any swirl design in their body. They are 4¼" tall and have a short ⅜" pedestal above the foot with a small ridge at the top edge. Most of the perfumes have stoppers which have a tall octagonal-shaped top with a ground end. The length of these stoppers is 4¼". A few perfumes will be found with the shorter 3¾" flat ruffled top stopper as seen in the previous picture. However, the perfume with a flat stopper is not normally found in vanity sets with the puff boxes shown here, but is used with the flat oval puff box shown on page 122. Some of the perfumes will have the New Martinsville trademark embossed in the center of the bottom of the foot.

The two different style puff boxes shown here both have the same tall octagonal-shaped knob. The larger jar is flat with a flat lid and is 4¼" in diameter. The smaller jar is 3¾" in diameter.

Numerous trays were made for these vanity sets. The frosted pink one shown on the top row is oval. It is decorated to match the rest of the set and measures 4¾" wide by 8½" long. The round tray on the bottom row is 7¼" in diameter. It is not decorated, but its accompanying perfumes and puff box have an elegant floral wheel cutting. The green triangular-shaped tray has rounded corners and the length of each side is 7".

	Crystal	Pink/Green Amber	Black/Cobalt Jadite	Amethyst Blue
Perfume, plain taper	$15.00-18.00	$27.00-30.00	$50.00-55.00	$35.00-40.00
Puff box, 4¼"	$10.00-12.00	$18.00-20.00	$20.00-25.00	$18.00-20.00
Puff box, 3¾"	$10.00-12.00	$18.00-20.00		$18.00-20.00
Tray, oval	$7.00-9.00	$8.00-10.00		$9.00-11.00
Tray, round	$7.00-9.00	$8.00-10.00		$9.00-11.00
Tray, triangular	$8.00-10.00	$10.00-12.00		$12.00-14.00

Top Row: The oval puff box and pink perfume on the left with the handpainted floral decorations are part of a vanity set. The tall tapered perfume has a plain body with a flat ruffled stopper and is the same as the ones described on page 121. The oval puff box has two compartments. The large compartment on the bottom has three divisions. A round area in the center is for powder and a recessed groove on each side is designed to hold lipstick. A separate small round covered area on the top of the lid is designed for eye makeup or cold cream. The puff box is 3¾" wide by 6¾" long.

The small pinkish-amber perfume in the center is a variation of the No. 1926 perfume shown on page 120. The two styles are identical, except the one pictured here has a vertically paneled body. These perfumes are often found with the New Martinsville trademark embossed on the bottom of the foot.

The crystal and red vanity set was produced during the early 1930's and is called "Judith." The stoppers are the same shape as those used with the "Judy" set shown on the next page. The set consists of two colognes, a puff box and an oval tray. Sets will usually be found with colored cologne stoppers and puff box lid, crystal bottoms and a crystal tray. Commonly found colors of the tops are jadite and black. The 3½" high round cologne base has an embossed small diamond pattern with an alternating clear area of embossed circles on each side. The heart-shaped stopper is 2½" long. Both the lid and base of the puff box have an all-over embossed small diamond pattern. The jar is 3¼" in diameter and the lid has a heart-shaped finial which matches the shape of the cologne stoppers. The matching 8¾" two-handled oval tray has several rows of diamond stipples on the underside around its outside edge. The underside of the center area has fine lines radiating from the middle.

Bottom Row: During the 1930's, New Martinsville advertised a No. 18/2 four-piece vanity set. The set consisted of a diamond-shaped puff box, two colognes and a mirror tray. The set is commonly found with pieces having crystal bases and colored stoppers, but solid colored sets may also be found. The cologne base is 3" tall and the stopper is 3¼" long. It does not have a long dauber. There are two sizes of puff boxes. The smaller one is used in the vanity set, and the larger one does not appear to have any matching accessories. The small puff box is 3¼" wide and 5½" long. The large puff box is 3¾" wide and 6¼" long.

	Crystal with Colored Top	Pink/Green Amber
Cologne, No. 18/2	$18.00-20.00	$22.00-25.00
Cologne, "Judith"	$22.00-27.00	
Perfume, No. 1926		$27.00-30.00
Perfume, plain taper		$27.00-30.00
Puff box, oval 2-part		$20.00-25.00
Puff box, "Judith"	$15.00-18.00	
Puff box, small diamond	$12.00-14.00	$15.00-18.00
Puff box, large diamond		$20.00-25.00

Top Row: According to original early 1930's ads, this style of "brilliant diamond" vanity set was available in "all crystal, all rose, or all green ... as well as the popular combinations of crystal with jade green or black stoppers and covers ... with an extremely attractive decorated mirror plateau 7 x 14 inches to make it doubly beautiful." The set was named "Geneva" by Hazel Weatherman. The cold cream and make-up jars were offered separately. The footed perfume base is 4¼" tall and the stopper is 3¼" long. The powder jar is 3¾" in diameter. The base is the same as the one used with the "Judy" set shown on the bottom row, but the lid has a finial matching the perfume stoppers. The cold cream jar is 2½" in diameter and 2½" high. The smaller make-up jar is 2¼" in diameter and 1¾" tall.

Bottom Row: The first vanity set with the small embossed diamond design has been called "Judy" by Hazel Weatherman. The shape of the perfume base is the same as in the sets above and the stoppers, lid, and tray are the same as those used with the "Judith" set on the previous page. Solid color sets in crystal, pink, green and amber may also be found.

The cologne bottles to the vanity set on the right (called "Leota" by Hazel Weatherman) have wide concentric ribs with beehive stoppers. The bottoms are 3½" high and the stoppers are 2" long. The puff box is 3¾" in diameter. The base has vertical ribs, and the lid has horizontal concentric ribs.

Crystal with Colored Tops

Cologne, "Geneva"	$18.00-20.00
Cologne, "Judy"	$18.00-20.00
Cologne, "Leota"	$18.00-20.00
Jar, cold cream	$7.00-9.00
Jar, make-up	$7.00-9.00
Puff box, "Geneva"	$12.00-14.00
Puff box, "Judy"	$12.00-14.00
Puff box, "Leota"	$12.00-14.00

Top Row: The left side features "Leota" pieces shown in the previous photo which have been modified by adding vertical ribbing to produce a checked design. These vanity sets have plume-style stoppers and may be found in all crystal, all pink, all green or in crystal with black or jadite stoppers and lids. The lid of the puff box has concentric ribs and a plume-shaped finial.

The pink cologne on the right has the traditional New Martinsville fancy plume stopper. It is 6" tall with its stopper in place.

Bottom Row: The Moondrops cologne and puff box are shown on this row. New Martinsville introduced the Moondrops line in 1932 and the shape proved attractive and sold well. Colors that may be found are ruby, cobalt, ice blue, light green, dark green, jadite, pink, amber, amethyst, black and crystal.

The cologne is a very heavy 4¾" tall glass bottle with a rocket-like stem. "Moondrops" are prominently embossed on the lower area of the body between the points of attachment of the rocket legs. The plume-style stopper is 2" long.

The base of the 3¾" diameter puff box has three rectangular feet which extend downward from the sides and meet in the center of the bottom. There are two embossed "Moondrops" positioned on the body between each foot. The slightly domed lid has interior panels and a plume finial.

	Crystal	Crystal/ Colored Tops	Pink/Green Amber	Light Blue	Cobalt/Ruby Black/Jadite
Cologne, checked	$10.00-12.00	$12.00-14.00	$20.00-30.00		
Cologne, large plain			$20.00-25.00		
Cologne, Moondrops	$45.00-55.00		$50.00-60.00	$125.00-150.00	$175.00-200.00
Puff box, checked	$10.00-12.00	$12.00-14.00	$14.00-16.00		
Puff box, Moondrops	$45.00-55.00		$85.00-95.00	$95.00-110.00	$145.00-165.00

PADEN CITY PERFUMES AND VANITY SETS

The Paden City Glass Manufacturing Company was founded in Paden City, West Virginia in 1916. Production of colored glassware started in the early 1920's. Brilliantly colored vanity sets were one of the company's major products. These sets were often wheel cut or handpainted.

The perfumes shown in this photo are all the same style. They have a smooth tapered body which is connected to a small raised ridge on their round foot by a 1" hexagonal stem. The height of the bottle is 4½". The 3¾" long stopper has a flat round top which is ground in the center.

The puff box has a small round foot. It is 4" in diameter and the knob on the lid is attached with a short hexagonal-shaped stem.

The 4½" by 10" tray is oval and has thick ribs which are perpendicular to the long sides.

	Crystal	Pink/Green Amber	Cobalt	Mulberry
Perfume	$18.00-20.00	$25.00-30.00	$50.00-55.00	$35.00-40.00
Puff box		$14.00-16.00	$18.00-22.00	$14.00-16.00
Tray		$9.00-11.00	$16.00-18.00	$10.00-12.00

Top Row: The tall No. 500-5 perfumes on the left have a smooth tapered 5¼" tall body which is joined to a round foot by a long hexagon stem. The flat top of the stopper is separated from the ground fitting by a ¾" long hexagon stem. The stopper is 4" long, and its top is ground smooth. Colors usually found are amber, green, blue, and mulberry.

The smaller No. 502-5 perfumes on the right use the same stopper as the larger ones. The 4¼" tall body has 1¾" long embossed vertical panels circling the lower part and is joined to the foot via a ⅜" high stem. The colors are the same as above.

The No. 503-5 puff box is 4" in diameter and has a small foot with an embossed star in the center. The lid has a small knob with a hexagon stem connecting it to a small raised area on the top.

Bottom Row:

The vanity set on the left is from the late 1920's and is part of the No. 191 line, more commonly known as "Party Line." Sets will be found in pink, green and blue.

The 4½" tall perfume bottom is flat and has four large concentric rings near the base. The stopper is 4¾" long. It has a ground flat top which is connected to the ground fitting by a hexagon-shaped stem which is ¾" long.

The 4" diameter puff jar is footed and has four concentric ribs near the bottom of the body. The lid has four concentric ribs near the point where the knob attaches. The round flat knob is attached to the lid with a short hexagon-shaped stem.

The 5" by 9½" tray is rectangular, but has twelve scalloped sides. The footed green No. 201-4 puff box is 4" in diameter. It has an embossed star in the bottom and an embossed diamond pattern around the lower half of the body. Colors produced were green, amber, blue and mulberry.

The perfume on the right is Paden City's No. 499 1 oz. bottle. The body is smooth and tapers to a pedestal which rises ⅜" above the foot. The stopper is 4⅜" long. The top is ground and the sides are octagon-shaped. Colors which have been found are blue, green, amethyst, amber and black.

For information and pricing on the "Sunset" vanity set, see page 128.

	Crystal	Pink/Green Amber	Blue/Black Mulberry
Perfume, "Party Line"		$35.00-40.00	$55.00-65.00
Perfume, No. 500-5	$15.00-18.00	$25.00-30.00	$50.00-60.00
Perfume, No. 502-5	$15.00-18.00	$25.00-30.00	$50.00-60.00
Perfume, No. 499	$15.00-18.00	$22.00-27.00	$45.00-55.00
Puff box, "Party Line"		$20.00-25.00	$27.00-32.00
Puff box, No. 201-4	$12.00-14.00	$18.00-20.00	$22.00-25.00
Puff box, No. 503-5	$12.00-14.00	$18.00-20.00	$22.00-27.00
Tray, No. 449		$18.00-22.00	$25.00-30.00

"Sunset" vanity set with ruby stoppers, lid and tray.

Reprint of perfumes and puff boxes from an early 1930's Paden City catalogue.

127

Top Row: The Paden City No. 215 vanity set, which has been named "Sunset" by Hazel Weatherman is shown on the left. This set was available in all crystal or in combinations of crystal bottoms and colored lids and stoppers. Colors advertised were amber, cobalt, ruby, forest green, pink, and black. The type of tray was optional. A tray could be chosen which matched the color of the tops or an oval mirror tray was available if the customer desired.

The flat bottom cologne has a vertically ribbed body which is 3" tall. Its stopper is fan-shaped and measures 3¼" long. The sides of the flat bottom puff box flare outward, and its vertical ribs form a sawtooth edge. The lid has a large flat, rayed knob which covers most of its surface. A short sawtooth edge rests over the edge formed by the ribs on the bottom. The tray is the same as the one used with the set on the previous page.

The No. 700 blue puff box is 4¾" in diameter. It is round with straight sides and has a small foot. The lid is flat and has a round flat knob which is attached with a hexagonal-shaped stem.

The perfumes on the right are Paden City's No. 503. They are very similar to the Cambridge perfume shown on page 74, but the beehive on these stoppers is not as tall. The base of the perfume is short and the body is round. The bottle is 3" tall and the stopper is 3" long.

Bottom Row: The vanity set on the left is embossed with a diamond-shaped pattern. It was called "Moon Set" by Hazel Weatherman, and the set normally consists of the three pieces shown and a mirror tray. Numerous colors of lids and stoppers may be found. These include cobalt, ruby, green, pink, amethyst, amber and black.

The colognes are round with a flat bottom. The base is 3" tall and the stoppers are 3¾" long. The puff box is 4¼" in diameter. The base has a flat bottom, and the lid has a long pointed finial which matches the size of the cologne stoppers.

The 3¾" diameter puff box on the right is crystal with a metal lid. It is very similar to the Cambridge Caprice puff box shown on page 84. The easiest way to tell the difference is to look for rays in the bottom. The Paden City powder has rays, but the Cambridge one does not.

	Crystal	Green/Pink Amber	Blue/Black Amethyst	Colored Top/ Crystal Bottom
Cologne, "Moon Set"				$25.00-35.00
Cologne, "Sunset"	$10.00-20.00			$25.00-35.00
Perfume, No. 503		$27.00-32.00	$40.00-45.00	
Puff box, "Moon Set"				$22.00-27.00
Puff box, "Sunset"	$9.00-11.00			$22.00-27.00
Puff box, 4¾" No. 700		$18.00-20.00	$18.00-20.00	
Puff box, Caprice style	$20.00-25.00			
Tray, No. 499		$12.00-14.00	$18.00-20.00	

L.E. SMITH VANITY SET

L.E. Smith began producing glass in Mt. Pleasant, Pennsylvania in 1907. Initial efforts were concentrated on jars, percolator tops, automobile lenses and kitchenware items. Eventually, production expanded to include tableware and giftware items. Lines produced in the mid-1920's included all colors, but Smith is probably best recognized for its efforts in the area of black glass. Today the firm still produces numerous giftware items - many of them from the old molds.

According to a 1932 ad, the L.E. Smith "Colonial" design dresser set sold for $1.00. It is usually found in crystal with black, green, or pink stoppers and lids. However, occasionally solid color sets will be found in crystal, black, pink or green, and sets have been found in flashed colors over a crystal base. In addition to the pieces shown, the set came with an oval two-handled tray. The height of the cologne and stopper is 5¾". The top part of the stopper and the finial of the puff box are disc-shaped. The powder jar is 4" in diameter and 3½" high.

	Crystal	Flashed Colors	Crystal with Colored Tops	Pink/ Green	Black
Cologne	$8.00-10.00	$10.00-12.00	$14.00-16.00	$20.00-25.00	$20.00-30.00
Puff box	$7.00-9.00	$7.00-9.00	$9.00-11.00	$10.00-12.00	
Tray	$4.00-5.00				$8.00-10.00

STEUBEN PERFUMES

Frederick Carder and Thomas Hawkes established the Steuben Glass Works in Corning, New York in 1903. In 1918, Steuben was incorporated as a division of Corning Glass. Production of high quality art glass was their primary interest. One of the earliest products was aurene, which is an art glass product with a lustrous metallic finish. Gold and blue are the most frequently found colors, but red and green also exist. Perfume bodies with this treatment were often supplied to DeVilbiss for finishing as perfumizers and perfume droppers. Most of these will not have a Steuben signature, but may bear the "DeVilbiss" mark.

The perfume dropper pictured is 6½" tall and it has a 5" long glass stopper with a metal cap. The atomizer is 9¾" tall. It has a wheel cut floral design on top of the foot and is signed "DeVilbiss" on the underside.

Steuben aurene gold perfume dropper finished by DeVilbiss $70.00-80.00
Steuben aurene gold perfumizer, signed "DeVilbiss" $350.00-450.00

TIFFIN AND U.S. GLASS VANITY SETS

The United States Glass conglomerate was formed in 1891 through the union of 18 different glass houses. The object of the combination was survival in the tough economic times. The loose organization was only moderately successful in solving all the problems, and most of the members had disappeared by the Depression. However, as a result of the union, a new plant was built in Tiffin, Ohio for the production and decoration of quality hand made glassware. This plant produced some of the most delicate and elaborately decorated glassware of the era.

The vanity set shown on the top row has been name "Chipperfield" by Hazel Weatherman. Although this set has been attributed to the Indiana Glass Company, the colors are not consistent with those made by Indiana. Both the colors and shapes of the vanity set shown on the bottom row match those produced by U.S. Glass. Until further documentation becomes available, the set will be considered as a possible U.S. Glass product. The set has been found in crystal, crystal with colored stoppers and lids, pink and blue.

Notice the insert in the vanity set on the bottom row has special molded areas for rouge and lipstick.

	Crystal	Crystal/ Black Tops	Pink	Blue
Perfume	$12.00-14.00	$40.00-45.00	$30.00-35.00	$40.00-45.00
Puff Box	$8.00-10.00	$20.00-25.00	$20.00-22.00	$20.00-25.00
Tray with insert			$25.00-30.00	

Top Row:

(a) Perfume, hexagonal stem, flat
    stopper with fully polished top
    surface, gold decorated topaz, 6" $40.00-50.00

(b) Perfume, straight taper of
    body to foot, cone-shaped stopper,
    transparent blue, 7¾" $70.00-80.00

(c) Perfume, thick hexagonal stem,
    large pear-shaped body, pointed
    stopper, transparent topaz, 8" $45.00-55.00

(d) Perfume, long stem with balls
    separated by ridge, stopper with wide
    disc topped by small point,
    frosted topaz $85.00-95.00

(e) Perfume, hexagonal stem, pointed
    stopper, gold decorated transparent
    topaz, 6½" $40.00-50.00

(f) Perfume, large disc at top of body,
    narrow waist, tapered stem with
    single ridge, mushroom stopper,
    transparent amberina, 6" $125.00-150.00

Bottom Row:

(a) Perfume, satin blue with
    wheel cut wheat design,
    mushroom stopper, 4¼" $27.00-32.00

(b) Atomizer, satin blue with
    wheel cut wheat design, 6" $30.00-35.00

(c,e) Perfume, six-sided,
    transparent green, 3½" $30.00-35.00

(d) Puff box, eight-sided,
    transparent green, 3½" $10.00-12.00

(f) Perfume, six-sided,
    frosted green with handpainted
    decoration, 3½" $35.00-45.00

(a) Perfume, No. 5759
gold decorated transparent blue,
cone top stopper $75.00-85.00
(b) Perfume, handpainted amberina,
hexagon stem, flat stopper ground
and polished over entire
top surface $110.00-135.00

(a) Perfume, gold decorated black.............$80.00-90.00
(b) Perfume, amberina, body tapers
to ridged stem above foot, flat stopper
ground and polished on
top surface $110.00-130.00

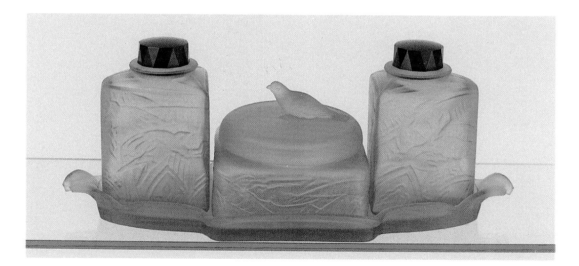

The "Tweety Bird" vanity set has a powder puff and cologne bottles which are marked "Dermay, Inc., 5th Ave, N.Y." on their underside. The 4" tall cologne bottles may have either Bakelite or metal screw lids. They are triangular - flat on one side and curved to fit the tray on the other sides. The puff box is 4" square. Its lid has a small bird finial, and there is a bird embossed on each side of the bottom. The scalloped tray has two upraised handles. It is 4½" wide in the center and 11¼" long. Colors which have been found are frosted pink, frosted green and frosted blue.

	Frosted Pink/Green	Frosted Blue
Cologne	$20.00-25.00	$27.00-32.00
Puff box	$35.00-40.00	$40.00-45.00
Tray	$12.00-15.00	$15.00-18.00

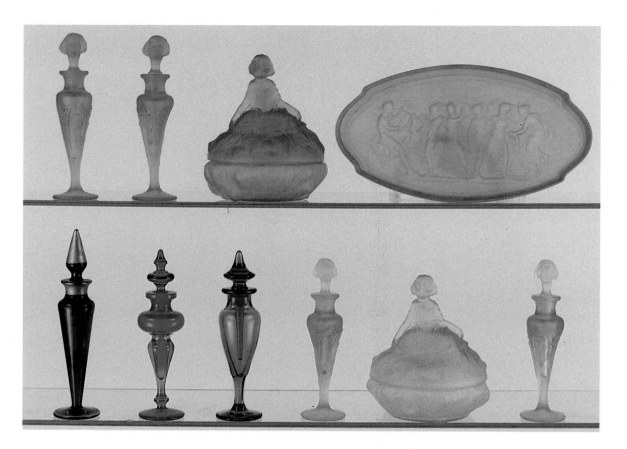

Top Row:

(a,b) Perfume, "Dancing Girl,"
    embossed figures of girls dancing
    on sides of body, top of stopper in
    form of girl's head,
    frosted blue, 6¾" $175.00-225.00

(c) Powder jar, "Dancing Girl,"
    frosted blue, 5" $75.00-85.00

(d) Tray, "Dancing Girl,"
    frosted blue, 5¾" x 10" $40.00-50.00

Bottom Row:

(a) Perfume, straight tapered body
    to foot, cone stopper, gold decorated
    by Lotus, cobalt, 7¾" $70.00-80.00

(b) Perfume, large disc at top of body,
    narrow waist, tapered stem with single
    ridge near foot, stopper with wide
    disc topped by small point,
    amberina, 7" $125.00-150.00

(c) Perfume, hexagon stem,
    pointed stopper,
    transparent blue, 7" $45.00-55.00

(d,f) Perfume, "Dancing Girl,"
    frosted pink, 6¾" $175.00-195.00

(e) Powder jar, "Dancing Girl,"
    frosted pink, 5" $55.00-65.00

"Flower Garden with Butterflies" vanity set, transparent pink

"Flower Garden with Butterflies" was a major tableware line produced by U.S. Glass during the late 1920's. Each piece is covered with an intricate floral design in which small butterflies are hidden. The line included the vanity set pictured and was sometimes sold with another style puff box which is shown in the photo on page 136. The flat puff box has the pattern in the center of the bottom but is plain on the side. The stopper used in these perfumes is the same swirl style used with the "Milady" perfumes shown on page 137. Two styles of trays may be found with this set. Both have the pattern design in the bottom. One type is the same oval shape that is used with most of the other Tiffin dresser sets, and the other style is rectangular. Colors made include pink, green, blue-green, blue, canary, crystal, amber and black.

	Crystal	Amber	Pink/Green Blue-Green	Canary	Blue/Black
Atomizer			$175.00-195.00		$195.00-225.00
Perfume, 7½"	$75.00-85.00	$95.00-110.00	$120.00-140.00	$120.00-140.00	$195.00-225.00
Puff box, flat	$20.00-25.00	$35.00-40.00	$40.00-45.00	$45.00-55.00	$85.00-95.00
Tray, 5¾" x10"	$18.00-20.00	$30.00-35.00	$35.00-40.00	$45.00-50.00	$60.00-70.00
Tray, 7¾" x 11¾"	$20.00-22.00	$30.00-35.00	$40.00-45.00	$50.00-55.00	$85.00-90.00

Left: Tiffin No. 5764 vanity set, frosted blue with handpainted floral design by Cozy Nook Studio.
Right: "Flower Garden with Butterflies" footed puff box, transparent green.

The No. 5764 vanity set shown on the left was produced between 1926 and 1935. The perfumes are similar in shape to some produced by Fenton. However, the body of the Fenton cologne is rounded evenly on both the top and bottom halves. The Tiffin perfume slopes out sharply, almost horizontally to the widest point. From there it tapers with a gentle rounding to a ridge at the top of the stem. Also, the Fenton cologne has no ridge at the top of its stem. The end of the Tiffin stopper has a small disc below a larger disc which is topped by a small point. The height of the base is 3½" and the length of the stopper is 3¾".

The frosted blue puff box is Tiffin's No. 9309. It is 4¾" in diameter. The footed puff box is from the "Flower Garden with Butterflies" line. It may be found used in the vanity set on the previous page in place of the flat puff box.

	Crystal	Amber	Green/Pink Blue-Green	Canary	Blue Black
Perfume, No. 5764			$25.00-30.00		$30.00-35.00
Puff box, No. 9309			$15.00-18.00		$20.00-25.00
Puff box, "Flower Garden with Butterflies"	$20.00-25.00	$30.00-35.00	$40.00-45.00	$50.00-55.00	$70.00-90.00

The vanity sets shown on the next page are all the same style. They have been named "Milady" by Hazel Weatherman. They will be found in both frosted and transparent colors and with numerous handpainted decorations.

The perfume body is 3½" high and is accented with a slight vertical swirl. The stopper is 4½" long and has a swirl design around the center area of the top. The part above this is cone-shaped.

The puff box is 4" in diameter and has a plain bottom. The lid has a swirl design on top which matches the pattern on the perfume, and the swirled knob matches the top of the perfume stopper.

The tray is 5¾" wide by 10" long and has a swirl design in the bottom which fans out from the center to the sides.

A variation of the commonly found "Milady" set is illustrated in the picture at the top of page 137. This set has a tray with a molded puff base and molded rings into which the perfumes fit. Also there are no swirls in the bottom of the tray. A stack section fits onto the puff base. This section has an embossed holder for make-up and lipstick. The regular lid fits over this insert.

	Crystal/ Crystal Frosted	Pink/Green Amber	Blue-Green Canary	White Milk Glass	Blue
Perfume	$18.00-20.00	$35.00-40.00	$40.00-45.00	$35.00-40.00	$40.00-45.00
Puff box	$12.00-14.00	$18.00-20.00	$18.00-20.00	$18.00-20.00	$20.00-22.00
Tray	$8.00-10.00	$10.00-12.00	$10.00-12.00	$12.00-14.00	$15.00-18.00
Tray with molded puff box					$25.00-30.00

Variation of "Milady" vanity set with puff box base molded to tray, frosted blue.

"Milady" vanity sets.

"Milady" perfumes and puff boxes.

WESTMORELAND VANITY SETS

Top Row: English Hobnail No. 555 colognes and powder jars.
Bottom Row: Hobnail No. 77 puff boxes.

The Westmoreland Specialty Company began production in Grapeville, Pennsylvania in 1890. Production in the early years was concentrated on glass jars and some pressed tableware patterns. By the 1920's, Westmoreland was producing various reproductions of earlier style lamps, candlesticks, and novelty items. Colorful handmade giftware items became a specialty, and many of the molds were in use until Westmoreland closed in the mid-1980's. Even then, some of the molds were bought by independent glass houses and are still in use today.

Top Row: The colorful English Hobnail line was introduced in 1925. A dresser set is comprised of the 5 oz. toilet bottles and two sizes of puff boxes - 5" and 6". The toilet bottle is available with two different size openings, but the one with the narrow neck is found more often. Some toilet bottles will be found with enamel labels such as "Mouthwash," "Alcohol," etc. For example of these, see the toiletries section. Pieces were produced in colors through the mid-1930's. Crystal and white milk glass items were made as late as the 1960's.

Bottom Row: Westmoreland's Hobnail pattern puff boxes have hobs on the side of the bottom and the top of the lid. The elongated round knob is also covered with hobs. The powder was made in crystal, pink and green during the late 1920's through the early 1930's. Production during the early 1970's consisted of white milk glass, "Moonstone" and Belgian blue colors. Belgian blue is a blue opalescent color.

	Crystal/ Milk Glass	Pink/Green Amber	Light Blue Cobalt	Moonstone Belgian Blue
Cologne, English Hobnail	$14.00-16.00	$25.00-30.00	$40.00-50.00	
* Puff box, English Hobnail	$10.00-12.00	$20.00-25.00	$40.00-50.00	
Puff box, Hobnail	$10.00-12.00	$20.00-25.00		$20.00-25.00

* Produced in ruby for LeVay, 1980's.

Westmoreland gold decorated Paneled Grape vanity set.

Westmoreland's white milk glass Paneled Grape is a very popular pattern among collectors. The vanity set consists of two 6" tall cologne bottles, a puff box, and an oval tray with two fancy scroll handles. Two different puff boxes may be found with this set - the one shown in the photo above and the one shown on the bottom right in the bottom photo on page 141.

The set is commonly found without decoration, with gold decoration on the grapes, and with the desirable "Roses and Bow" decoration which is illustrated on page 141.

	White Milk Glass	Gold Decorated	Roses and Bow Decoration
Box, 4" square	$14.00-16.00	$20.00-25.00	$30.00-35.00
Cologne	$18.00-20.00	$25.00-30.00	$45.00-55.00
Puff box	$14.00-16.00	$25.00-30.00	$40.00-45.00
Tray, 8¼" x 13¼"	$10.00-12.00	$15.00-18.00	

The No. 1902 bath set is shown on the left of the top two rows. The white milk glass set has the popular handpainted "Roses and Bow" decoration. The dresser set on the right is Westmoreland's Depression Era Lotus pattern. The colognes are currently being made in both satin and transparent colors from the original molds. The new colors we have seen are amberina, black, cobalt, and pink. The puff box has not been reproduced.

Paneled Grape puff boxes are pictured in the center of the middle row and one the right side of the bottom row. The No. 500 vanity set with a dainty floral decoration is shown on the left side of the bottom row. Westmoreland frequently referred to this pattern as "Old Quilt."

	Pink/ Green	Blue/ Black	White Milk Glass	Decorated White Milk Glass
Cologne, No. 500			$18.00-20.00	$25.00-30.00
Cologne, No. 1902		$20.00-25.00	$12.00-15.00	$18.00-20.00
Cologne, Lotus	$45.00-55.00			
Puff box, No. 500			$10.00-12.00	$16.00-18.00
Puff box, No. 1902		$18.00-20.00	$9.00-11.00	$15.00-18.00
Puff box, Lotus	$35.00-40.00			
Tray, oval		$8.00-10.00	$8.00-10.00	
Tray, No. 500			$9.00-11.00	

Handpainted daisies on "Soft Blue Mist" No. 1902/42 bath set.

(a) Westmoreland's No. 1902 bath set with "Roses and Bow" decoration; (b) No. 1921 Lotus vanity articles.

Row 1: (a) No. 1902 bath set, black; (b) No. 1881 Paneled Grape puff box, black; (c,d) Lotus colognes.
Row 2: (a) No. 500 dresser set, white milk glass with handpainted flowers; (b) No. 1881 puff box, light green opaque glass; (c) No. 1881 puff box, white milk glass with "Roses and Bow" decoration.

MISCELLANEOUS PERFUMES AND VANITY SETS

The perfume bodies in this photo are all the same shape. The necks are very thick, and the 4½" long bodies taper to a ridge just above the foot. The lower 1⅝" of the bodies are embossed with vertical ribs. Two styles of stoppers are used. The top of one type has a wide disc which is topped by a nipple-like tip. The very tip of the nipple is ground flat and the stopper is 4⅝" long. The other style stopper has a flat top and is 4" long. This is one of the few perfume stoppers without a ground top.

Both puff boxes are the same style. They are 4" in diameter with a 2¼" diameter foot which is about 3/16" high. The lid is slightly domed and has a round knob on a slightly raised ridge. The knob is attached to the ridge with a smooth stem.

The pink tray has a plain bottom and is 7¼" in diameter. The blue tray is also 7¼" in diameter and has an embossed flower in the center of the bottom. The flower is outlined by a ring of beads.

	Pink/Green Amber	Blue
Perfume	$25.00-30.00	$40.00-45.00
Puff box	$10.00-12.00	$18.00-20.00
Tray, embossed	$9.00-11.00	$14.00-16.00
Tray, plain	$8.00-10.00	

Top Row:

(a) Perfume, amber with short 4"
tapered body and small ridge above
foot, octagonal-shaped
top of stopper $25.00-30.00

(b) Perfume, iridized amber with
paneled 4¼" long body, 3½" long
stopper with octagonal top $22.00-27.00

(c) Perfume, blue with elongated 7"
tall body, probably experimental,
3½" long stopper with flat top $45.00-55.00

(d) Perfume, blue with long
narrow body which distends to
inner tube-shaped base, top of 5"
long stopper has several discs and
small pointed tip $45.00-55.00

(e) Perfume, frosted crystal with
handpainted floral decoration,
bell-shaped body flares out at foot,
stopper has pointed,
ribbed top $20.00-25.00

Bottom Row:

(a) Cologne, amber
Daisy and Button $25.00-30.00

(b,d) Cologne, crystal with diamond,
quilted pattern $12.00-15.00

(c) Puff box, crystal with diamond
quilted pattern $8.00-10.00

(e) Cologne, crystal, round body
with large teardrop stopper $8.00-10.00

The vanity set on the left is crystal frosted with fired-on white bodies. It is decorated with handpainted roses and bows. The set is probably not very old.

The hobnail set on the right has a bell-shaped cologne bottle and a squatty puff box which bows out around the middle. Sets are rather common in crystal, crystal frosted, and white milk glass. Other colors such as transparent pink and green are harder to find.

	Crystal/ Crystal Frosted	Milk Glass	Pink/Green
Cologne, footed	$5.00-7.00		
Puff box, footed	$5.00-7.00		
Cologne, hobnail	$9.00-11.00	$10.00-12.00	$14.00-16.00
Puff box, hobnail	$8.00-10.00	$8.00-10.00	$10.00-12.00

143

The crystal "Beaded Medallion" vanity set shown above has been found with paper "Made in Czechoslavakia" labels. The 7" tall 8-sided colognes are made of heavy glass. The puff box is 3¾" in diameter and the tray is 8" wide by 14¼" long. The perfume to the right has a rosebud stopper and is 5½" tall.

Cologne, "Beaded Medallion" $8.00-10.00
Puff box, "Beaded Medallion" $7.00-9.00
Tray, "Beaded Medallion" $7.00-8.00
Vanity set, "Beaded Medallion" $30.00-37.00
Cologne, rosebud..$18.00-20.00

The vanity set with the Colonial lady finial has been named "Antoinette." The top of the stoppers and the lid to the puff box have Colonial lady finials. The lady's skirt is completed by the body of the perfumes and the base of the puff box. For more information, see page 34.

Perfume $25.00-30.00
Puff box $25.00-30.00

The crystal perfume on the left with the lavender stopper is of unknown origin. The other three bottles were made in Czechoslavakia.

(a) Perfume, crystal with lavender stopper $35.00-45.00
(b) Perfume, ebony with dancing nudes $145.00-175.00
(c) Perfume, pink with tall starburst stopper $60.00-75.00
(d) Perfume, crystal with figural lady on stopper $35.00-45.00

Miniature Czechoslavakian perfumes are illustrated in the bottom picture. They are about 2" - 2¼" tall and all have long stoppers. For more information on Czechoslavakian perfumes, see the bibliography reference for Ruth Forsythe's book *Made in Czechoslavakia*. The perfume on the right side was not made in Czechoslavakia. It is 3¼" tall and has a cut decoration near the top of the body. The long stopper has a sterling metal top with a blue enamel insert.

(a) Crystal, pink stopper $16.00-18.00
(b) Green $35.00-40.00
(c) Pink $35.00-40.00
(d) Green head, black base with crystal dauber $175.00-200.00
(e) Lavender $37.00-42.00
(f) Light blue $35.00-40.00
(g) Black, crystal stopper $40.00-45.00
(h) Crystal with cut design (not Czech) $70.00-85.00

Top Row:
(a) Puff box, crystal diamond-shaped $5.00-7.00
(b) Puff box, amber $10.00-12.00
(c) Vanity set, crystal with black tops $27.00-32.00
     Cologne $10.00-12.00
     Puff box $7.00-10.00

Bottom Row:
(a) Vanity set, green, marked on
     bottom "Made in Japan".....................$31.00-37.00
(b) Cologne, crystal with black design $8.00-10.00
(c) Vanity set, ruby,
     "Irice, Made in Japan"
     Atomizer $15.00-17.00
     Cologne, flared base $12.00-14.00
     Cologne, rounded base $12.00-14.00

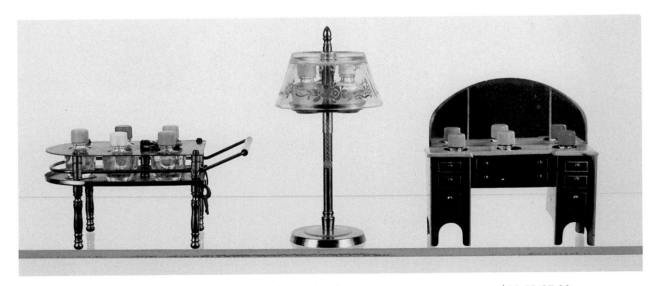

(a) Piano with five miniature cologne bottles $20.00-25.00
(b) Lamp with three miniature cologne bottles $18.00-22.00
(c) Dresser with three miniature cologne bottles.....................................$20.00-25.00

Top Row: The cobalt "Evening in Paris" perfume and talc bottles were used by Bourjois as early as the 1930's. Some items were still available in Sear's catalogues in the late 1950's.

    (a) Vanity set, ultramarine $32.00-38.00
        Atomizer, 4" $12.00-14.00
        Cologne, 8¼" $10.00-12.00
    (b) "Evening in Paris," cobalt bottles
        Eau de Toilette, 5½" $8.00-10.00
        Cologne, 5½" $8.00-10.00
        Talcum powder, 5" $8.00-10.00
        Cologne, 4½" $7.00-8.00

Bottom Row: The tray to the green vanity set has indents into which the atomizer and cologne fit.

    (a) Vanity set, green $37.00-44.00
        Atomizer, 3⅜" $12.00-14.00
        Cologne, 5½" $12.00-14.00
        Puff box, 5¼" $7.00-9.00
        Tray, 5" x 11¾" $6.00-7.00
    (b) Cologne, square crystal body with blue stopper $20.00-25.00
    (c) Cologne, square crystal body with pink stopper $20.00-25.00
    (d) Cologne, crystal, "R. Lalique" $45.00-50.00

MISCELLANEOUS VANITY SETS

The sets in the above picture were made in England. Notice many English dresser sets include candleholders and more than one size puff box. Cologne bottles are commonly absent.

Top Row:
Candleholder $7.00-9.00
Pin Tray $4.00-5.00
Puff box, large $10.00-12.00
Puff box, small $8.00-10.00
Tray $7.00-9.00

Bottom Row:
Candleholder $7.00-9.00
Puff box, large $10.00-12.00
Puff box, small $8.00-10.00
Ring tree $5.00-7.00
Tray $7.00-9.00

NEXT PAGE
Top Photo:
The items shown here were made by the Baccarat Glass Company of Luneville, France. The company was founded in 1765 and is still in production. Many of the Baccarat items bear the company logo on the underside.

Top Row:
(a) Covered dish $60.00-70.00
(b) Atomizer $40.00-45.00
(c) Cologne $55.00-60.00
(d) Covered box $85.00-95.00

Bottom Row:
(a) Candleholder $27.00-32.00
(b) Hat pin tray $50.00-60.00
(c) Vanity dish $30.00-35.00

Bottom Photo:
Top Row:
(a) Tumble-up $65.00-75.00
(b) Toilet bottle $40.00-45.00
(c) Cologne $40.00-45.00

Bottom Row:
(a) Puff box, 3¾" $35.00-40.00
(b) Soap dish, 2" x 4½" $25.00-30.00
(c) Vanity box, 2¾" $35.00-40.00

MISCELLANEOUS ATOMIZERS

(a) Jadite, tall, 6¾" $50.00-60.00
(b) Jadite, short disc-shape, 3¾" $45.00-55.00

(a) Amber with floral etching, 6½" $35.00-45.00
(b) Pink, 6½" $35.00-40.00
(c) Lavender with gold encrusted decoration,
    marked "Czechoslavakia," 7½" $85.00-100.00
(d) Amber with embossed zigzag design, 7" $30.00-35.00
(e) Flashed rose, signed "DeVilbiss," 6½" $85.00-95.00
(f) Crystal with cut design, 6" $25.00-30.00
(g) Green with frosted band decoration, 4¾" $15.00-22.00
(h) Blue with enameled flowers, 4½" $32.00-40.00

BARBER BOTTLES

Top Row:
(a) Fenton vaseline Vertical Stripe,
    made for L.G. Wright, 1960 ....$70.00-80.00
(b) Fenton cranberry Vertical Stripe,
    made for L.G. Wright, 1960 ....$85.00-95.00
(c) Fenton blue satin Daisy and Fern,
    made for L.G. Wright, 1960 ....$70.00-75.00
(d) Fenton amber satin with flowers,
    made for L.G. Wright, 1960 ....$55.00-60.00
(e) Blue vertical Coin Spot,
    circa 1900, maker unknown.............$110.00-125.00
(f) Fenton amethyst satin with flowers,
    made for L.G. Wright, 1960 ....$55.00-65.00

Bottom Row:
(a) Fenton cranberry Coin Dot
    Mellon Rib, 1953 ....$110.00-120.00
(b) Fenton custard Hanging Hearts,
    1953 ....$60.00-70.00
(c) Fenton cased rose, made for
    L.G. Wright, 1960 ....$90.00-100.00
(d) Fenton cobalt Christmas Snowflake,
    made for L.G. Wright, 1960 ....$70.00-80.00
(e) Fenton cranberry Stars and Stripes,
    1953 ....$125.00-150.00
(f) Hobbs Hobnail, marked,
    circa 1900 ....$75.00-85.00

COTTON BALL HOLDERS AND PIN TRAYS

	Pink/Green	Amber
Seated German shepherd pin tray	$25.00-30.00	$30.00-37.00

Two styles of the Paden City "Bunny" cotton ball dispensers were made - ears up and ears back. All colors of the "ears up" variety are hard-to-find. The most common colors of the "ears back" version are frosted crystal and frosted pink.

	Frosted Crystal	Frosted Pink	Frosted Blue	White Milk Glass
"Bunny," ears back	$40.00-45.00	$60.00-70.00	$85.00-95.00	$85.00-95.00
"Bunny," ears up		$100.00-150.00		

MANICURE SETS AND BATHROOM ACCESSORIES

The fancy covered heart-shaped manicure sets are marked "E.W. Inc., Chicago, Ill." on their underside. The heart is 5½" wide and 6" long. The green heart has a frosted base and a light acid etched design on the cover. The round green manicure also has the same mark on the bottom. Both styles may be found in green, pink and black.

	Green/Pink	Black
Manicure, heart-shaped	$35.00-45.00	$45.00-55.00
Manicure, round	$28.00-35.00	

The soap holder with the nude figural is 6" long and 4" high. It is commonly found in frosted pink and green. It has been extensively reproduced in both colors and is also being made in new colors. The blue bath salts bottle with the nude figural stopper is 6" tall.

	Frosted Green/Pink	Blue
Soap holder (old)	$35.00-40.00	
Bath salts bottle		$65.00-70.00

TOILET ARTICLES

The jadite Jeannette set shown on the top row was sold as a five-piece set. There are four bottles with black Bakelite caps and different labels and a 10 oz. tumbler.

Top Row:
(a) Jadite Jeannette decorated
   bath bottles, ea. $28.00-30.00
(b) Jadite Jeannette tumbler, 10 oz. $25.00-28.00

Bottom Row:
(a,b) Green opaque bath bottles,
   plastic lid, 4" $12.00-14.00

Bottom Row:
(c) Crystal bottles, handpainted decoration,
   set of four with ground stoppers
   on round, black glass tray $40.00-45.00
(d) Light blue English Hobnail
   "Peroxide" bottle $35.00-40.00
(e) Pink English Hobnail
   "Mouthwash" bottle $35.00-40.00

NEXT PAGE, TOP PHOTO:

Top Row:
(a) Green satin Fenton San Toy
   No. 16-17-54,
   four-piece bathroom set $150.00-175.00
(b) Crystal satin Fenton puff box
   on diamond-shaped tray $40.00-45.00

Bottom Row:
(a) Jadite three-piece set $50.00-60.00
(b) Jadite/Black three-piece set,
   marked "Made in Japan" $40.00-50.00

NEXT PAGE, BOTTOM PHOTO;

Top Row:
(a) Pink floral etched bottles, ea. $25.00-30.00
(b) Pink transparent bottle,
   three-piece set $45.00-55.00

Bottom Row:
(a,b) Pink bottles, Cambridge, ea. $35.00-40.00
(c)   Green Cambridge five-piece set ...$100.00-135.00
(d,e) Pink crackle glass pinch bottles
   with ground glass anchor
   finial stopper, ea. $25.00-35.00

154

Top Row:
(a) Green Cambridge "Old Spanish"
   style bottle, 5" $20.00-25.00
(b) Blue Consolidated Catalonian
   bottle, 5" $15.00-18.00
(c) Green Consolidated Catalonian bottle,
   paper label, "Catalonian, a reproduction
   of OLD SPANISH GLASS," 5" $20.00-25.00
(d) Green three-piece bathroom set with
   black ground glass stoppers, set $50.00-65.00

Bottom Row:
(a) Bathroom set, crystal bottles with
   embossed labels, plastic tops,
   wooden tray, set $40.00-45.00
(b) Crystal bottle $18.00-20.00

Top Row:
(a) Pink large four-footed cold cream
   jar with metal lid, "Dubarry-Richard
   Hudnut" label, 4½" $14.00-16.00
(b) Aqua Richard Hudnut
   bath salts jar $20.00-25.00
(c) Blue Richard Hudnut bath salts jar .. $20.00-25.00
(d) Pink Richard Hudnut bath salts jar .. $20.00-25.00

Top Row:
(e) Blue Kress vanity jar, metal lid $18.00-20.00
(f) Green vanity jar, plastic lid $18.00-20.00

Bottom Row:
(a) Amber travel set $40.00-45.00

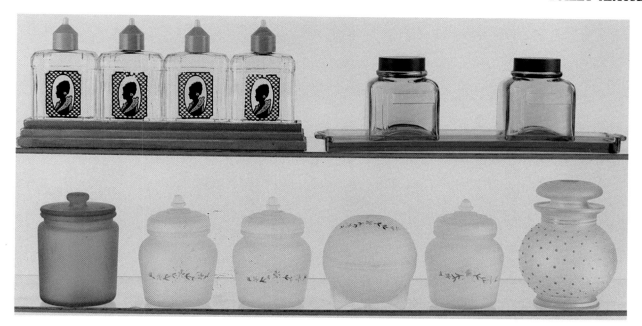

Top Row:
(a) Crystal decorated bottles,
   wooden tray, set $40.00-45.00
(b) Green rectangular bottles, rectangular
   glass tray and set of four bottles ...$100.00-125.00

Bottom Row:
(a) Blue frosted Hocking jar $27.00-30.00
(b-e) Crystal frosted set with
   floral decoration $20.00-25.00
(f) Crystal frosted jar with pink trim $10.00-12.00

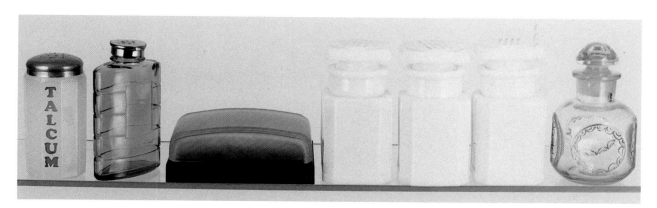

Left to right:
(a) Clambroth talcum powder bottle $10.00-12.00
(b) Cobalt "Evening in Paris"
   talcum bottle $18.00-20.00
(c) Soap dish, black glass base $18.00-20.00

(d) White milk glass
   three-piece bathroom set $45.00-55.00
(e) Green handpainted bottle,
   circular indents in sides $22.00-25.00

Decorative fruit-shaped powder room accessories made by Fostoria are pictured in this photograph.

Left to right:
(a) Melon, #2690, 8" $20.00-25.00
(b) Pear, #2699, 7⅝" $22.00-25.00
(c) Pear, #2699, 7⅝" $22.00-25.00

The cold cream jar may have either a celluloid or glass lid. It is not easy to find, but the Akro trademark found on the underside of the base aids in identification. Look for this jar in both marbleized and solid colors.

Akro Agate cold cream jar $35.00-45.00
Akro Agate shaving mug $35.00-40.00

Top Row:
(a,b) White opalescent swirl bottles,
    original label reads
    "Wrisley's White Cloud Cologne" $10.00-12.00
(c) Pink bottle set, ground glass stoppers,
    round 2-handle tray $85.00-100.00
(d) Jadite cold cream jar, glass lid...........$40.00-45.00
(e) Black cold cream jar, glass lid............$30.00-35.00

Bottom Row:
(a) Crystal frosted puff box, hand
    decorated, marked "DeVilbiss" $18.00-22.00
(b) Crystal frosted bath jar,
    matches above puff box $18.00-22.00
(c) Alacite type oval mirror frame, 7⅛" ...$80.00-85.00
(d) Black swan bath set $35.00-45.00

Top Row:
(a,b) Crystal with colored dot bath bottles with glass stoppers, 2½" sq., ea. $4.00-5.00
(c) Crystal bath bottles with black cattail design, 2½" sq. with rectangular glass stoppers,
    three-piece set with black tray...$45.00-55.00
(d) Black Ardena Velva lotion bottle from Elizabeth Arden, 4¾" high with glass stopper $40.00-45.00
(e) Old Spanish glass type lotion bottle with glass stopper, pink, 4" high $10.00-15.00
(f) Jadite Quinlan facial oil bottle from Kathleen Mary Quinlan of New York,
    3¼" high with glass stopper $35.00-40.00

Bottom Row:
(a,b,c) Bath bottles, green stretch glass with gold trim, ea..$18.00-25.00
(d) Bath set, aqua blue, 4 bottles, 2" wide x 2½" long x 3¼" high with celluloid lids;
    rectangular tray 2½" wide x 11½" long, set $150.00-175.00
(e) Cologne bottle, green with embossed flowers and metal lid $10.00-12.00

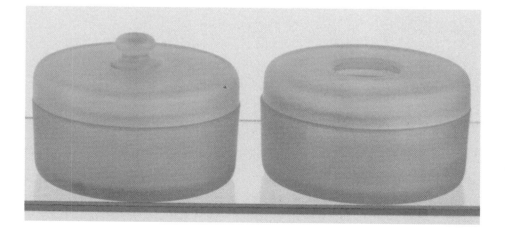

Tiffin frosted topaz puff box $18.00-20.00
Tiffin frosted topaz hair receiver $20.00-25.00

The items in this picture were made by the Westmoreland Glass Company.

Left to right:
(a) Ruby treasure chest $14.00-18.00
(b) Handpainted black trinket box $20.00-25.00
(c) Handpainted white milk glass trinket box...$18.00-20.00

Left to right:
(a) Cut cranberry bottle with gold decoration, Czechoslavakia $50.00-60.00
(b) Delphite hair oil bottle $125.00-150.00
(c) Topaz bottle with blown stopper, France $50.00-60.00
(d) Blue Bulging Loops puff box, Consolidated Glass and Lamp Company $80.00-85.00

TOLIET ARTICLES, TOWEL BARS, SOAP DISHES

All items in this picture were made by the Cambridge Glass Company of Cambridge, Ohio.

Top Row:
(a) Helio puff box and cover $45.00-55.00
(b) Helio pomade box and cover $40.00-50.00
(c) Helio pin tray, 3¾" $25.00-30.00
(d) Ebony soap dish and cover $50.00-60.00
(e) Ebony brush vase $30.00-35.00
(f) Primrose ring holder $32.00-37.00

Bottom Row:
(a) Azurite brush holder $30.00-35.00
(b) Azurite puff box and cover $40.00-50.00
(c) Azurite pomade box and cover $40.00-45.00
(d) Azurite pin tray, 3¾" $22.00-27.00
(e) Azurite soap dish $38.00-42.00
(f) Azurite cologne, with gold encrusted
    Basket motif from the the
    Dresden etching $90.00-125.00

NEXT PAGE, Top Photo

Top Row:
(a,b) Green Clambroth
      towel bar holder, pr. $20.00-25.00
(c) Green Clambroth cold cream jar $25.00-30.00
(d) Green Clambroth tumbler holder $14.00-16.00
(e) Green Clambroth soap dish $20.00-25.00

Center Row: **Price**
(a) Pink towel bar holder, Westite, pr. ... $40.00-45.00
(b) Pink toilet paper holder,
    Westite, pr. $40.00-45.00
(c) Pink clothes hook, Westite $28.00-30.00
(d) Green frosted tumbler and
    toothbrush holder $28.00-30.00

Bottom Row:
(a) Blue toothbrush holder $25.00-35.00
(b) Peacock blue soap dish, marked
    "Holt Soap Saver, Duro Hook Company,
    Chicago" $28.00-32.00
(c) White milk glass soap dish, marked
    "Holton Soap Saver, Patented
    Aug. 24, 1943,
    W. Jackson, Chicago" $18.00-20.00
(d) Green soap dish $28.00-32.00
(e) Green marbleized soap dish $28.00-32.00

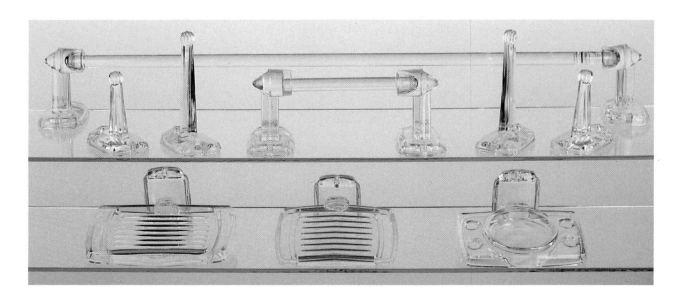

Top Row:
(a) Towel bar with glass holders $8.00-10.00
(b) Clothes hook, short $8.00-10.00
(c) Clothes hook, long $8.00-10.00
(d) Toilet paper holder
    with glass holders $15.00-18.00

Bottom Row:
(a) Soap dish $8.00-10.00
(b) Soap dish $8.00-10.00
(c) Soap dish/toothbrush holder $15.00-18.00

TOWEL BARS

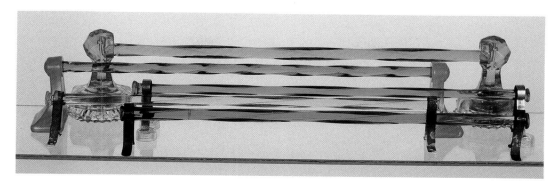

	Crystal	Pink/Green	Blue
Twisted towel bars with clip holders	$4.00-6.00	$20.00-25.00	$22.00-27.00

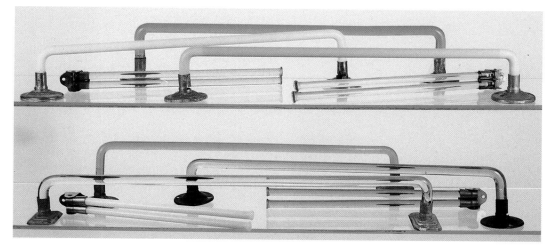

	Crystal	Pink/Green	Blue	White Milk Glass	Jadite
Curved towel bars	$4.00-6.00	$20.00-25.00	$22.00-27.00	$8.00-10.00	$18.00-20.00
Double rods for hand towels	$8.00-10.00	$30.00-40.00	$30.00-40.00	$8.00-10.00	$25.00-30.00

	Crystal	Pink/Green	Blue	White Milk Glass	Jadite
Straight towel bars with metal clips	$4.00-5.00	$18.00-22.00	$20.00-22.00	$4.00-6.00	$15.00-18.00

CABINET KNOBS AND DRAWER PULLS

Collectors are using various styles of cabinet knobs and drawer pulls to decorate the bathroom. The knobs and pulls shown on the top and third rows have large screw-in ends which are anchored with metal caps. If the caps are missing, as is often the case, the knobs can be glued in place.

	Crystal	Pink/Green	Amber	Black/Blue Lavender	White Milk Glass
Top Row:					
Knob, large hexagonal	$2.00-3.00	$4.00-6.00	$4.00-6.00	$6.00-7.00	$3.00-4.00
Knob, medium hexagonal	$2.00-3.00	$4.00-6.00	$4.00-6.00	$6.00-7.00	$3.00-4.00
Knob, small hexagonal	$2.00-3.00	$3.00-5.00	$3.00-5.00	$5.00-6.00	$2.00-3.00
Knob, round	$2.00-3.00	$4.00-6.00	$4.00-6.00	$6.50-7.50	$3.00-4.00
Second Row:					
Knob, large hexagonal, metal screw	$2.00-3.00	$4.00-6.00	$4.00-6.00	$6.00-7.00	$3.00-4.00
Knob, medium-size, metal screw	$2.00-3.00	$4.00-6.00	$4.00-6.00	$6.00-7.00	$3.00-4.00
Knob, small-size, metal screw	$2.00-3.00	$4.00-5.00	$4.00-5.00	$5.00-6.00	$3.00-4.00
Third Row:					
(a) Pull with round ends	$2.00-4.00	$10.00-12.00	$10.00-12.00	$12.00-15.00	$10.00-12.00
(b) Pull, anchor shape	$3.00-4.00	$5.00-9.00	$5.00-9.00	$14.00-16.00	$8.00-10.00
(c,d) Knob, elongated hexagonal	$3.00-4.00	$5.00-8.00	$5.00-8.00	$6.00-9.00	$4.00-5.00
(e,f) Knob, oval	$3.00-4.00	$5.00-8.00	$5.00-8.00	$6.00-9.00	$4.00-5.00
Bottom Row:					
Pull, ends with metal screws	$4.00-7.00	$10.00-14.00	$10.00-14.00	$12.00-18.00	

DOOR KNOBS

Collectors are searching for the attractive glass ends, and the door knobs shown here are priced with two glass knobs. Sometimes handles will be found with a single glass knob and one metal end. These are valued at half of the price indicated below.

Top Row:

(a) Crystal, oval with cut design $25.00-35.00
(b) Green $80.00-85.00
(c) Dark amber $75.00-85.00
(d) Light amber $75.00-85.00
(e) Light amber, small size $50.00-60.00

Bottom Row:

(a) Topaz with cut center $75.00-90.00
(b) Amethyst $20.00-35.00
(c) Jadite $100.00-125.00
(d) Topaz $75.00-90.00
(e) Topaz, cut center, medium-size $65.00-85.00

Above Photo:
Left:
Night light, frosted green glass base
with metal ballerina finial $55.00-60.00

Right:
Bookend night light, flashed green $45.00-55.00

Left Photo:
Reprint of boudoir lamps from an early 1940's Levin Bros. catalogue from Terre Haute, Indiana.

SOUTHERN BELLE LAMPS

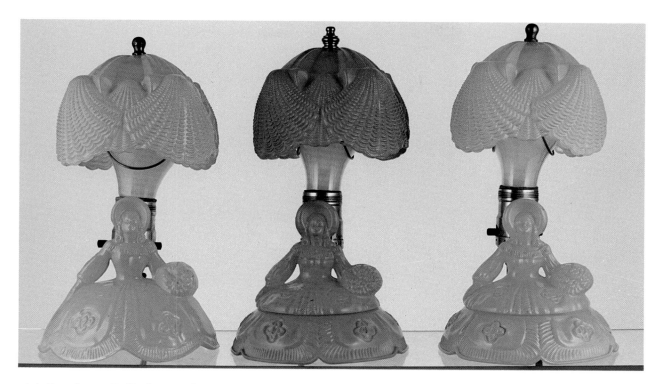

(a) Southern Belle lamp, fired-on pink. Southern Belle lamp/powder box: (b) fired-on blue, (c) fired-on pink.

The Southern Belle lamp is perhaps the most frequently found of all the fired-on bedroom lamps. There are several different mold variations of the basic lamp, but all feature the same characterization of a young girl in a sunbonnet with a ruffled hoop dress. The girl is holding a bouquet in her left hand and her right arm is extended downward.

Two different style lamps are shown in the photo. The pink lamp on the left is the type which is usually found. The lamp/powder box combinations are harder to find. Both styles are available in fired-on pink or blue. The lamp will also be found infrequently in frosted crystal and frosted green.

Glass shades for these lamps clip onto the light bulb. Their shape is a rounded square and shells which flare to the center of each side form the corners.

The frosted green Southern Belle has been found in night light form also. The night light was produced by placing the figural top over a plaster lamp base.

	Pink/ Blue	Frosted Crystal	Frosted Green
Lamp, Southern Belle	$30.00-37.00	$25.00-30.00	$55.00-60.00
Lamp/Powder Box, Southern Belle	$45.00-55.00		

HUMAN FIGURAL VANITY LAMPS

Left to right: "Harpist," (a) fired-on blue, (b) caramel slag, (c) fired-on pink.

The "Harpist" lamp has a seated lady who is strumming a harp. Several styles of metal fittings were used with the "Harpist." As a result, this lamp is found with different shades. Two styles of glass shades are shown in the photo above. The fired-on pink and blue lamps are from the 1930's, and the slag base is from an Imperial production in the 1960's.

The lamp with the seated lady with the flowing skirt is called "Portrait Lady." She has her arms extended downward away from her sides and a basket is by her right arm. Her glass shade clips to the light and is cone-shaped with a large beaded edge. Fired-on blue lamps have also been found.

"The Dreamer" has her head tilted. Her palms are together and her head is resting on her hand. The floral design on the shade matches the design around the base of the lamp.

The "Spanish Dancing Couple" also has a ruffled shade with an embossed cameo design which matches the style around the bottom of the base. This dancing couple will also be found in fired-on blue.

The "Oriental Lady" nodder lamp has a weighted figural head which rocks. Both arms are bent upward at the elbows and her hands are supporting a fan behind her head.

The "Chinese Coolie" is taking a break from work in the rice paddy. He appears to be seated against a wall and has one hand resting on his knee. The other hand is clutching a bundle of rice. The flared shade depicts assorted oriental scenes.

The base of the fired-on blue lamp on the right side of the bottom photo is formed by a seated "Oriental Girl." Her arms are by her side and she is holding a basket in her left hand.

	Fired-on Pink	Fired-on Blue	Slag Colors
"Harpist"	$50.00-55.00	$50.00-55.00	$30.00-35.00
"Portrait Lady"	$45.00-55.00	$50.00-55.00	
"Dreamer"	$50.00-55.00	$55.00-60.00	
"Spanish Dancing Couple"	$35.00-45.00	$35.00-45.00	
"Oriental Lady"	$125.00-135.00	$125.00-135.00	
"Chinese Coolie"	$40.00-47.00	$47.00-55.00	
"Oriental Girl"	$35.00-45.00	$35.00-45.00	

Left to Right: (a) "Portrait Lady," fired-on pink; (b) "Dreamer," fired-on pink; (c) "Spanish Dancing Couple," fired-on pink.

Left to right: (a) "Oriental Lady," fired-on blue; (b) "Chinese Coolie," fired-on pink; (c) "Oriental girl," fired-on blue.

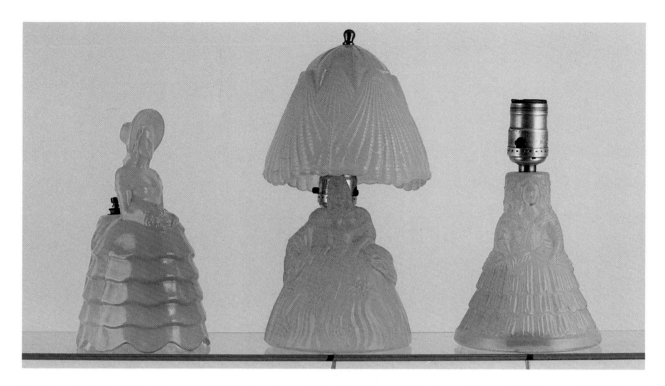

Left to right: (a) "Sunbonnet Girl," fired-on pink; (b) "Tara," fired-on blue; (c) "Flower Girl," fired-on pink.

The "Sunbonnet Girl" has been found both as a vanity lamp and a night light. The night light version is pictured above, and the vanity lamp is shown at the top of the next page. A switch protrudes through the hole and a small bulb illuminates the base of the night light.

"Tara" will also be found in fired-on pink. Her shade is an elongated Southern Belle shade with the larger shells almost producing a veil.

The "Flower Girl" has a long flared basketweave dress and her one hand is clasping a fan. There are embossed flowers above both sides of her head.

The "Lovers" lamp was produced by adding four tiny feet to the lid of the "Lovers" powder jar. We have not seen a glass shade used with this lamp. Colors which have been found are frosted green, frosted pink and frosted crystal.

The "Prima Donna" vanity lamp is pictured with its original flared glass shade. The lamp was adapted from the powder jar of the same name by adding five small feet to the bottom of the lid. In addition to fired-on pink, the lamp will be found in fired-on white and fired-on blue colors.

The three lamps shown in the bottom photo on the opposite page were all made from powder jars. The first two utilize the lids of jars with a metal base. "Spring Nymph" - the green flashed and crystal frosted combination - is a night light. "Camellia" is a combination lamp/night light.

	Fired-on White	Fired-on Pink/Blue	Frosted Crystal	Frosted Pink/Green
"Sunbonnet Girl" lamp		$25.00-35.00	$20.00-25.00	$30.00-40.00
"Sunbonnet Girl" night light		$35.00-37.00	$22.00-28.00	$40.00-45.00
"Tara"		$40.00-45.00		
"Flower Girl"		$35.00-40.00		
"Lovers"			$30.00-35.00	$50.00-60.00
"Prima Donna"	$25.00-35.00	$30.00-37.00		
"Victorian Lady"				$60.00-75.00
"Camellia"				$125.00-150.00
"Spring Nymph"			$100.00-125.00	$125.00-150.00

Left to right: (a) "Lovers," frosted green; (b) "Sunbonnet Girl," frosted crystal; (c) "Prima Donna," fired-on pink.

Left to right: (a) "Victorian Lady," frosted pink with metal base and shade; (b) "Camellia," frosted green with metal base; (c) "Spring Nymph," flashed green and frosted crystal combination.

Left to right: "Reclining Nude": (a) white Clambroth; (b) transparent green, (c) pink opaque.

As may be seen from the picture, the "Reclining Nude" base was used with different fixtures to produce a lamp. The base was also sold as a matchholder ashtray with a different metal attachment in the center.

The "Dancing Couple" is listed in an early 1940's Sear's catalogue. The retail price with "an eggshell, rose, or blue paper shade with lace design" was $1.39.

The "Reclining Nude with Harp" figural base has been found in numerous colors and with several different lamp fixtures. Older lamps were made in frosted crystal, frosted blue, frosted pink, white milk glass and flashed colors. The caramel slag color base shown was produced by Imperial in the 1960's. Shades are invariably frosted crystal. The frosted and flashed lamps will usually have frosted crystal shades with lightly flashed colors which match the color of the base.

	Crystal Frosted	Opaque Colors	Frosted Green/Pink	Transparent Green
"Reclining Nude"		$40.00-60.00		$40.00-45.00
"Dancing Couple"	$20.00-25.00	$35.00-40.00		
* "Reclining Nude with Harp"	$30.00-35.00	$25.00-35.00	$75.00-100.00	
"Delilah II"	$35.00-40.00		$45.00-55.00	
"Rin Tin Tin"	$35.00-40.00		$45.00-55.00	

* Flashed colors, $60.00-75.00

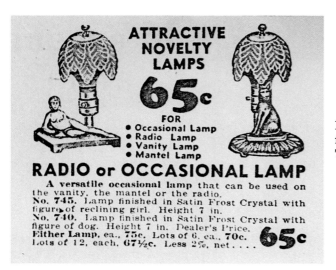

Paramount Salesman Supplies catalogue ad from 1938 featuring "Delilah II" and "Rin Tin Tin" figures.

Left: "Dancing Couple," frosted crystal. Right: "Dancing Couple," white milk glass.

Left to Right: "Reclining Nude with Harp": (a) frosted pink; (b) frosted crystal; (c) white milk glass; (d) caramel slag.

Left to Right: (a) "Organ Grinder," fired-on pink; (b) "Dutch Couple," flashed blue; (c) "Performing Ballerinas," fired-on pink.

The "Organ Grinder" has his pet monkey on his shoulder. The lamp has also been found in fired-on blue and comes with fittings to accept a flared shade.

The "Dutch Couple" lamp is usually found in frosted crystal with flashed colors. We have seen blue and pink. The matching scenic Dutch shades are frosted crystal with flashed highlights.

The "Performing Ballerinas" are usually found with the gaudy fixture with prisms and the shade shown in the photo. Besides fired-on pink, it has also been found in fired-on blue.

The Clown lamp has a carousel shade with horses, giraffes, elephants and camels prancing about the side. The lamp was made in alacite, fired-on colors and crystal frosted with pink or blue flashed colors. However, the flashed colors are easily destroyed by washing, and most of the lamps found today are merely crystal frosted.

The "Sleeping Mexican" has been found in fired-on pink, fired-on blue, and crystal frosted with flashed colors. The flashed-on lamp is quite attractive as long as none of the color has been destroyed through washing. Notice the flashed and fired-on shades are different styles.

	Frosted Crystal	Frosted Crystal with Flashed Colors	Fired-on Pink/Blue
"Organ Grinder"			$35.00-40.00
"Dutch Couple"	$25.00-30.00	$45.00-55.00	
"Performing Ballerinas"			$30.00-37.00
* Clown	$30.00-35.00	$45.00-55.00	$40.00-45.00
"Sleeping Mexican"	$25.00-30.00	$75.00-85.00	$30.00-37.00

* Alacite color, $75.00-90.00

Left: Clown, frosted crystal.   Right: "Sleeping Mexican," fired-on blue.

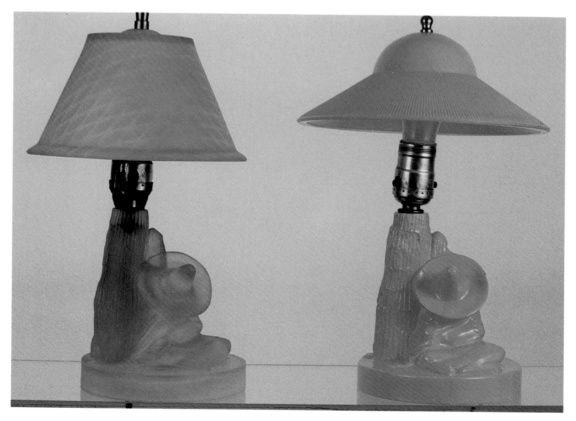

Left: "Sleeping Mexican," flashed colors over frosted crystal.
Right: "Sleeping Mexican," fired-on pink.

LAMPS WITH ANIMAL FIGURES

	Frosted Pink	Fired-on Pink	Fired-on Blue
(a) "Panther"	$75.00-85.00		
(b) "Scotty Twins"		$55.00-60.00	$55.00-60.00
(c) Scotty pups in a basket		$75.00-85.00	$75.00-85.00

	Frosted Crystal	Flashed Colors
(a) "Squirrels"	$60.00-75.00	$100.00-125.00
(b) "Playful Scotties"	$45.00-55.00	

	Fired-on Pink	Fired-on Blue	Frosted Crystal with Metal Base
(a) "Begging Scotty"	$85.00-95.00	$85.00-95.00	
(b) Metal Scotties			$60.00-75.00

	Clambroth	Fired-on Pink/Blue
(a) "Scotty on a Cube"	$30-37	
(b) "Scotty with a Ball"		$100-125

CELESTIAL AND WORLD'S FAIR LAMPS

The Saturn lamp with the concentric ring base has been reproduced since the mid-1980's by Sarsparillo Deco Designs Limited. The frosted lamps with painted decorations are priced with their paint in good condition.

Saturn Lamp	Crystal	Transparent Green	Frosted Crystal	Frosted Green/Pink
(a) Concentric Ring base			$90.00-100.00	$90.00-110.00
(b) Waffle Base	$60.00-75.00	$200.00-225.00		
(c) Ring and Rib Base	$60.00-75.00	$180.00-200.00		

World's Fair Lamp
$200.00-250.00

NAUTICAL LAMPS

(a) Crystal frosted torchiere with anchor...$30.00-35.00
(b) Fired-on blue sailboat $35.00-40.00
(c) Crystal frosted with red maritime designs...$35.00-45.00
(d) Clambroth lighthouse shade with metal sailboat $45.00-50.00

(a) Crystal frosted sailboat and cylinder...$50.00-60.00
(b) Enameled sailboat with metal rigging $40.00-50.00

TORCHIERE AND CATHEDRAL LAMPS

(a) Cathedral, frosted crystal with black base $45.00-50.00
(b) Church, frosted crystal accented with bright enamel, black base $100.00-125.00

(a) Torchiere, flashed orange, rural scene, wire spring held light $25.00-30.00
(b) Torchiere, flashed orange with black screw base..$40.00-45.00

U.S. GLASS (TIFFIN) FIGURAL LAMPS

(a) Colonial Lady..$100.00-140.00
(b) Parrot...$125.00-145.00
(c) Santa Claus...$700.00-800.00

(a) Lovebirds, red..$150.00-175.00
(b) Lovebirds (Consolidated Glass Co.).....................$150.00-175.00
(c) Lovebirds, green...$135.00-165.00

ALADDIN DRAPED LADY

Frosted crystal $600.00-800.00
Blue opalescent $2,500.00-3,000.00

McKEE LAMPS

The torchiere lamp without the black base has been reproduced since the mid-1980's.

    (a) Torchiere, crystal frosted with black top and base $125.00-150.00
    (b) Torchiere, topaz frosted with black lid $150.00-225.00

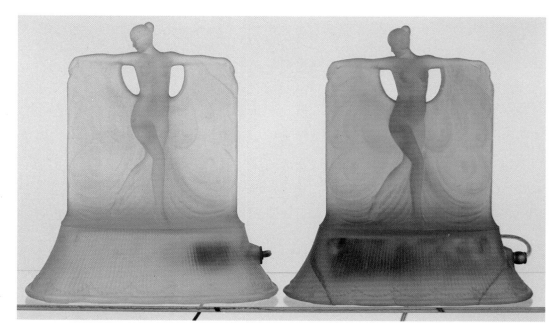

    (a) Danse de Lumiere, pink $500.00-600.00
    (b) Danse de Lumiere, green $550.00-650.00

HEISEY, McKEE AND "VALENTINE" LAMPS

	Crystal	Colored
Left Photo: (a) Heisey Electro-portable glass shade holder, 7½" satin glass shade with No. 1 cutting	$475.00-550.00	$550.00-650.00
(b) Heisey No. 201 candle lamp	$250.00-300.00	
Right Photo: McKee, pressed glass, transparent topaz	$100.00-125.00	$200.00-300.00

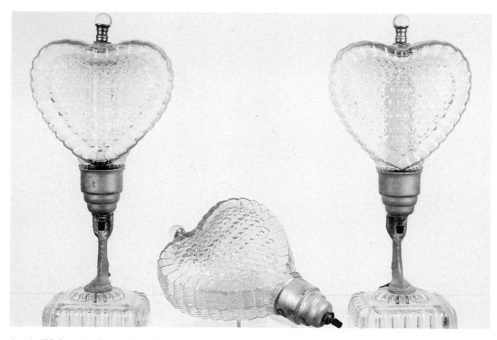

(a,c) "Valentine" vanity lamp $85.00-100.00
(b) "Valentine" bed lamp $75.00-95.00

NIGHT LIGHTS

(a) Covered wagon, crystal frosted $125.00-145.00
(b) Football, opaque beige marbleized $85.00-95.00
(c) Football, frosted amber $100.00-110.00

The above photo illustrates various designs of Aerolux figural night lights. According to information on the box, they were made by the Aerolux Light Corporation of New York. They advertised their lights, "as not like the light of the filament bulb commonly used in the home, but like the light of a firefly ... soft, cool, delicate ... so very soft even a child may gaze at it for hours without eyestrain. It is a charming home decoration as well as a safe night light for child or adult."

(a,b,c) Floral lights $40.00-45.00
(d) Scotty light $50.00-60.00

DeVILBISS PERFUME LAMPS

These DeVilbiss perfume lamps have a metal container just below the top cover in which perfume may be placed. Most lamps have a multi-colored glass insert with nude figures in graceful motion.

Round, short, 7" $100.00-200.00
Round, tall, 12" $200.00-250.00
Square, short, 8½" $100.00-150.00

Colorful DeVilbiss perfume lamps, shown lighted in nocturnal setting.

DeVilbiss perfume lamps as they appear in normal daylight.

ART GLASS AND PERFUME LAMPS

All the perfume lamps have a small indent at the top into which perfume may be placed. Numerous lamps have been found with paper labels indicating they were sold by the Irving R. Rice Company (Irice) of New York.

The two lamps in the bottom photo on the opposite page are not perfume lamps. They are examples of colored satin finish 1920's and 1930's art glass vanity lamps.

Top Row:
(a) Perfume lamp, blue Czechoslavakia, 4" $50.00-75.00
(b) Perfume lamp, crystal with prisms, Czechoslavakia, has Irice paper label, 5¼" $75.00-100.00
(c) Perfume lamp, blue, Czechoslavakia, 4" $50.00-75.00

Bottom Row:
(a) Perfume lamp, frosted pink, Czechoslavakia, 5¼" $50.00-75.00
(b) Perfume lamp, crystal, Czechoslavakia, 5¾" $45.00-55.00
(c) Perfume lamp, Hanging Heart pattern, Imperial, 4¾" $100.00-125.00

Next Page, Top:
Right: Flashed yellow perfume lamp $40.00-50.00
Left: Cambridge azurite perfume lamp $125.00-145.00

Bottom Photo:
(a) Blue and satin crystal lamp, 9" $100.00-125.00
(b) Mottle color lamp, 11½" $250.00-275.00

Perfume lamp, azurite, Cambridge.   **Perfume lamp, flashed yellow.**

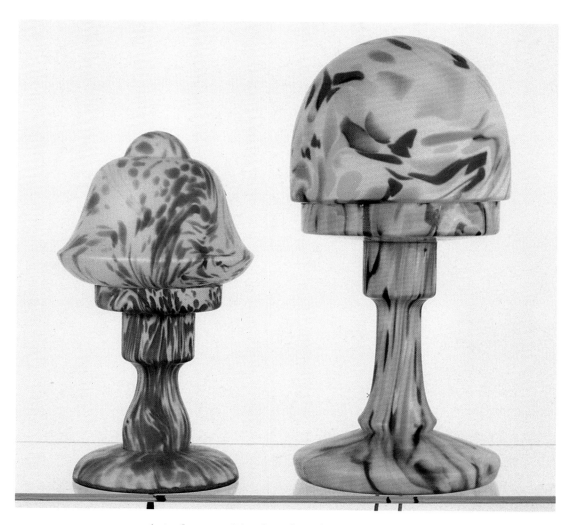

Art glass multi-colored satin finish lamps.

TORCHIERE LAMPS

(a) Vanity lamp, pink flashed with celluloid base, 11½" $15.00-18.00
(b) Bed lamp, pink flashed with celluloid holder, 10" $10.00-15.00
(c) Bed lamp, blue flashed with metal holder, 10"..$20.00-25.00
(d) Vanity lamp, blue flashed, 10½"..$20.00-25.00

The two lamps on the left side have the same style shade. Each is turned a different direction so both the front and back may be illustrated.

(a) Pink flashed, crystal base, 12½" $20.00-22.00
(b) Blue flashed, blue flashed base, 11½" $20.00-25.00
(c) Crystal frosted shade with embossed lovebirds, 9¼" $60.00-75.00
(d) Pink opaque with enameled flowers, 10¾" $50.00-55.00

(a) Crystal frosted shade with crystal base, 11½" $12.00-14.00
(b) Pink frosted shade and base with handpainted flowers, 11" $30.00-40.00
(c) Green frosted, black decoration, 10½" $25.00-35.00
(d) Crystal frosted, 7¾" $20.00-25.00

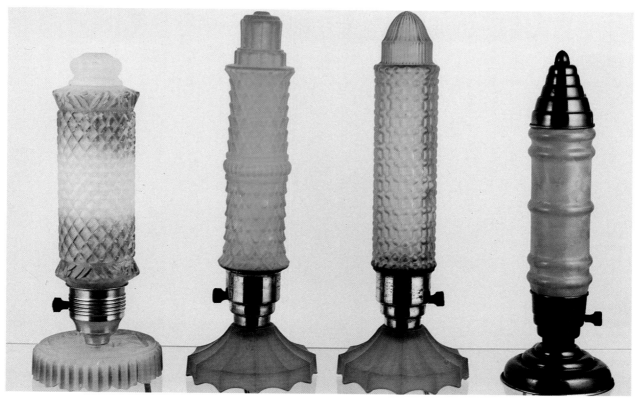

(a) Crystal frosted with green flashed decoration, 11½" $20.00-25.00
(b) Blue frosted, flat top, 12¼" $25.00-30.00
(c) Blue frosted, cone top, 12½" $25.00-30.00
(d) Amber wood grain with metal cap and base, 11½" $20.00-30.00

MISCELLANEOUS VANITY LAMPS

(a) Crystal frosted with
    Chinese pagoda and tree $18.00-20.00
(b) Pink frosted with
    embossed flowers $25.00-30.00

(a) Pink flashed with large embossed hanging flowers $10.00-14.00
(b) White flashed with gold accented embossed stars $10.00-14.00
(c) White opaque with green flashed vertical ribs $14.00-16.00

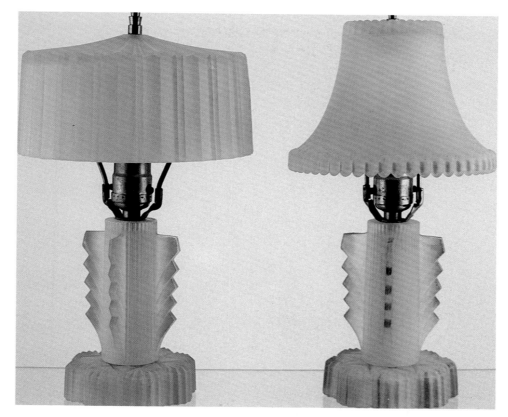

(a) Crystal frosted with flashed pink trim, round shade $25.00-35.00
(b) Crystal frosted with blue flashed trim, flared shade........................$25.00-35.00

(a) Crystal frosted with blue flashed trim....................................$8.00-10.00
(b) Crystal with light blue flashed film $18.00-20.00
(c) Opaque pink base with large flowers $20.00-25.00

HOUZEX AND NEW MARTINSVILLE VANITY LAMPS

The Houzex Convex Glass Company of Point Marion, Pennsylvania produced numerous colorful opaque glass lamps. Many of these lamps are identified today through the location of their paper label which may be found on the underside of the lamp. The lamps in the above photo were all made by Houzex. In addition, all these shapes will be found in opaque green. For other examples of lamps produced by Houzex, see page 196.

Positive identification of all the lamps on the opposite page is not possible at this time. Both Houzex and New Martinsville, as well as several other companies produced this style lamp.

	Opaque Green	Opaque Topaz	Opaque Blue
(a,b) Short bulbous base, tall shade	$35.00-45.00	$50.00-55.00	$55.00-60.00
(c) Short bulbous base, short shade	$35.00-45.00	$50.00-55.00	$55.00-60.00
(d) Tall narrow body	$18.00-20.00	$25.00-30.00	$30.00-40.00

NEXT PAGE,
Top Photo:

(a) Opaque green, four-footed, ribbed shade $30.00-35.00
(b) Opaque green, square step base, frosted green shade with square sawtooth rim $35.00-40.00
(c) Frosted chartreuse, handled base with ribbed pattern, ribbed shade with
    scalloped rim, New Martinsville $30.00-35.00

Bottom Photo:

(a) Green opaque, handled base with square feet, shade with square sawtooth rim, 9½" $30.00-35.00
(b) Frosted green, base and shade with vertical ribs, shade clips to bulb, 11½" $30.00-35.00

GLOBE SPECIALLTY COMPANY AND HOUZEX LAMPS

The lamps in this photo bear the paper label of the Globe Specialty Company, Chicago, Illinois.

    (a) Orange marbleized $30.00-35.00
    (b) Green marbleized $30.00-35.00
    (c) Blue marblieized $30.00-35.00
    (d) Red/brown marbleized $25.00-30.00
    (e) Green marbleized $25.00-30.00

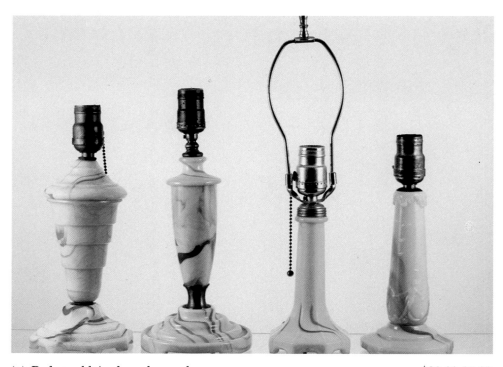

    (a) Red marbleized, maker unknown $30.00-35.00
    (b) Brown marbleized, Houzex $30.00-35.00
    (c) Brown marbleized, Houzex $20.00-35.00
    (d) Brown marbleized with dancing nudes at base of body, Houzex $40.00-50.00

AKRO AGATE LAMPS

The Akro Agate Company of Clarksburg, West Virginia was a prolific maker of slag glass boudoir lamps. These lamps were assembled from parts and many combinations resulted. At times, slag pieces were combined with crystal or metal pieces to produce slightly different shapes. Occasional solid colored lamps may also be found. Green and blue lamps are shown on page 199. Crystal lamps and wall lamps were also made, but collectors have not shown much interest in these.

Collectors regard the bell-shaped Akro slag shades very highly. Many of these shades have not withstood the abuse from high wattage bulbs, therefore, numerous lamps are begging for original shades. The current value of a shade is about $85.00 to $95.00. Lamps in the photo that are shown with shades are priced with shades. To obtain the value of the base, this value should be subtracted from the indicated price. Also, this value should be added to the price of lamps shown without shades to determine the value of a complete lamp.

    (a) Square base, pineapple design body, shade $125.00-150.00
    (b) Round thick base, ribbed flower pot body, shade...........................$125.00-150.00
    (c) Small round ribbed base, handled body, shade $135.00-175.00

(a) Square base, tubular body $20.00-25.00
(b) Round footed base, handpainted wood insert in body $25.00-30.00
(c) Square base, handled inset and pineapple design insert
    used in body $30.00-35.00
(d) Crystal $12.00-18.00
(e) Round base, metal feet, tubular body $20.00-25.00

(a) Metal base, flared embossed body..$18.00-22.00
(b) Metal base, cone body, shade $150.00-175.00
(c) Round footed base, metal and celluloid $18.00-22.00

(a) Cream square base, green pineapple design body $75.00-100.00
(b) Square base, flower pot body, shade $125.00-150.00
(c) Round thick base, narrow metal and embossed glass body $40.00-45.00

(a) Square base with mirror, wall lamp $18.00-25.00
(b) Blue, pineapple body, square black wood base $75.00-100.00

CAMBRIDGE LAMPS

(a) Azurite with gold band $100.00-125.00
(b) Mulberrry with glass shade; beaded prisms $500.00-600.00
(c) Mulberry $110.00-135.00

(a) Gold Krystol Apple Blossom, metal base $110.00-135.00
(b) Primrose, black and gold band decoration $85.00-95.00
(c) Crystal Mt. Vernon body, blue mirror base $50.00-60.00
(d) Emerald $45.00-50.00

FENTON LAMPS

(a) French opalescent Coin Dot, metal base, tall shade..........................$45.00-55.00
(b) French opalescent Coin Dot, dual light, metal base.........................$60.00-85.00
(c) French opalescent, Spiral Optic, marble base $45.00-55.00

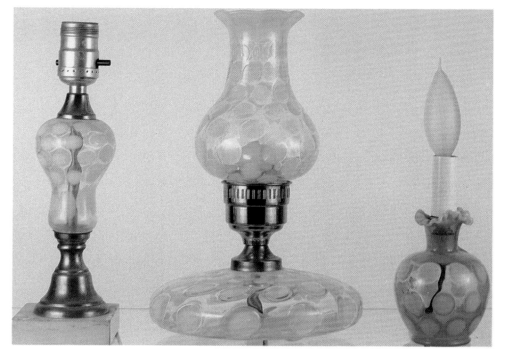

(a) French opalescent Coin Dot body on metal inset
    with marble base $20.00-30.00
(b) French opalescent Coin Dot $125.00-155.00
(c) Blue opalescent Coin Dot..$25.00-30.00

Left Photo:
(a) Topaz satin, 18" $95.00-110.00
(b) Blue opalescent, 18" $145.00-195.00

Right Photo:
(a) Cranberry Coin Dot....................................$225.00-250.00
(b) Cranberry Hobnail, 17½" $225.00-275.00

WESTMORELAND LAMPS

	Pink/Green	Amber	Blue
(a) Dolphin, No. 1049/1	$75.00-85.00	$75.00-85.00	
(b) Colonial No. 185	$50.00-60.00	$50.00-60.00	
(c) Rib optic	$45.00-55.00	$40.00-50.00	$65.00-75.00
(d) Lotus No. 1921	$85.00-100.00	$75.00-95.00	

(a) Pink Waterford No. 300/8 .... $85.00-100.00
(b) Crystal Waterford No. 300/8 .... $35.00-45.00

(a) Cobalt, English Hobnail, No. 555, 9¼" $140.00-150.00
(b) Cobalt, English Hobnail, No. 555/1, 6¼" $140.00-150.00
(c) Medium blue, English Hobnail, No. 555, 9¼" $85.00-95.00
(d) Light blue, English Hobnail, No. 555, 9¼" $85.00-95.00

(a) Pink, English Hobnail, No. 555, 9¼" $75.00-85.00
(b) Pink, English Hobnail, No. 555/1, 6¼" $65.00-75.00
(c) Green, English Hobnail, No. 555, 9¼" $75.00-85.00
(d) Green English Hobanail, No. 555/1, 6¼" $65.00-75.00
(e) Dark green English Hobnail, No. 555, 9¼" $75.00-85.00
(f) Aqua English Hobnail, No. 555, 9¼" $85.00-95.00

(a) White milk glass, English Hobnail, No. 555, 9¼" $45.00-55.00
(b) White milk glass, English Hobnail, No. 555/1, 6¼" $35.00-45.00
(c) Amber, English Hobnail, No. 555, 9¼" $50.00-60.00
(d) Crystal, English Hobnail, No. 555, 9¼" $30.00-35.00
(e) Crystal, English Hobnail, No. 555/1, 6¼" $27.00-35.00

Left:
Custard, English Hobnail,
No. 55/1, 6¼" $75.00-95.00
Right:
Green, English Hobnail, 7" $85.00-100.00

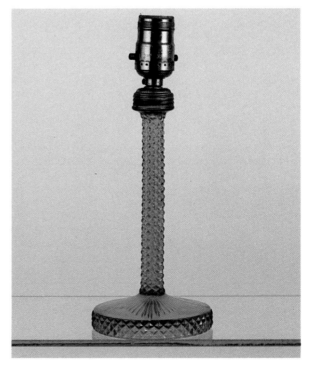

Amber, English Hobnail,
stick lamp, 8" $35.00-45.00

MISCELLANEOUS COLORED LAMPS

Left: American Pioneer ball lamp, green, 6¼" $95.00-110.00
Right: American Pioneer tall lamp, green, 8½" $85.00-95.00

Dolphin lamp, pink $95.00-110.00

(a) Black, 7¾" $35.00-45.00
(b) Black, combination lamp, cigarette holder, ashtray $40.00-45.00
(c) Black, 8½" .... $35.00-$45.00

	Pink/Green	Amber	Red
(a) Hexagonal, 8½"	$20.00-27.00	$20.00-27.00	
(b) Pseudo rombic, 8"	$45.00-55.00	$45.00-55.00	$95.00-125.00
(c) Arches, 8½"	$45.00-55.00	$35.00-45.00	
(d) Diamond cut rib, 8¼"	$45.00-55.00	$40.00-45.00	

Left: Topaz $45.00-55.00
Right: McKee Mayflower, green $40.00-50.00

Pink Waffle $55.00-60.00

STICK LAMPS

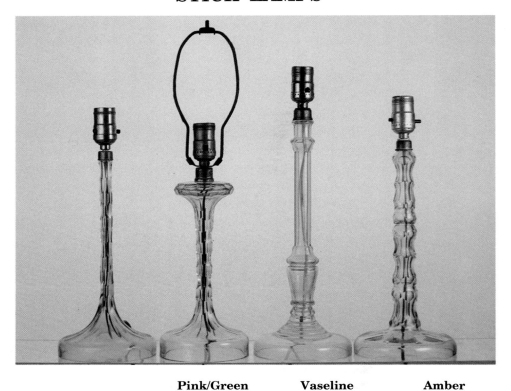

	Pink/Green	Vaseline	Amber	Blue
(a) Honeycomb, 14½"	$40.00-45.00	$50.00-55.00	$40.00-45.00	$55.00-60.00
(b) Hex optic, 12½"	$60.00-65.00		$50.00-55.00	
(c) Oriental scene etched above base, 5½"		$60.00-70.00		
(d) Scalloped body, 14½"	$40.00-45.00	$50.00-65.00	$40.00-45.00	

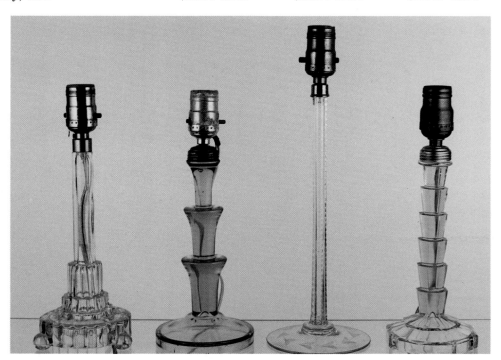

	Pink/Green	Vaseline	Amber	Blue
(a) Tower, 9½"	$20.00-25.00			
(b) Step, 9"	$35.00-40.00			
(c) Zipper, 12"	$35.00-40.00	$35.00-40.00	$30.00-35.00	$35.00-40.00
(d) Tearoom, 9"	$60.00-75.00			

SPOOL LAMPS

A tall slender lamp, often called a "Spool" lamp was made by the Jefferson Glass Company of Follansee, West Virginia. Some lamps were made with combinations of different styles of spools. Pink, amber, jadite and lavender are the colors which have been found.

	Lavender	Amber/Pink	Jadite
(a,b) Flared spool, 12"	$50.00-60.00	$40.00-50.00	$40.00-45.00
(c) Smooth and flared spool combination, 11½"	$50.00-55.00	$50.00-55.00	
(d) Inverted cone spool, 10½"		$50.00-55.00	$50.00-55.00

(a) Clambroth and opaque green $45.00-55.00
(b) Alacite-type $30.00-35.00

Floral embossed ball $20.00-25.00

CLOCKS

Row 1: (a) McKee Tambour Art Glass clock, pink; (b) McKee Tambour Art Glass clock, canary.

Row 2: (a) McKee Tambour Art Glass clock, amber; (b) "Twin Ballerina" clock, flashed pink, movement by Sessions, 8½" high by 13½" long.

	Crystal Flashed Colors	Pink/ Amber	Canary	Blue/Black Jadite
(a) McKee, 14" long	$100.00-135.00	$200.00-225.00	$210.00-250.00	$295.00-325.00
(b) "Twin Ballerina"	$100.00-150.00			

Next Page, Top Photo:

Top Row:

(a) Clock, blue, pressed pattern on rounded sides with embossed flowers and birds; embossed nudes and urn on front below face, 3½" high $75.00-85.00

(b,d) Candlestick, black, 5" $10.00-14.00

(c) Clock, black, Fostoria, works made by the New Haven Clock Co., U.S.A., 6" high $100.00-125.00

Bottom Row:

(a,c) Candlestick, green, Fostoria, 5" $8.00-12.00

(b) Clock, green, Fostoria, 3¼" high $70.00-75.00

(d) Clock, topaz, "Foreign," 3½" high, 6" long $50.00-65.00

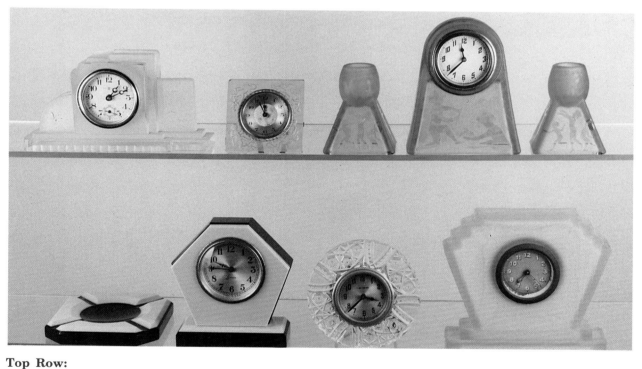

Top Row:
(a) Clock, crystal frosted $100.00-125.00
(b) Clock, crystal frosted, gold decorated square body $50.00-65.00
(c,e) Candlestick, green satin, Fostoria Cupid pattern $15.00-18.00
(d) Clock, green satin, Fostoria Cupid pattern $150.00-200.00

Bottom Row:
(a) Ashtray, green/black opaque $18.00-20.00
(b) Clock, green/black opaque $100.00-125.00
(c) Clock, crystal, round pressed glass body $25.00-35.00
(d) Clock, green frosted, "Foreign" $100.00-125.00

Top Row:
(a) Clock, crystal, "Belfor, Western Germany" $25.00-30.00
(b) Clock, frosted green, "Foreign," elongated 8-sided base, pinwheel-shaped body,
    5½" high, 6½" long $100.00-125.00
(c) Clock, black, Fostoria, etched design, 5¼" high $125.00-150.00

Bottom Row:
(a) Clock, black, embossed floral design, advertising on face,
    "James Davis - Highest Art in Wallpaper - Chicago, St. Paul," 5½" tall $125.00-150.00
(b,d) Vase, green, 5½" $10.00-12.00
(c) Clock, green, "Foreign," 6" high, 5" long $85.00-95.00

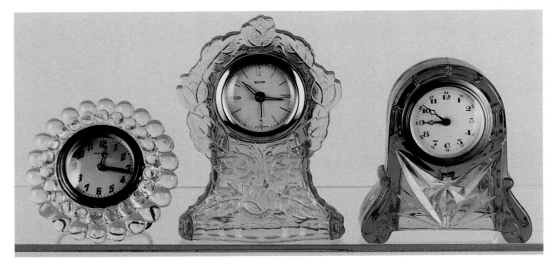

(a) Clock, crystal, New Haven works, 4¼" diameter $25.00-30.00
(b) Clock, pink, embossed leaf design, 6½" high $85.00-95.00
(c) Clock, pinkish-amber, 4¾" high $75.00-80.00

PART V:
GUEST SETS

The various companies which made the items shown in this section called them by several names - guest set, night set, night cap set and tumble-up. Night set may also be spelled nite set. Identification of the maker of many of the sets is complicated by the similarity in the appearance of some of the sets made by different companies. In the pictures, sets with similar shapes have been grouped together as much as possible when the maker is unknown. Sets which can be identified are grouped together by company of manufacture.

The bedside set pictured below consists of a lid and tray. It was sold with the gift box shown and the recipients had to provide their own tumbler.

Glass cover and tray $20.00-25.00

CAMBRIDGE HANDLED GUEST SETS

Row 1: Guest sets: (a) amber with ribbed handle; (b) crystal with Rosepoint etching; (c) green with ribbed handle.
Row 2: Guest sets: (a) green with plain handle; (b) green with # 704 plate etching.

In the mid-1920's, the Cambridge Glass Company of Cambridge, Ohio began production of colored glass "guest sets." The bedside sets shown here consist of a handled pitcher and tumbler which also serves as a cover for the jug. Most often colored sets will be found without etchings, but various etchings can also be found with some diligent searching. Crystal sets with major Cambridge pattern etchings such as Rosepoint are very difficult to find.

The pitcher to this set holds 38 oz. and is 7" tall. The bottom of the jug has a small foot and is 4" in diameter. Notice the pitcher may have either a plain or ribbed applied handle. The total height of the pitcher with the tumbler inserted is 7⅜". The height of the tumbler is 3⅜". The top diameter of the tumbler is 2¼" and the sides slope out gently at the base to form a small foot to prevent the tumbler from sliding down into the pitcher when it is used as a cover.

	Crystal	Green/Pink	Amber	Cobalt
Handled, #103 plain, 38 oz.	$25.00-30.00	$50.00-60.00	$45.00-50.00	$75.00-85.00
Handled, Rosepoint etch	$175.00-225.00			
* Handled, #704 etch	$30.00-40.00	$65.00-90.00	$65.00-90.00	

* With etched tumbler, add 20%.

CAMBRIDGE GUEST SETS

Row 1: (a) Guest set, 4-piece #489, pink with Cleo etching; (b) guest set #489 jug and cover, amber with Hunt Scene etching; (c) guest set #489 jug and cover, Moonlight blue; (d) guest set #489 jug, Royal blue with crystal applied handle.
Row 2: 4-piece Guest Set #488: (a) amber; (b) pink with No. 726 etching; (c) green with floral etching.

Two styles of 4-piece guest sets were made by Cambridge. The top row pictures the #489 guest set with a ribbed 22 oz. pitcher and ribbed tumbler. The lid to this jug is slightly domed and has an open loop finial. The jug is 5" tall - 6¾" with the lid. The ribbed tumbler is 3⅛" high and the sides curve outward slightly.

The smooth 22 oz. jug of the #488 set is 5" tall and 6" high with the lid. The lid to this set has a solid flat knob. The tumbler is 3⅜" high and sometimes has slight vertical panels.

The tray to both sets is usually the same, however, a different tray was found with the green set on the bottom row. The common tray is 5¾" wide and 9¾" long. This tray is easily confused with a similar tray used with Paden City bedside sets. The handles of the Paden City trays generally curve upward more than those of the Cambridge trays. Also, the Paden City trays are smooth with a rolling curvature on the upper surface at the junction of the handle and tray. The Cambridge trays have a sharp molded edge at this junction. The flat tab handled tray used with the green floral etched set is 6¼" wide and 11" long.

	Green/Pink Amber	Royal Blue Cobalt/Mulberry	Moonlight Blue	Carmen
No. 489, no etching	$50.00-60.00	$85.00-110.00	$85.00-95.00	$95.00-125.00
No. 489, Cleo etching	$100.00-125.00		$125.00-150.00	
No. 489, Hunt Scene etching	$95.00-110.00			
No. 488, no etching	$50.00-60.00	$85.00-110.00	$85.00-95.00	$125.00-145.00
No. 488, floral etching	$55.00-70.00			

	Etched	Plain
Tumbler only, #489 set	$14.00-20.00	$6.00-8.00
Tumbler only, #488 set	$14.00-20.00	$6.00-8.00
Tray, deep handed		$10.00-15.00
Tray, flat tab handled		$15.00-18.00

FENTON GUEST SETS

Row 1: Fenton No. 401 guest sets: (a) topaz; (b) Celeste blue; (c) Florentine pearl; (d) Florentine green.
Row 2: (a) Guest set, pink with floral etching; (b) guest set, flashed mulberry; (c) guest set, pink with wicker holder; (d) guest set, cobalt; (e) guest set, pink with decal decoration and advertising on tumbler.

Fenton's No. 401 stretch glass guest sets from the early 1920's are pictured on the top row. The tumbler is 3" high and has curved sides. The water bottle is 5¾" tall, and the overall set with the tumbler in place measures 6½".

Various colored night sets with the same measurements are shown on the bottom row. These may not have been made by Fenton. The pink tumbler shown on the set on the right side has been found on more than one style base. It is etched with a floral design and bears the ad, "Sparklett's California's Finest Drinking Water, The Aristocrat of Drinking Waters."

	* Pink/Green	Flashed Colors	Stretch Glass Colors	Cobalt
Fenton No. 401	$16.00-20.00	$12.00-18.00	$30.00-45.00	$45.00-55.00

* Set with Sparklett's advertising, $25.00-27.00.

OPALESCENT AND STRETCH GLASS GUEST SETS

Top Row:	Height of Tumbler	Height of Water Bottle	Combined Height	Price
(a) Turquoise opalescent	3"	5⅝"	6½"	$80.00-90.00
(b) Blue opalescent	3"	5⅝"	6½"	$85.00-100.00
(c) Green opalescent	3"	5⅝"	6½"	$75.00-85.00
(d) French opalescent	3½"	6½"	7"	$65.00-85.00
(e) Pink opalescent	3½"	6½"	7¼"	$70.00-90.00

Bottom Row: Fenton No. 200 stretch glass guest sets with applied handles.

	Height of Tumbler	Height of Water Bottle	Combined Height	Price
(a) Marigold iridescent with cobalt handle	3¾"	7"	8"	$175.00-200.00
(b) French opalescent with clear handle	3¾"	7"	8"	$200.00-225.00
(c) Topaz stretch glass with cobalt handle	3¾"	7"	8"	$225.00-250.00

DIAMOND OPTIC AND SWIRL GUEST SETS

Left to right: (a) Fenton's No. 1502 Diamond Optic pattern night set with tray, top for water bottle and two tumblers; (b) Opalescent twin rib night set with original Wrisley's bath salts label.

The pink guest set on the left is Fenton's No. 1502 Diamond Optic pattern. It is unusual to find this set with the glass cover for the water bottle since most sets have the associated tumbler used as the cover.

The opalescent night bottle on the right is being reproduced by a national importer. This set still has its original label and was made by Fenton for Wrisley. The new sets are shown on page 253.

    (a) Twin rib No. 1502 Diamond Optic, pink, set $50.00-65.00
    (b) Twin rib opalescent, with original label $75.00-95.00

Next Page: The three tumble-ups on the left side of the top row were made by Fenton. Both the tumbler and the water bottle have two ribs around the base. The three sets on the right side of the top row have a swirled neck which descends to a diamond optic pattern on the lower body. A very similar diamond optic night set was listed in the catalogue of the West Virginia Specialty Company in the early 1980's. This later tumble-up was produced in crystal and flashed colors. The overall height of both night sets is the same - 6⅞". However, the tumbler of the newer set is only 3" tall and the tumbler to the old set is 3¼" tall.

The pink and green sets on the left side of the bottom row have a palm optic looped swirl design. The larger set on the right appears to be Fostoria's No. 1697 Spiral Optic pattern.

	Height of Tumbler	Height of Water Bottle	Combined Height	Price
Top Row:				
(a) Aqua twin rib	3⅛"	5⅞"	6¾"	$45.00-50.00
(b) Pink twin rib	3⅛"	5⅞"	6¾"	$18.00-25.00
(c) Green twin rib	3⅛"	5⅞"	6¾"	$18.00-25.00
(d) Pink diamond optic	3¼"	5¾"	6⅞"	$20.00-25.00
(e) Crystal diamond optic	3¼"	5¾"	6⅞"	$12.00-14.00
(f) Green diamond optic	3¼"	5¾"	6⅞"	$22.00-27.00

	Height of Tumbler	Height of Water Bottle	Combined Height	Price
Bottom Row:				
(a) Pink palm optic	3⅜"	5¾"	7"	$20.00-25.00
(b) Green palm optic	3⅜"	5¾"	7"	$20.00-25.00
(c) Marigold iridescent swirl	3⅛"	6"	7"	$18.00-22.00
(d) Pink handpainted swirl	3"	6"	7"	$25.00-28.00
(e) Pink swirl	3"	6"	7"	$25.00-28.00
(f) Pink Spiral Optic	3⅛"	6⅝"	7¾"	$30.00-32.00

HEISEY GUEST SETS

Row 1: (a) Guest set, crystal; **(b)** guest set, stained blue with gold encrusted decoration; **(c)** guest set, crystal with "Thistle" decoration.

Row 2: (a) Guest set, crystal with floral and zigzag line decoration; **(b)** guest set, crystal with floral decoration; **(c)** guest set, crystal with floral decoration.

The A.H. Heisey Company of Newark, Ohio produced a handled one quart guest set. The set was made primarily in crystal and cut with various decorations, but also can be found in alexandrite and in stained colors with gold decoration. The bottoms of the tumblers and the bottoms of the jugs are usually marked with a diamond "H". The tumbler is 3⅜" tall and has a ridge about an inch from the bottom to prevent it from slipping into the jug when it is used as a cover. The #517 jug is 6" tall.

Guest set, crystal $50.00-65.00
Guest set, alexandrite, (not shown) $250.00-250.00
Guest set, crystal with floral decoration $125.00-145.00
Guest set, blue stained and gold decorated $245.00-275.00

HANDLED GUEST SETS

The first two sets on the top row were produced by the Imperial Glass Company of Bellaire, Ohio. They are both style No. 650 with Cut No. 2. The tumbler is 3⅝" tall and has a ridge at the base. The jug is 6¾" tall and has a small foot at the base. The set was made in pink, crystal and green.

The two sets with concentric ribs are pink and a deep pinkish-amber. The tumbler has a ridge at its base and is 3¼" tall. The pitcher measures 7" in height.

The amber guest set is similar in appearance to the Imperial and tall Cambridge sets, however, its foot is not as prominent. The height of the tumbler is 3⅜" and the jug is 7" tall.

The crystal and green sets on the bottom row are possibly New Martinsville. The shape of the jug is right, but the tumbler differs from the ones shown in the catalogues. The jug is 6½" tall. The tumbler is 3¼" tall and has a ridge ½" from the bottom.

	Crystal	Crystal Decorated	Pink/Green Amber
Guest set, Imperial	$25.00-35.00	$35.00-40.00	$70.00-90.00
Guest set, ribbed	$20.00-30.00		$85.00-95.00
Guest set, Row 2, No. 1	$20.00-30.00		$60.00-85.00
Guest set, New Martinsville	$20.00-30.00	$40.00-50.00	$70.00-90.00

LIBBEY NIGHT SETS

Of the dozens of different decorated crystal tumble-ups, those made by Libbey are most easily identified. The top edges of both the tumbler and bottle have a noticeable ridge which Libbey describes as a "Safe-edge lip" which defies chipping. The tumbler is 3⅛" tall and the bottle is 5⅝" high. Overall combined height is 7" with the tumbler inverted on the base.

Many of the Libbey night sets were decorated with simple gold lines or standard stencil designs, but some will be found with elaborate wheel cut or handpainted enameled decorations.

	Crystal with Gold Bands	Crystal with Stencil Design	Crystal with Wheel Cut Design	Crystal Handpainted
Night set, 7"	$12.00-14.00	$14.00-15.00	$8.00-14.00	$14.00-16.00

NEW MARTINSVILLE GUEST SETS

Most of the colored New Martinsville guest sets date from the mid-1920's to the early 1930's. The height of the "Wise Owl" set is 4¾". The pitcher is 4½" high and the tumbler measures 2¼".

The No. 728 guest sets are pictured on the second row. The pitchers may be found with or without vertical panels. The blue and green sets have panels, but the iridescent set in the center has none. The pitcher is 4¾" tall and measures 6" with its lid. The paneled tumbler is 2¾" high and the plain tumbler is 3¼" tall. The tray has heavy ribs and is 6" wide by 9¼" long. The pitcher will sometimes be found with handpainted or etched decorations.

	Crystal	Pink/Green Amber	Blue Amethyst	Green Clambroth	Iridized Colors
* "Wise Owl"	$40.00-45.00	$85.00-95.00		$120.00-125.00	
No. 728		$45.00-55.00	$70.00-80.00		$60.00-70.00
No. 728 decorated		$55.00-65.00	$75.00-85.00		

* With wheel cut or handpainted decoration, add 20%.

PADEN CITY GUEST SETS

The Paden City Glass Manufacturing Company of Paden City, West Virginia produced much colorful glassware during the late 1920's and early 1930's when these guest sets were made. Colored sets will often be found with gold or etched decorations. The tumblers and tray will usually be decorated to match the pitcher. Applied handles may be either roped or plain. Some pitchers have wide rib optic panels and others are smooth. The pitcher is 5" tall and measures 6¼" with its cover. The tumbler is 3⅛" tall and the tray is 5⅝" wide and 9⅞" long. For a comparison to the similar Cambridge trays, see the section on Cambridge guest sets (page 215).

	Pink/Green Amber	Vaseline Amethyst	Cobalt
Plain	$50.00-60.00	$85.00-110.00	$125.00-145.00
Gold decorated	$50.00-60.00	$75.00-85.00	$125.00-145.00
Etched	$55.00-70.00	$85.00-110.00	$135.00-165.00

U.S. GLASS NIGHT CAP AND GUEST SETS

The three-piece U.S. Glass Company guest sets shown on the top row were made in the late 1920's. The set has a flat bottom, bulbous-sided jug which is 5½" tall. The tumbler is 3" tall and has a wide ridge in the center to prevent it from sliding into the jug when it is used as a cover. The jug rests on an eight-sided tray which has bar-like handles. The tray has a star in the bottom and is 5¼" wide and 10" long.

The items shown on the bottom row were called night cap sets in the U.S. glass catalogues. Two sizes were produced and many crystal ones were flashed and hand decorated. The smaller set has a 3" tumbler and the bottle is 5⅞" tall. The larger set, shown on the right, is flashed blue and has a handpainted yellow and blue parrot. Its tumbler is 3¼" tall and the bottom is 6⅛" high. Besides the flashed colors and decorations shown, sets in either size may be found in both transparent and frosted pink, green, canary and crystal.

	Pink/Green Canary	Flashed Colors	Flashed Colors with Fancy Paint
Guest set, handled with tray	$85.00-95.00		
Night cap set, short	$20.00-25.00	$18.00-22.00	$25.00-30.00
Night cap set, tall	$22.00-27.00	$22.00-25.00	$30.00-32.00

225

MISCELLANEOUS NIGHT SETS

The first two sets on the top row were made by Cambridge. The thin transparent colored Cambridge and Paden City tumble-ups are very similar in appearance. The major difference upon close examination is in the definition of the mold seams. Mold seams are very apparent on the Paden City tumble-ups and are virtually indistinguishable on the Cambridge ones.

Top Row:
(a) Night bottle, Cambridge No. 237, Azurite, 7"..$200.00-250.00
(b) Night bottle, Cambridge No. 726 etching, 7"..$45.00-55.00
(c) Night set, Hocking Block Optic, transparent green, 7"...$32.00-37.00
(d) Night set, Hocking Rib Optic, transparent green, 7"..$18.00-20.00
(e) Night set, Hocking Rib Optic with etched tumbler, 7"...$25.00-27.00

Bottom Row:
(a) Night set, Fostoria Rogene,
    both tumbler and bottle have ground bottoms, 7¾"..$45.00-55.00
(b) Night set, Paden City floral etching, pink, 7"..$45.00-55.00
(c) Night set, Macbeth-Evans Crystal Leaf, green, 6½"...$40.00-50.00
(d) Night set, Macbeth-Evans Crystal Leaf, pink, 6½"...$40.00-50.00

MISCELLANEOUS COLORED NIGHT SETS

The style tumble-up shown in the above photo is found frequently in opaque colors. Jadite and opaque turquoise are especially prevalent. The transparent blue and ruby sets are not as common. The tumbler has gently curved sides and is 2⅞" high. The base is 5⅞" tall and the combined height with the tumbler in place is 6⅞".

Top Row:
(a) Blue transparent $35.00-40.00
(b) Yellow opaque $30.00-35.00
(c) Black opaque $40.00-45.00
(d) White opaque $40.00-45.00
(e) Yellow opaque base with black tumbler $32.00-37.00
(f) Ruby $50.00-60.00

Bottom Row:
(a) Jadite $20.00-25.00
(b) Jadite with handpainted flowers $25.00-28.00
(c) Dark turquoise opaque $27.00-30.00
(d) Medium turquoise opaque $25.00-27.00
(e) Light turquoise opaque $25.00-27.00
(f) Powder blue opaque $27.00-30.00

The tumblers of the handled sets on the top row are straight-sided and the pitcher has a spout. The opaque turquoise handleless water set on the right is similar in shape, but the bottom has no spout and the sides of the tumbler are curved.

	Height of Tumbler	Height of Water Bottle	Combined Height	Price
Top Row:				
(a) Pink handled with decoration	2⅞"	5¼"	6"	$60.00-70.00
(b) Jadite, handled	2⅞"	5¼"	6"	$60.00-70.00
(c) Amber, handled	2⅞"	5¼"	6"	$50.00-60.00
(d) Opaque turquoise	2⅞"	5⅜"	6¼"	$45.00-50.00
Bottom Row:				
(a) Green decorated	3½"	5¾"	7"	$20.00-25.00
(b) Mulberry	3½"	5¾"	7"	$25.00-35.00
(c) Green	3½"	5¾"	7"	$20.00-25.00
(d) Blue decorated	3½"	5¾"	7"	$45.00-55.00
(e) Topaz	3½"	5¾"	7"	$30.00-35.00

BELL-SHAPED BEDROOM SETS

The three tumble-ups with bell-shaped bases which have tumblers with curved sides on the right side of the top row appear to be from Westmoreland's No. 1800 Line. Many of these sets will have either wheel cut or handpainted decorations. The tumbler is 3¼" tall and the bottle is 5½" high. A slight variation of the basic style is offered by the other tumble-ups with a similar shape. The careful observer will be able to detect slight differences in either the shape of the tumbler or in the overall measurements. A similar set with a swirled pattern is shown on the left side of the bottom row.

	Height of Tumbler	Height of Water Bottle	Combined Height	Price
Top Row:				
(a) Crystal, decorated	2⅞"	5½"	6¼"	$8.00-14.00
(b) Crystal, decorated	3"	5½"	6⅜"	$8.00-14.00
(c) Crystal, decorated	3⅛"	5⅝"	6½"	$8.00-14.00
(d) Crystal, decorated	3¼"	5½"	6½"	$8.00-14.00
(e) Crystal, decorated	3¼"	5½"	6½"	$8.00-14.00
(f) Flashed, handpainted	3¼"	5½"	6½"	$25.00-30.00
Bottom Row:				
(a) Pink, swirled	3⅛"	5⅝"	6½"	$25.00-30.00
(b) Green, decorated	2¾"	5½"	6"	$25.00-30.00
(c) Pink, plain	3⅛"	5½"	6½"	$20.00-25.00
(d) Crystal, silver/blue bands	3"	5½"	6¼"	$8.00-10.00
(e) Pebbled pink over crystal	3⅛"	5⅝"	6⅜"	$10.00-12.00
(f) Flashed amber iridescent	2⅞"	5⅝"	6¼"	$10.00-12.00

Westmoreland No. 1800 Line	Crystal	Green/Pink	Flashed Colors
Night set, plain	$6.00-8.00	$20.00-25.00	$10.00-12.00
Night set, wheel cut	$8.00-10.00	$25.00-27.00	
Night set, handpainted	$8.00-10.00	$25.00-27.00	$17.00-27.00

PANELED NIGHT SETS

All of the night sets shown in this photo have vertical paneled bodies. The large-size sets are harder to find than the smaller ones.

	Height of Tumbler	Height of Water Bottle	Combined Height	Price
Top Row:				
(a) Pink, plain	3⅜"	6"	7⅛"	$20.00-25.00
(b) Blue, plain	3"	5½"	6½"	$30.00-35.00
(c) Amberina/crystal	3"	5½"	6½"	$65.00-80.00
(d) Pink, handpainted	3"	5½"	6½"	$22.00-27.00
(e) Amber, plain, large	3⅛"	6½"	7⅝"	$35.00-40.00
Bottom Row:				
(a) Green plain	3⅛"	6⅛"	6⅞"	$20.00-25.00
(b) Pink decorated	3⅛"	6⅛"	6⅞"	$25.00-30.00
(c) Crystal decorated	3⅛"	6⅛"	6⅞"	$8.00-10.00
(d) Mulberry iridized	3⅛"	5⅞"	6⅞"	$25.00-35.00

IRIDIZED NIGHT SETS

The night sets pictured on this page have an iridescent finish applied over a crystal body.

	Height of Tumbler	Height of Water Bottle	Combined Height	Price
Top Row:				
(a) Cranberry flashed	3⅛"	6"	7"	$15.00-18.00
(b) Light blue, flashed	3⅛"	6"	7"	$15.00-18.00
(c) Marigold flashed	2¾"	5¾"	6⅜"	$18.00-20.00
(d) Cranberry flashed	3⅛"	6"	7"	$25.00-30.00
(e) Marigold flashed	3⅜"	6"	7½"	$18.00-20.00
Bottom Row:				
(a) Marigold flashed	3⅛"	6"	7"	$18.00-20.00
(b) Dark cranberry flashed	3⅛"	6"	7"	$28.00-32.00
(c) Marigold flashed and handpainted	3⅛"	6"	7"	$15.00-18.00
(d) Pearl iridized	3⅛"	6"	7"	$15.00-18.00
(e) Cranberry flashed	3⅛"	6"	7"	$25.00-28.00

DECORATED CRYSTAL NIGHT SETS

	Height of Tumbler	Height of Water Bottle	Combined Height	Price
Top Row:				
(a) Crystal decorated	3"	6⅛"	7¼"	$10.00-12.00
(b) Crystal decorated	2"	6⅛"	7⅛"	$8.00-10.00
(c) Crystal decorated	3⅛"	5¾"	7"	$8.00-10.00
(d) Crystal decorated	3⅛"	6"	7"	$8.00-10.00
Bottom Row:				
(a) Crystal decorated	3⅛"	6"	7"	$8.00-10.00
(b) Crystal decorated	3⅛"	6"	7"	$10.00-12.00
(c) Crystal decorated	3⅛"	6"	7"	$8.00-10.00
(d) Crystal decorated	3⅛"	6"	7"	$8.00-10.00
(e) Crystal decorated	3"	5¾"	6⅝"	$8.00-10.00

Next Page, Top Photo:

	Height of Tumbler	Height of Water Bottle	Combined Height	Price
Top Row:				
(a) Crystal, needle etch	3¼"	6½"	7¾"	$8.00-10.00
(b) Crystal, etched/silver	3¼"	6½"	7¾"	$12.00-16.00
(c) Crystal decorated	3¼"	6"	7"	$8.00-10.00
(d) Crystal decorated	3¼"	6"	7"	$8.00-10.00
(e) Crystal decorated	3¼"	6½"	7"	$10.00-12.00
Bottom Row:				
(a) Crystal decorated	3¼"	6½"	7"	$10.00-12.00
(b) Crystal decorated	3¼"	6½"	7"	$10.00-12.00
(c) Crystal decorated	3¼"	6½"	7"	$8.00-10.00
(d) Crystal decorated	3¼"	6½"	7"	$8.00-10.00
(e) Crystal decorated	3¼"	6½"	7"	$10.00-12.00

The tumble-ups in this photo are all the same style but have different decorations. The tumbler is 3⅛" tall, has straight sides and a very flat bottom. The water bottle is 6" high and the combined height with the tumbler in place is 6⅞".

Crystal, decorated $10.00-12.00

MISCELLANEOUS NIGHT SETS

The first two night sets on the top row were made by the West Virginia Specialty Company in the early 1980's. The first tumble-up has a gold 30th Anniversary decoration and a paper label with the identifying mark "Handmade, West Virginia Glass Company, Weston, W. Va." The company still produces night sets with numerous decorations in both crystal and flashed-on colors.

Night Set	Height of Tumbler	Height of Water Bottle	Combined Height	Price
Top Row:				
(a) Crystal, 30th Anniversary	3"	5⅞"	6⅞"	$8.00-12.00
(b) Crystal, band decoration	3"	5⅞"	6⅞"	$8.00-10.00
(c) Crystal, gold/enamel decoration	3⅛"	6"	7"	$8.00-10.00
(d) Crystal	3⅛"	6"	7"	$8.00-10.00
(e) Crystal, gold/enamel decoration	3⅛"	5⅞"	6⅞"	$12.00-14.00
Bottom Row:				
(a) Crystal heavy crackle glass (overshot)	3⅝"	6⅝"	7"	$15.00-18.00
(b) Crystal frosted, handpainted	3¾"	7"	8⅛"	$18.00-22.00
(c) Crystal frosted, handpainted	3¾"	7"	8⅛"	$18.00-22.00
(d) Crystal, orange flashed	4⅜"	7¼"	8⅜"	$30.00-35.00

	Height of Tumbler	Height of Water Bottle	Combined Height	Price
Top Row:				
(a) Crystal frosted, enamel decorated tumbler	3"	6½"	7⅜"	$10.00-14.00
(b) Green frosted with enamel decoration	3"	5⅝"	6⅞"	$25.00-30.00
(c) Green frosted	3"	5⅝"	6⅞"	$18.00-20.00
(d) Pink frosted with enamel decoration	3"	5⅝"	6⅞"	$25.00-27.00
Bottom Row:				
(a) Ruby	3"	5½"	5¾"	$40.00-50.00
(b) Crystal with color bands	3"	5½"	5¾"	$10.00-14.00
(c) Crystal/cranberry flashed	3"	5½"	5¾"	$8.00-12.00
(d) Pink	3"	5½"	5¾"	$20.00-27.00

The green 4-piece set on the top row has a separate lid and rests on a 4½" wide by 9½" long rectangular tray. The handled pitcher is 5" tall. Its complete height with the lid is 6½". The tumbler is 3⅜" high. The tumble-ups shown on the bottom row are miniatures.

	Height of Tumbler	Height of Water Bottle	Combined Height	Price
Top Row:				
(a) Green 4-piece				$85.00-100.00
(b) Pink owl	2"	5½"	6"	$75.00-85.00
Bottom Row:				
(a) Crystal decorated	1¾"	3½"	4½"	$20.00-30.00
(b) Crystal decorated	1¾"	3½"	4¾"	$20.00-30.00
(c) Custard opaque	2¼"	4⅝"	4¾"	$40.00-60.00

TALL AND RIBBED GUEST SETS

The four pink guest sets on the top row were produced by the Dunbar Flint Glass Corporation of Dunbar, West Virginia in the early 1930's. These sets are usually pink and may be frosted. The sets are often decorated with wheel cuttings, applied gold or handpainting. The tumbler has curved sides and is 3" tall. The water bottle is 8" tall and the combined set is 8¾" tall.

The taller green set on the top row has a flared 3½" tumbler. The water bottle has concave sides and is 9" tall. The whole set is 10¼" high.

The first three night sets on the bottom row have wheel cut floral decorations. The water bottles are 8" tall and have bands around the shoulder. The tumblers are 3" tall and the set measures 8¾".

	Height of Tumbler	Height of Water Bottle	Combined Height	Price
Top Row:				
(a) Pink frosted	3"	8"	8¾"	$20.00-25.00
(b) Pink/gold band	3"	8"	8¾"	$25.00-30.00
(c) Pink, cut design	3"	8"	8¾"	$25.00-30.00
(d) Pink frosted, handpainted	3"	8"	8¾"	$25.00-30.00
(e) Green	3½"	9"	10¼"	$30.00-35.00
Bottom Row:				
(a) Pink, cut floral design	3"	8"	8¾"	$30.00-32.00
(b) Pink, cut floral design	3"	8"	8¾"	$30.00-32.00
(c) Pink, cut floral design	3"	8"	8¾"	$30.00-32.00
(d) Pink	2½"	7⅞"	8½"	$28.00-30.00
(e) Pink, handpainted	3"	8¼"	9"	$30.00-32.00

The tumble-ups on the top row are all the same style. Both the tumbler and the water bottle have ridges near the bottom. The tumbler is 4" tall and flares slightly toward the top. The water bottle is 6⅝" tall, and the combined height of the base and the tumbler is 8¼".

The shapes of the water bottles on the bottom row are the same. However, the bottle to the first set is much taller than the other three. The tumbler to the first set is also larger and its ribs are deeper. The smaller tumblers are merely slightly wavy, rather than ribbed. The second night set is crystal. The pink color is from the original bath salts which are still intact. The paper seal on the top provides the information, "Nite Set Bath Salts, $1.25. One Tablespoon Softens and Delightfully Perfumes the Bath. Cont. 24 oz. Mfd. by Trylon Products Corp., Chicago, U.S.A."

	Height of Tumbler	Height of Water Bottle	Combined Height	Price
Top Row:				
(a) Pink	4"	6⅝"	8¼"	$25.00-28.00
(b) Amber iridescent	4"	6⅝"	8¼"	$14.00-18.00
(c) Crystal	4"	6⅝"	8¼"	$8.00-12.00
(d) Light blue iridescent	4"	6⅝"	8¼"	$20.00-22.00
(e) Crystal/gold and floral decoration	4"	6⅝"	8¼"	$14.00-16.00
Bottom Row:				
(a) Amber iridescent	3⅞"	7½"	8"	$14.00-18.00
(b) Crystal (original contents)	3½"	7"	7⅜"	$20.00-22.00
(c) Green	3½"	7"	7⅜"	$20.00-25.00
(d) Pink	3½"	7"	7⅜"	$20.00-25.00

The two sets on the left side of the top row are similar. However, there are slight differences between the two. The blue tumbler flares out at the rim, and the water bottle has ribs in the neck. The green tumbler is more barrel-shaped and there are no ribs in the neck of the water bottle. The tumble-ups on the bottom row are all the same style.

	Height of Tumbler	Height of Water Bottle	Combined Height	Price
Top Row:				
(a) Blue	3¼"	5¾"	6¾"	$30.00-35.00
(b) Green	3¼"	5⅞"	6¾"	$30.00-32.00
(c) Green	4¼"	6¾"	7⅞"	$28.00-30.00
(d) Pink	3½"	7"	8½"	$28.00-30.00
(e) Green	3½"	7"	8½"	$28.00-30.00
Bottom Row:				
(a) Pink frosted	3"	5½"	6⅜"	$16.00-18.00
(b) Pink	3"	5½"	6⅜"	$20.00-22.00
(c) Lavender etched	3"	5½"	6⅜"	$14.00-18.00
(d) Cranberrry flashed	3"	5½"	6⅜"	$14.00-18.00

HANDLED DECORATED CRYSTAL GUEST SETS

The picture on this page illustrates various styles of handled crystal guest sets with wheel cuttings.

Top Row: (a) The jug has a ground bottom and the sides of the tumbler are cut to match the design on the pitcher. (b,c) The jug has a ground bottom. The sides of the tumbler are plain, but there is a cutting on its base. (d) This set has a tumbler with a cut design on both its sides and base.

	Height of Tumbler	Height of Water Bottle	Combined Height	Price
(a) Guest set, handled	3"	6¼"	6⅝"	$30.00-35.00
(b) Guest set, handled	3"	6¼"	6⅝"	$30.00-35.00
(c) Guest set, handled	3¼"	6½"	7"	$30.00-35.00
(d) Guest set, handled	3⅛"	6¾"	6½"	$40.00-45.00

Bottom Row:
All three jugs have wheel cut designs. The tumblers to the first two sets are only cut on the base, but the third set has a tumbler with a cut design on both the sides and the base.

	Height of Tumbler	Height of Water Bottle	Combined Height	Price
(a) Guest set, handled	3¼"	6⅝"	7"	$40.00-42.00
(b) Guest set, handled	3⅛"	6½"	6¾"	$32.00-37.00
(c) Guest set, handled	3½"	6½"	7"	$30.00-35.00

GUEST SETS WITH GOLD AND ENAMELED DECORATIONS

Top Row: The crystal bottle with the ribbed sides has a glass stopper in addition to the matching tumbler.

	Height of Tumbler	Height of Water Bottle	Combined Height	Price
(a) Crystal, handled, gold decorated	3"	7"	7¾"	$50.00-55.00
(b) Crystal ribbed bottle, gold decorated	4¼"	8¼"	9"	$85.00-87.00
(c) Crystal bottle, gold decorated	3⅜"	7½"	8¾"	$45.00-50.00

Bottom Row:
The crystal set with the enameled basket decoration has six matching tumblers. The indicated price is for the complete set.

	Height of Tumbler	Height of Water Bottle	Combined Height	Price
(a) Crystal pitcher with gold and enameled basket	3½"	6¾"	7¼"	$125.00-165.00
(b) Green pitcher with silver overlay design	3¼"	5½"	6½"	$55.00-65.00

HANDLED GUEST SETS

	Height of Tumbler	Height of Water Bottle	Combined Height	Price
(a) Handled, amethyst	3⅜"	7"	7½"	$60.00-70.00
(b) Handled, crystal stretch	2"	6¾"	7"	$40.00-45.00
(c) Red opaque with black applied handle	2½"	4⅜"	5¼"	$50.00-55.00

Next Page, Top Photo:

	Height of Tumbler	Height of Water Bottle	Combined Height	Price
Top Row:				
(a) Amber with enameled lady	3⅜"	6½"	7⅞"	$65.00-75.00
(b) Pink transparent	3⅜"	6⅞"	7¾"	$60.00-70.00
(c) Crystal	2⅝"	6¾"	7¼"	$35.00-40.00
Bottom Row:				
(a) Crystal	3⅛"	5"	5⅞"	$20.00-30.00
(b) Green transparent	3⅛"	5"	5⅞"	$45.00-48.00
(c) Crystal Fostoria No. 2104 with floral etching	3"	6"	6¾"	$50.00-60.00

Next Page, Bottom Photo:

The guest sets in this photo were made in the 1960's and 1970's. They are cased glass, which means they have a colored outer layer applied over an interior white milk glass base.

	Height of Tumbler	Height of Water Bottle	Combined Height	Price
Top Row:				
(a) Red	3½"	6"	7½"	$25.00-30.00
(b) Green	3½"	6"	7½"	$20.00-22.00
Bottom Row:				
(a) Green	3½"	5"	6½"	$20.00-22.00
(b) Blue	3½"	5"	6½"	$25.00-30.00
(c) White	3½"	5"	6½"	$18.00-20.00

CRYSTAL GUEST SETS

	Height of Tumbler	Height of Water Bottle	Combined Height	Price
Top Row:				
(a) Crystal etched	3⅜"	6"	7"	$18.00-20.00
(b) Crystal etched with footed base	2⅜"	6½"	7⅛"	$14.00-18.00
(c) Crystal, needle etched	4⅛"	7½"	8¼"	$18.00-20.00
(d) Crystal footed with needle etched design	3"	7½"	7⅞"	$14.00-18.00
Bottom Row:				
(a) Crystal, Farberware holder	2⅞"	5½"	6½"	$20.00-25.00
(b) Same as above, without holder	2⅞"	5½"	6½"	$16.00-18.00
(c) Crystal pressed glass	3"	6⅝"	7⅝"	$30.00-35.00
(d) Crystal pressed Daisy and Button with 5½" tray	3¼"	6"	7"	$35.00-40.00

The guest sets in this photo are all heavy crystal with hand cut decorations. The one on the top left has a paper label which reads "Waterford Glass Limited, Republic of Ireland." The paper label on the large bulbous set on the top row provides the information, "Fostoria, Made in Rumania."

	Height of Tumbler	Height of Water Bottle	Combined Height	Price
Top Row:				
(a) Crystal Waterford	3½"	8½"	8¾"	$100.00-150.00
(b) Crystal with elaborate cut floral design	3¾"	6¾"	7⅞"	$75.00-85.00
(c) Crystal Fostoria	4"	8¾"	9¼"	$45.00-55.00
(d) Crystal with cut floral design	3¼"	5¾"	6⅞"	$35.00-45.00
Bottom Row:				
(a) Crystal cut	3⅜"	7"	7⅜"	$25.00-30.00
(b) Crystal footed	3½"	7¼"	7¾"	$40.00-50.00
(c) Crystal cut	3¾"	6⅜"	7"	$40.00-50.00
(d) Crystal cut	3⅜"	6"	6½"	$25.00-27.00

	Height of Tumbler	Height of Water Bottle	Combined Height	Price
Top Row:				
(a) Crystal etched	2⅞"	5½"	5⅞"	$12.00-14.00
(b) Crystal, needle etched	2⅞"	5½"	5⅞"	$12.00-14.00
(c) Crystal with silver overlay	2⅞"	5½"	5⅞"	$35.00-45.00
(d) Crystal etched	2⅞"	5½"	5⅞"	$12.00-14.00
Bottom Row:				
(a) Crystal with gold band	2⅞"	5½"	5⅞"	$14.00-18.00
(b) Crystal etched	3⅛"	4¼"	5½"	$14.00-18.00
(c) Crystal etched	2⅜"	4⅞"	5½"	$20.00-22.00
(d) Crystal with enameled floral decoration	3½"	4⅜"	5"	$18.00-20.00
(e) Crystal with frosted bands	3½"	4⅜"	5"	$18.00-20.00

GUEST SETS WITH FLASHED DECORATIONS

	Height of Tumbler	Height of Water Bottle	Combined Height	Price
Top Row:				
(a) Crystal footed, cranberry flashed	3⅝"	5⅝"	7"	$40.00-50.00
(b) Crystal footed, blue flashed	3⅝"	5⅝"	7"	$45.00-65.00
(c) Crystal, amber flashed	3½"	6¼"	6⅞"	$40.00-45.00
(d) Crystal, blue flashed	3⅞"	7½"	8½"	$100.00-125.00
(e) Crystal, cranberry flashed	3⅜"	7"	7½"	$75.00-85.00
Bottom Row:				
(a) Crystal hobnail, cranberry flashed	3¾"	7⅞"	8"	$60.00-70.00
(b) Crystal, cranberry flashed	5"	6¾"	8½"	$40.00-60.00
(c) Crystal, cranberry flashed	3½"	6¼"	7⅜"	$40.00-50.00
(d) Crystal, cranberrry flashed	3⅞"	7¾"	8"	$60.00-65.00

	Height of Tumbler	Height of Water Bottle	Combined Height	Price
Top Row:				
(a) Crystal, cranberry flashed	3¼"	6½"	6⅞"	$145.00-185.00
(b) Crystal, cobalt flashed	3½"	6½"	7⅛"	$125.00-165.00
(c) Crystal, cranberry flashed with ground flat bottom tumbler	3⅝"	6½"	7¼"	$120.00-150.00
Bottom Row:				
(a) Crystal, cranberry flashed	3½"	6½"	7¼"	$75.00-85.00
(b) Crystal, cobalt flashed	3½"	6½"	7¼"	$75.00-85.00
(c) Crystal cranberry flashed, base has glass stopper	3¼"	8"	8¾"	$80.00-90.00
(d) Crystal, cranberry flashed	3¼"	6⅝"	7"	$80.00-90.00

	Height of Tumbler	Height of Water Bottle	Combined Height	Price
(a) Crystal cut, flashed amber	3½"	6⅜"	7½"	$150.00-180.00
(b) Crystal cut, flashed green	3⅜"	6⅞"	7½"	$150.00-180.00
(c) Crystal cut, flashed cranberry	3⅝"	7"	7¾"	$85.00-95.00
(d) Crystal with floral cutting, flashed amber panels	3⅜"	6⅝"	7½"	$45.00-55.00

MISCELLANEOUS GUEST SETS

The tumble-ups in this picture have enameled decorations and were made in Czechoslavakia.

	Height of Tumbler	Height of Water Bottle	Combined Height	Price
Top Row:				
(a) Crystal, enameled floral design and green bands	3⅝"	6⅜"	7¼"	$20.00-22.00
(b) Crystal, blue enamel with gold	3½"	7"	7⅝"	$18.00-22.00
(c) Crystal, enameled	3¾"	9½"	10"	$20.00-22.00
(d) Crystal with intricate enameled design	3½"	7½"	8"	$20.00-25.00
(e) Crystal with enameled flowers	3¼"	6¼"	6⅞"	$18.00-20.00
Bottom Row:				
(a) Crystal with enameled flowers	3⅝"	6¾"	7½"	$20.00-22.00
(b) Crystal with enameled flowers	3⅝"	7¼"	7⅝"	$25.00-27.00
(c) Crystal, flashed lavender with handpainted flowers	3⅜"	7½"	7¾"	$24.00-28.00

	Height of Tumbler	Height of Water Bottle	Combined Height	Price
Top Row:				
(a) Cobalt transparent	3⅛"	5⅜"	5¾"	$40.00-60.00
(b) Blue opaque with gold bands	4⅛"	8"	8¾"	$50.00-60.00
(c) Cobalt with enamel decoration	3⅜"	6¼"	7⅜"	$40.00-60.00
(d) Mulberry	3⅝"	7¼"	8"	$50.00-55.00
Bottom Row:				
(a) Green opaque with enameled decoration and 6⅞" tray	3½"	6½"	7½"	$28.00-35.00
(b) Mulberry with gold band	4"	7"	8"	$50.00-55.00
(c) Clambroth	3¾"	6¾"	7¼"	$28.00-35.00
(d) Green with gold bands and 7¼" tray	3½"	6¼"	6½"	$40.00-45.00

	Height of Tumbler	Height of Water Bottle	Combined Height	Price
Top Row:				
(a) Orange/Yellow Vasart	4⅛"	7½"	8½"	$20.00-25.00
(b) Pink/White opaque blend	3½"	6⅜"	7½"	$20.00-27.00
(c) Green/White opaque swirl blend	3½"	6⅜"	7½"	$20.00-27.00
(d) Crystal frosted	3⅝"	7⅛"	7½"	$20.00-22.00
Bottom Row:				
(a) Green cased	3¼"	7¼"	7½"	$30.00-35.00
(b) Opaque multi-colored art glass style	3⅝"	7½"	7⅞"	$80.00-85.00
(c) Ebony with oriental lady watering plant decoration	3½"	7⅛"	7⅞"	$40.00-45.00
(d) Milk glass with enamel design, base has glass stopper	3⅞"	7¼"	8"	$40.00-50.00

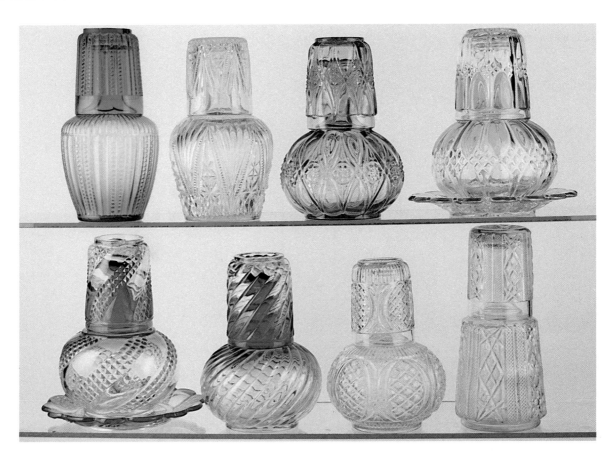

	Height of Tumbler	Height of Water Bottle	Combined Height	Price
Top Row:				
(a) Blue "Zipper" pattern	3⅝"	7½"	8¼"	$80.00-90.00
(b) Crystal, pressed design, flashed yellow	3¼"	7½"	7¾"	$60.00-80.00
(c) Pink, pressed design, tumbler has "Belge" molded on bottom	3⅞"	6¾"	7⅝"	$85.00-90.00
(d) Crystal, flashed yellow, 7" tray, tumbler signed "Belqique"	3⅞"	6¾"	7⅝"	$150.00-185.00
Bottom Row:				
(a) Crystal, flashed cranberry, 7" tray, signed "Baccarat"	4"	6⅞"	7⅞"	$225.00-275.00
(b) Crystal, flashed cranberry, signed "Baccarat"	3⅞"	6⅞"	7½"	$200.00-225.00
(c) Crystal, pressed design	3½"	6⅞"	7¼"	$50.00-60.00
(d) Crystal pressed design with light topaz flashing	3⅞"	8"	8⅝"	$60.00-80.00

All the tumble-ups in the above photo are currently being produced for a midwest importer. The opalescent ones on the left are a copy of originals produced by Fenton for Wrisley. Both styles are commonly found at local flea markets in the $10.00 to $15.00 range. Some problems exist for collectors when the seller becomes confused and represents and prices these new items as old.

Books on Antiques and Collectibles

Most of the following books are available from your local book seller or antique dealer, or on loan from your public library. If you are unable to locate certain titles in your area you may order by mail from COLLECTOR BOOKS, P.O. Box 3009, Paducah, KY 42002-3009. Add $2.00 for postage for the first book ordered and $.25 for each additional book. Include item number, title and price when ordering. Allow 14 to 21 days for delivery. All books are well illustrated and contain current values.

Books on Glass and Pottery

1810	American Art Glass, Shuman	$29.95
1517	American Belleek, Gaston	$19.95
2016	Bedroom & Bathroom Glassware of the Depression Years	$19.95
1312	Blue & White Stoneware, McNerney	$9.95
1959	Blue Willow, 2nd Ed., Gaston	$14.95
1627	Children's Glass Dishes, China & Furniture II, Lechler	$19.95
1892	Collecting Royal Haeger, Garmon	$19.95
2017	Collector's Ency. of Depression Glass, Florence, 9th Ed.	$19.95
1373	Collector's Ency of Amercian Dinnerware, Cunningham	$24.95
1812	Collector's Ency. of Fiesta, Huxford	$19.95
1439	Collector's Ency. of Flow Blue China, Gaston	$19.95
1961	Collector's Ency of Fry Glass, Fry Glass Society	$24.95
1813	Collector's Encyclopedia of Geisha Girl Porcelain, Litts	$19.95
1664	Collector's Ency. of Heisey Glass, Bredehoft	$24.95
1915	Collector's Ency. of Hall China, 2nd Ed., Whitmyer	$19.95
1358	Collector's Ency. of McCoy Pottery, Huxford	$19.95
1039	Collector's Ency. of Nippon Porcelain I, Van Patten	$19.95
1350	Collector's Ency. of Nippon Porcelain II, Van Patten	$19.95
1665	Collector's Ency. of Nippon Porcelain III, Van Patten	$24.95
1447	Collector's Ency. of Noritake, Van Patten	$19.95
1038	Collector's Ency. of Occupied Japan, 2nd Ed., Florence	$14.95
1719	Collector's Ency. of Occupied Japan III, Florence	$19.95
2019	Collector's Ency. of Occupied Japan IV, Florence	$14.95
1715	Collector's Ency. of R.S. Prussia II, Gaston	$24.95
1034	Collector's Ency. of Roseville Pottery, Huxford	$19.95
1035	Collector's Ency. of Roseville Pottery, 2nd Ed., Huxford	$19.95
1623	Coll. Guide to Country Stoneware & Pottery, Raycraft	$9.95
1523	Colors in Cambridge, National Cambridge Society	$19.95
1425	Cookie Jars, Westfall	$9.95
1843	Covered Animal Dishes, Grist	$14.95
1844	Elegant Glassware of the Depression Era, 3rd Ed., Florence	$19.95
2024	Kitchen Glassware of the Depression Years, 4th Florence	$19.95
1465	Haviland Collectibles & Art Objects, Gaston	$19.95
1917	Head Vases Id & Value Guide, Cole	$14.95
1392	Majolica Pottery, Katz-Marks	$9.95
1669	Majolica Pottery, 2nd Series, Katz-Marks	$9.95
1919	Pocket Guide to Depression Glass, 6th Ed., Florence	$9.95
1438	Oil Lamps II, Thuro	$19.95
1670	Red Wing Collectibles, DePasquale	$9.95
1440	Red Wing Stoneware, DePasquale	$9.95
1958	So. Potteries Blue Ridge Dinnerware, 3rd Ed., Newbound	$14.95
1889	Standard Carnival Glass, 2nd Ed., Edwards	$24.95
1941	Standard Carnival Glass Price Guide, Edwards	$7.95
1814	Wave Crest, Glass of C.F. Monroe, Cohen	$29.95
1848	Very Rare Glassware of the Depression Years, Florence	$24.95

Books on Dolls & Toys

1887	American Rag Dolls, Patino	$14.95
1749	Black Dolls, Gibbs	$14.95
1514	Character Toys & Collectibles 1st Series, Longest	$19.95
1750	Character Toys & Collectibles, 2nd Series, Longest	$19.95
2021	Collectible Male Action Figures, Manos	$14.95
1529	Collector's Ency. of Barbie Dolls, DeWein	$19.95
1066	Collector's Ency. of Half Dolls, Marion	$29.95
1891	French Dolls in Color, 3rd Series, Smith	$14.95
1631	German Dolls, Smith	$9.95
1635	Horsman Dolls, Gibbs	$19.95
1067	Madame Alexander Collector's Dolls, Smith	$19.95
2025	Madame Alexander Price Guide #15, Smith	$7.95
1995	Modern Collectors Dolls, Vol. I, Smith	$19.95

1516	Modern Collector's Dolls V, Smith	$19.95
1540	Modern Toys, 1930-1980, Baker	$19.95
2033	Patricia Smith Doll Values, Antique to Modern, 6th ed.,	$9.95
1886	Stern's Guide to Disney	$14.95
1513	Teddy Bears & Steiff Animals, Mandel	$9.95
1817	Teddy Bears & Steiff Animals, 2nd, Mandel	$19.95
2028	Toys, Antique & Collectible, Longest	$14.95
1630	Vogue, Ginny Dolls, Smith	$19.95
1648	World of Alexander-Kins, Smith	$19.95
1808	Wonder of Barbie, Manos	$9.95
1430	World of Barbie Dolls, Manos	$9.95

Other Collectibles

1457	American Oak Furniture, McNerney	$9.95
1846	Antique & Collectible Marbles, Grist, 2nd Ed.	$9.95
1712	Antique & Collectible Thimbles, Mathis	$19.95
1880	Antique Iron, McNerney	$9.95
1748	Antique Purses, Holiner	$19.95
1868	Antique Tools, Our American Heritage, McNerney	$9.95
2015	Archaic Indian Points & Knives, Edler	$14.95
1426	Arrowheads & Projectile Points, Hothem	$7.95
1278	Art Nouveau & Art Deco Jewelry, Baker	$9.95
1714	Black Collectibles, Gibbs	$19.95
1666	Book of Country, Raycraft	$19.95
1960	Book of Country Vol II, Raycraft	$19.95
1811	Book of Moxie, Potter	$29.95
1128	Bottle Pricing Guide, 3rd Ed., Cleveland	$7.95
1751	Christmas Collectibles, Whitmyer	$19.95
1752	Christmas Ornaments, Johnston	$19.95
1713	Collecting Barber Bottles, Holiner	$24.95
2018	Collector's Ency. of Graniteware, Greguire	$24.95
1634	Coll. Ency. of Salt & Pepper Shakers, Davern	$19.95
2020	Collector's Ency. of Salt & Pepper Shakers II, Davern	$19.95
1916	Collector's Guide to Art Deco, Gaston	$14.95
1753	Collector's Guide to Baseball Memorabilia, Raycraft	$14.95
1537	Collector's Guide to Country Baskets, Raycraft	$9.95
1437	Collector's Guide to Country Furniture, Raycraft	$9.95
1842	Collector's Guide to Country Furniture II, Raycraft	$14.95
1962	Collector's Guide to Decoys, Huxford	$14.95
1441	Collector's Guide to Post Cards, Wood	$9.95
1716	Fifty Years of Fashion Jewelry, Baker	$19.95
2022	Flea Market Trader, 6th Ed., Huxford	$9.95
1668	Flint Blades & Proj. Points of the No. Am. Indian, Tully	$24.95
1755	Furniture of the Depression Era, Swedberg	$19.95
1424	Hatpins & Hatpin Holders, Baker	$9.95
1964	Indian Axes & Related Stone Artifacts, Hothem	$14.95
2023	Keen Kutter Collectibles, 2nd Ed., Heuring	$14.95
1212	Marketplace Guide to Oak Furniture, Blundell	$17.95
1918	Modern Guns, Id. & Values, 7th Ed., Quertermous	$12.95
1181	100 Years of Collectible Jewelry, Baker	$9.95
1965	Pine Furniture, Our Am. Heritage, McNerney	$14.95
1124	Primitives, Our American Heritage, McNerney	$8.95
1759	Primitives, Our American Heritage, 2nd Series, McNerney	$14.95
2026	Railroad Collectibles, 4th Ed., Baker	$14.95
1632	Salt & Pepper Shakers, Guarnaccia	$9.95
1888	Salt & Pepper Shakers II, Guarnaccia	$14.95
1816	Silverplated Flatware, 3rd Ed., Hagan	$14.95
2027	Standard Baseball Card Pr. Gd., Florence	$9.95
1922	Standard Bottle Pr. Gd., Sellari	$14.95
1966	Standard Fine Art Value Guide, Huxford	$29.95
1890	The Old Book Value Guide	$19.95
1923	Wanted to Buy	$9.95
1885	Victorian Furniture, McNerney	$9.95

Schroeder's Antiques Price Guide

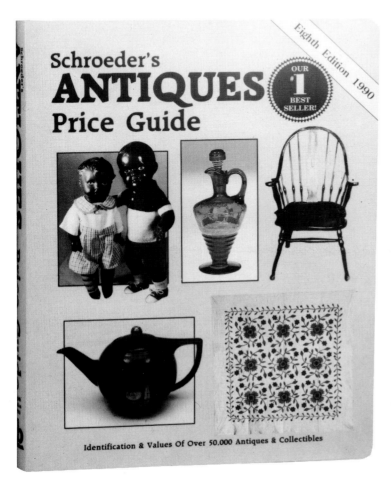

Schroeder's Antiques Price Guide has climbed its way to the top in a field already supplied with several well-established publications! The word is out, *Schroeder's Price Guide* is the best buy at any price. Over 500 categories are covered, with more than 50,000 listings. But it's not volume alone that makes Schroeder's the unique guide it is recognized to be. From ABC Plates to Zsolnay, if it merits the interest of today's collector, you'll find it in Schroeder's. Each subject is represented with histories and background information. In addition, hundreds of sharp original photos are used each year to illustrate not only the rare and the unusual, but the everyday "fun-type" collectibles as well -- not postage stamp pictures, but large close-up shots that show important details clearly.

Each edition is completely re-typeset from all new sources. We have not and will not simply change prices in each new edition. All new copy and all new illustrations make Schroeder's THE price guide on antiques and collectibles.

The writing and researching team behind this giant is proportionately large. It is backed by a staff of more than seventy of Collector Books' finest authors, as well as a board of advisors made up of well-known antique authorities and the country's top dealers, all specialists in their fields. Accuracy is their primary aim. Prices are gathered over the entire year previous to publication, from ads and personal contacts. Then each category is thoroughly checked to spot inconsistencies, listings that may not be entirely reflective of actual market dealings, and lines too vague to be of merit.

Only the best of the lot remains for publication. You'll find *Schroeder's Antiques Price Guide* the one to buy for factual information and quality.

No dealer, collector or investor can afford not to own this book. It is available from your favorite bookseller or antiques dealer at the low price of $12.95. If you are unable to find this price guide in your area, it's available from Collector Books, P. O. Box 3009, Paducah, KY 42001 at $12.95 plus $2.00 for postage and handling.

8½ x 11, 608 Pages $12.95

COLLECTOR BOOKS
A Division of Schroeder Publishing Co., Inc.